CONTENTS

*To Deborah, my devoted companion, and
to the seekers and the curious.*

ENDORSEMENTS

"Interviewing Jesus is powerful and engaging. David Collis delivers with a depth of understanding that transcends the literal and bridges scripture with a logical and practical conversation that enriches and feeds the Christian soul. David penetrates metaphysical motivations and delivers his interpretation with remarkable insight and savvy. A must read for anyone wishing to understand and explore the life of Jesus."

- Brent Baldwin author of *THINK WORLD CLASS*

"Interviewing Jesus is a title as fascinating as the content of this book. David's unique perspective on Christianity and the Bible will definitely not let you put this book down."

- Andreas Carlsson bestselling author of *LIVE TO WIN, FRAN IDÉ TILL SUCCÉ* and music composer & lyricist for Cirque du Soleil's Broadway show, *PARAMOUR*

"David Collis has written one of the most engaging and intimate portraits of the world's most mysterious figure. Who wouldn't want to sit with Jesus Christ and ask him every question you would ever want know about his life and ministry. "Interviewing Jesus; The Man" is a compelling page-turner I could not put down and it has found a permanent place next to our family bible."

- Desmond Child, Songwriter Hall Of Fame Inductee and Grammy Winning Co-writer of Bon Jovi's "Livin' On A Prayer."

"Interviewing Jesus is a compelling story that transports the reader to feel as though Jesus is alive and personally talking with David. The book is recommended reading for anyone wishing to expand their knowledge about Jesus, his life and his times."

- Kerry Palframan, Author of *SPIRIT TALK*

Sharon – let your light
continue to shine always !!?

INTERVIEWING JESUS – THE MAN

David Collis

DAVID COLLIS

M⊙tivational PRESS
LEADERS IN GLOBAL PUBLISHING

Published by Motivational Press, Inc.
1777 Aurora Road
Melbourne, Florida, 32935
www.MotivationalPress.com

Special thanks to David Collis for the use of his Mystery Symbols.
See more on davidcollis.com.

Manufactured in the United States of America.

ISBN: 978-1-62865-423-3

We become contemplatives when God discovers Himself in us. At that moment, the point of our contact with Him opens out and we pass through the center of our souls and enter eternity.

Thomas Merton

PREFACE

I believe the time is ripe for Jesus' life, words and ministry to be re-examined. *Interviewing Jesus* addresses a wide range of topics and introduces a number of alternative theories about Jesus, his times, his family, John the Baptist, the Father, his disciples and the meaning of his sayings.

The underlying theme of the book is encompassed in a fundamental question: Do we really know Jesus, or do think we know him when, in truth, we know very little about him? The New Testament emphasizes that the Father is personable and knowable, and by extension Jesus is too. But the historical material available for examination to determine this point was carefully tailored by early Christian and Christian Gnostic writers. Each had specific motives in constructing a theological narrative and each had reasons for depicting Jesus symbolically rather than historically. The primary source for Jesus' biographical story is the New Testament, but its writers glossed over, minimized and eliminated most of his history, motives and inspirations. This is the problem in seeing and understanding Jesus.

To write *Interviewing Jesus*, I investigated Greek, Roman and Jewish history and the development of early Christianity. I dovetailed this research into my study of other religions and spiritual disciplines, which I had conducted earlier. I felt the need to step into Jesus' sandals, throw on his tunic and gaze upon the world through his eyes in order to see, know and understand the man. I challenged myself to understand his words and deeds in their actuality, and I found that his sayings contain clues about his background. I peeled away the layers of theology to glimpse at his motives and back story and to identify the reasons for his actions.

I organized and catalogued his Wisdom Sayings thematically and contemplated how and when he composed them. Wisdom Sayings by definition contain wisdom, and wisdom is gained not through books alone but through life experiences. I compared his sayings to his ministry, which I then re-examined through the lens of Roman and Jewish history. I placed Jesus in context and I scoured the gospels for details. I found minute details that appeared out of place. I went from question to answer and back again as I sifted through his words, ministry, personality and historical setting. I discovered Jesus cannot be understood in isolation, nor can he be known from traditional theology. Seeing a divine being misses the point. Jesus has to be seen in the context of his humanity and his time. I also discovered that Jesus is more complicated and nuanced than the New Testament or any other ancient piece of literature suggests, and that he is more of an enigma – a puzzle to solve and a mystery to unravel – than a symbol to embody or a god to worship.

Jesus was born into this world. He walked along the ground, climbed mountains, sailed at least one sea and breathed air. He lived a life prior to his ministry. He had a family, ate food, drank wine, wore clothes, strapped on sandals, held tools in his hands, built things, told stories and composed a series of Wisdom Sayings. He laughed and cried and felt life's joys and sorrows. He suffered under Roman occupation and felt the turmoil caused by the illegitimacy of the royal and High Priest lineages. He was a man of action who rolled up his proverbial sleeves and did things. He was charismatic. He met and engaged people. He learned, read and was observant, and, at the very least, he was not afraid to experience and know the world.

Then everything changed, as if a light were switched on, and he left the comfort of his home and started his ministry. Jesus faced extraordinary challenges and overcame them through grit, determination, courage, intelligence and imagination. He was a real man who conducted a real ministry, who spoke real words through parables and aphorisms, and who masterfully wove his personal experiences into these stories without much notice.

The book is written as a dialogue because its informality, intimacy and authenticity allow the reader fast and simple access to surprising and thorny possibilities and ideas. A hypothetical conversation over coffee and a meal while watching a monsoon in the comfort of a living room or café seemed more appropriate than an academic presentation of proof, fact, argument and conclusion. In addition, the dialogue suggests Jesus is knowable and *one of us* and that is an essential feature of the conversation. At times, I introduced my personal experiences into the dialogue when I thought it necessary to present a similar occurrence, expand on a theme, introduce a new one, or move an idea or the conversation into new territory.

I also must confess that I did not always know the answer to the questions I asked Jesus. Though my knowledge of him and Christianity is extensive, at times I found it either incomplete or insufficient and was pushed to further contemplate and research for a plausible answer. I avoided any theological reason, answer or conclusion and did not revert back to any. The point of *Interviewing Jesus* was to remove the theological shroud and symbolic grandeur, and replace each with an unpolished gritty human image.

The more questions I asked, the closer I got to the clues; the more clues I discovered, the more I was able to reconstruct Jesus' history and intentions. Incrementally, a fuzzy portrait appeared. My research and curiosity allowed me to peek into Jesus' missing years, his personal history and his ministry with new eyes.

Even though I could not clearly see every detail, I knew where and how to look. By drilling down and boring deep, by putting two and two together, by comparing and contrasting and connecting historical dots, I discovered another side to Jesus. I cannot claim with absolute certainty that Jesus experienced what I state or that he said the words I uttered, but I made every attempt at the appearance of truth, possibility and probability. Each conclusion and inference about Jesus' life and his experiences presented in *Interviewing Jesus* are educated guesses resulting from my theories, deductive reasoning, intuitions and research.

Interviewing Jesus portrays and re-imagines a man of the Father who lived his life, at first, for himself and later for others. His life was a journey of self-discovery, transformation and self-sacrifice rather than a god performing divine acts and miracles.

I hope the reader's heart and mind will fill with awe and surprise as they did for me. His life, actions and words changed lives and redirected the course of history. He is an extraordinary individual who needs to be re-examined in light of his life and accomplishments.

David Collis

ACKNOWLEDGMENTS

I think of my life as an ongoing, romantic living odyssey. It is one thing to explore and discover the subject and the material for this book, it is quite another to write about it. *Interviewing Jesus* would not have been possible without the steadfast support and belief of my bride Deborah Mulvihill; the patient listening and encouragement of Otto Lacayo; the charity, kindness and love of Jim and Sandi Collis; the seasoned skill of my editor, Linda Jenkins; and the entrepreneurial conviction of my publisher, Justin Sachs.

I also want to express my deep appreciation to Brent Baldwin, Ann Boland, Andreas Carlsson, Desmond Child, Arnold Esser, Juliet Goff, John van Horn, Mary Ellen Korn, Mark McMahon, Stan Palasek, Kerry Palframan, Jennifer Perrette, Lynn Wiese Sneyd and Scott Sturgis for their contribution, willing support or spot-on advice.

There is a saying, "When the student is ready the master appears." In my case, when the book was taking shape pillars of support appeared. *Interviewing Jesus* left the harbor and sailed the open sea because of them, and for that I owe a debt of gratitude.

REFERENCE NOTES

Throughout *Interviewing Jesus*, I quote scripture, the lost Gospel Q, the Gospel of Thomas and other historical sources. In each case, the source is identified either in mid-sentence or at the end of the sentence.

I have used the following abbreviations:

JC = Jesus Christ

DC = David Collis

MT = Gospel of Matthew

MK = Gospel of Mark

LK = Gospel of Luke

JN = Gospel of John

THOM = Gospel of Thomas

Q = Lost Gospel Quill Document

I believe the biblical annotations are self-explanatory.

CHAPTER 1

GENESIS

A soft knock at the front door rings out and the door swings open.

David Collis: Hello, welcome to my home. Please come in. I want you to know I am deeply honored that you accepted my offer for this interview.

Jesus Christ: I'd like to walk the labyrinth in your front yard before we finish today.

DC: Would you like to walk it now?

JC: No. I can wait. The view of your mountains reminds me of Mount Hermon.

DC: The dark clouds looming over the tops will bring rain, thunder and lightning. That will be exciting. I'd like to conduct the interview here in the living room.

JC: I see your library over there and I'd like to look at it first.

DC: Please.

Jesus crosses the short distance and reviews the titles.

JC: History, warfare, human psychology, art, science, philosophy, Judaism and Christianity. I see you have books about me. We didn't have books; only scrolls and codices.

DC: I like books and I consider them friends.

JC: Shall we get started?

DC: Would you like coffee, tea or water?

JC: Water.

Moments later, as Jesus settles into his seat with a glass full of water.

DC: I'm going to open with a brief biographical description and overview and then begin the interview.

JC: All right.

DC: (as Narrator) Jesus of Nazareth was born to Mary and Joseph; he had four brothers – James, Joseph, Simon and Judas (MT 13:55) – and unnamed sisters. Throughout his life, he either moved or lived in various places: Bethlehem, Egypt, Nazareth, Capernaum, Tyre, and Sidon. At times, he was without a roof over his head; other times without a place to stay. He claims he was a prophet without honor in his hometown. Others, like the Apostle Paul, John the Baptist and other New Testament writers, claim he was God incarnate; the Son of God, the Logos made flesh, the Savior who washed away the sins of the world, the Sacrificial Lamb.

DC: (as Narrator, cont'd) The fourth century was pivotal in crystallizing Christianity into the Catholic religion we know today. Currently Jesus has over two billion worshippers, not including those from the past two millennia. His legacy contributed in shaping the Western world. He influenced the visual arts, literature, music, and architecture, not to mention the history of the Church, laws, ethics and morality. He is the central figure in one of the largest religions in the world.

DC: (as Narrator, cont'd) Who is this intriguing man? Much has been said about Jesus, much written and much blood spilled in his name. Perplexing questions persist: Was he human? Was he divinely inspired? Was he a simple servant in service of the Father and humanity? Or is he the Son of God as the New Testament proclaims and he is the Good News? Is he accurately portrayed or is there something missing? What do his ministry and Wisdom Sayings reveal about the man? Let's hear from Jesus the son of Joseph, the prophet from Nazareth.

DC: Thank you for coming. It is exciting to have you here.

JC: "Peace to this house." (LK 10:5)

DC: Thank you. Peace is an important pillar of your teaching. You say, "Blessed are the peacemakers, for they will be called the children of God." (MT 5:9) Immediately you equate action with the inclusion or identification with family; in other words, one belongs to a group.

JC: Peace is important. It is fragile, but it can become strong if nurtured and developed. It is sweet fruit for harvest.

DC: Is it an internal or external reality? Can it be achieved in society? The Messiah was expected to bring peace.

JC: Peace is known regardless of the demands placed on us by work or family, or by the turmoil and uncertainty in society.

DC: It appears peace was personal, but there was a social dimension to it as well. Did your society know peace?

JC: Partially. Our social reality was tense, peace was ultimately hollow and the hand of Rome was heavy. The Romans courted the wealthy and privileged with favor. If one was so graced, peace was experienced, but it came at a price. Peace in Galilee, on the other hand, was known differently.

DC: Just to confirm, during your time, two political jurisdictions existed. The Hasmoneans governed and ruled one area, and the Romans governed and ruled the other.

JC: That is correct. The one region was given to Herod and his lineage through Roman decree: Galilee, Idumea and Samaria. The other was governed by a Roman citizen loyal to and appointed by Caesar.

DC: That was Judea. You knew peace and I believe you knew it transcended external, material and social conditions.

JC: The peace I knew was not tethered to external conditions. It was an inward reality of the heart, of the mind, and of the Father. I taught my followers and disciples to know it and then to share it. Of course, my hope was that the Jews as a whole would know the peace I knew, but that proved overly ambitious.

DC: The Apostle Paul uses the word *peace* prolifically at the opening of his letters, and he uses it as a concept when he says, "And the peace of God, which transcends all understanding ..." (Philippians 4:7)

JC: I wasn't the only one who knew peace. Many did. When I came to know the Father, I came to know peace and I shared that peace with others. It was an essential element to my ministry.

DC: As this interview unfolds I'm going to ask you many things about your life and ministry. I want to know what motivated you and what inspired you. At times, I want to weave my story into the dialogue and share how I came to know you. Is that all right?

JC: Yes it is.

DC: Your life and ministry are intimately woven together. I want to mention something before we get started. Throughout this interview, I will refer to your collective body of sayings as Wisdom Sayings.

JC: I can accept that.

DC: Your Wisdom Sayings reflect both your life and ministry, and your ministry reflected the social dynamics of your time.

JC: I can't be removed from my era, nor can I be completely understood outside it. All my experiences, whether joyful and painful or sacred and profane, shaped my life and how I came to experience the Father. My ministry was an inevitable consequence.

DC: You felt you didn't have a choice?

JC: I had a choice, but my heart moved consistently in one direction. Following another path would not have felt right, nor would it have been satisfying or given me a sense of purpose.

DC: Is that Fate working?

JC: Some would agree with that.

DC: Did you always know what you wanted to do in life?

JC: No. It lay hidden, but then again life is hidden within mystery; one's purpose in life is not always clear. Time acts as the revealer.

DC: Some people know their purpose early and follow their path closely. Others are not as fortunate, but I can't believe you didn't know what you wanted to do with your life.

JC: Not at first. I had a heart for the divine, and a mind to peer into it and to know something about it, but I had to learn many lessons before I set out on my ministry. In that sense, it was a slow steady progression. When the time arrived, I was clear and I acted like Moses confronting the pharaoh. I was driven with purpose.

DC: Few details remain of your life prior to your ministry. We know you were born to Joseph and Mary sometime at the end of King Herod the Great's reign in 4 BCE and the beginning of the Roman occupation in 6 CE. It is said your family fled to Egypt; you were precocious in the ways of God, and you and your family celebrated Passover in Jerusalem. It is also written that you lived in the Galilee and were a carpenter or builder. Aside from these scant details, little written evidence remains of your life, especially between the ages of twelve and thirty. All in all, the New Testament canon is tight-lipped and fragmentary at best, and when it reveals something about you it appears to be driven theologically rather than historically. I am attempting to piece your history back together in the hopes of developing a more complete portrait of you.

JC: For what purpose?

DC: To understand what happened to you and what you experienced, and how events and circumstances affected your ministry and influenced your decisions.

JC: All right. I will share a few things. But first I'd like to know about your research. What did you do?

DC: I dug deep and investigated many strands. I learned ancient history, learned about ancient Mediterranean religions, investigated Roman and Jewish customs and practices, and read a vast array of religious and philosophic literature.

JC: Do you honestly believe you know me or my past from my sayings?

DC: I don't want to seem arrogant or prideful, but I think I understand more than the New Testament revealed. I believe I know another, more personal dimension of your story and history.

JC: How so?

DC: Your sayings reveal your character, thoughts and personality. I got to know you because of your sayings.

JC: Tell me what you discovered.

DC: I'd like to start by mentioning that it was important for me to separate you and your humanity from Christian theology. Christianity mixes the two together like leaven and yeast. I want to know your personal history and specific details. Unfortunately, traditional Christianity and Gnosticism offer very little in this regard. Most of your surviving first-century biography is prejudiced one way or another.

JC: What did you do?

DC: I contemplated and speculated. I imagined your life would crack open if I asked a series of leading questions. So I asked one question after another. The issue was how to draw out your history from the surviving accounts.

JC: What questions did you ask?

DC: What motivated you to start your ministry? Did you have a powerful supernatural experience beforehand? Why did you go to John the Baptist? What did you bring to the table before you went to John? What did your death mean to you? As I asked these questions, in the back of my mind I was thinking, "Your ministry reflects your missing years and your missing years reflect your ministry."

JC: Did you crack open my missing years?

DC: Partially.

JC: Tell me about that.

DC: New Testament scholars separated your sayings into two groups. The first group contained accepted and genuine sayings, while the other contained sayings your editors and biographers attributed to you for theological reasons.

JC: While I was on ministry it occurred to me that might happen. I had a gift to sense the future, and because of my intuition I habitually repeated myself in every town and village I visited and in every sermon I gave. I wanted my disciples and followers to remember my teachings and sayings.

DC: The early Christian writers told and edited your story through exaggeration, minimization and invention. They mixed *Midrash* into the storyline and combed through the Old Testament – that is our term for the Torah – for prophetic details and verses. They then inserted these verses into the gospel. If I counted correctly the Gospel of Matthew has thirty-seven such utterances alone.

JC: Would you say they created a new image of me?

DC: Yes, and one way they controlled the message was turning you into a symbol.

JC: Tell me about your understanding of symbolism in reference to the New Testament.

DC: One potent Jewish symbol adopted by the early Christians was the Messiah.

JC: The Messiah embodied a collective Jewish hope in desperate times and was prophesized in the Torah. Jewish people anticipated an anointed one who would lead the people back to God, restore the peace and the social equilibrium, and overthrow the Romans.

DC: The Messiah was also a person the people would naturally want to follow. I'd like to mention that the Christians stretched the meaning. I surmise years after your death, when they presented their message to the Hellenized world, few could appreciate the depth and meaning of the Jewish Messiah. To overcome this deficiency, Christian leaders felt the need to reinvent you, or re-symbolize you, in order to capture the heart and imagination of the Greco-Roman followers. The symbolism expanded to include the Lamb of God, the Son of God, and the Savior of the World. They needed to have a more robust, complete and comprehensive image of the man they transformed into a living God. They then fused this new image into a seamlessly woven mythic narrative.

JC: The symbols of which you speak were not unique to Christians. That was a cultural practice in my time. People were in the habit of searching for poetic terms to emphasize the importance of an event or person, and it didn't matter whether the event or person had positive or negative value. Significance was noted and symbolism applied either way.

DC: I noticed that pattern. I see it in the term *Abomination of Desolation*, which refers either to the Seleucid king Antiochus Epiphanes, who sacrificed a pig in the Holy of Holies of the Jewish Temple and turned the sacred space into a heathen space. I see it in any other heathen act of consequence committed inside the Jerusalem Temple, such as the placing of a statue of Zeus in it. I'm thinking out loud; I can think of a few others. A similar pattern developed within the Essene community. At some point in Essene history, a rift developed between two men over theology and practice and they subsequently separated. Some people stayed with the Teacher of Righteousness while others left with the Wicked Priest. The term *Teacher of Righteousness* shows the reverence and respect the main group had for their leader, while *Wicked Priest* reveals the group's disdain for the dissenter and traitor. Again, the point is to witness the invention of poetic terms. As I mentioned previously, the Christians coined the terms *Son of God*, *Lamb of God* and *Savior of the World*. They also amplified the significance of Messiah to mean God, not just one anointed by God, and conceived the term *Antichrist*, which means anyone in opposition to you and them. Clever!

JC: Each term is emotionally charged and is a quick identifier, but back to your earlier response: You don't agree with my post-resurrection symbolism.

DC: I've been involved, on and off, with Christianity since my early twenties, and as a young man I accepted the symbolism completely. As I matured, though, I questioned the meaning and intent of the Son of God, Lamb of God and Savior of the World. Eventually I saw through the symbols when I had an "ah-ha" moment. I realized you were a man who lived a life but that your last years were dedicated to the divine. You were not an abstract symbol. You were, however, a living sacrifice to the divine reality you knew. The weight of that revelation stunned me.

JC: Did your religious world crumble after that revelation?

DC: No. It happened to be one of many spiritual experiences I've had over the years. Each epiphany, each experience, each vision and revelation either peeled back or dissolved a layer of my world view, perceptions and beliefs, and opened me to see and know new possibilities.

JC: Your eyes were open and you removed that which no longer served you because you had eyes to see something different.

DC: Yes. I watched despondently as each Christian symbol broke apart before my eyes – Son of God, Messiah, Lamb of God and Savior of the World. I was not inspired or swayed by them any longer. I was grateful to them. They served a purpose by grounding and providing me with a sense of the divine, but over time they lost their significance for me. If I were to go back to them and believe in them as before I would consider it a step backward, a hindrance and detriment to my growth and evolution.

JC: What happened after this insight?

DC: Oddly, after some time, I found myself deeply interested in your personal story. I wanted to know what happened to you and I realized John the Baptist played a pivotal role in your development. I then found myself intrigued by your life before and after your time with John. Each part captivated me.

JC: Explain how that captivated you.

DC: Let me explain that I first had to strip away the stratified layers of Christianity I had spent years learning. Theology acts like a lens that focuses on Christian tenets, beliefs, doctrines, rites, ritual and scripture. Unfortunately, it inhibits and prevents the discovery of your humanity, history and personality. To get at the heart of the real historical Jesus and to understand your motives and intentions, I had to set aside Christian theology. It is much easier to appreciate and understand the theological Jesus than it is to know the historical Jesus.

JC: Now I understand the reason for this interview. What do you hope to gain?

DC: I want to appreciate your psychology and personal story. I want to know your inspirations, interests and motivations. I want to know the events that transformed you, what excited you and what upset you. I want to know what compelled you to initiate and conduct your ministry. Why would you embark on such an ambitious project in the first place? I want to know this and I want to reassemble as much of your life as possible. Unfortunately, the New Testament canon hampers my intentions, or so it seems. Your entire story is crafted specifically and theologically; it is directed to an explicit end. I do not have the tolerance nor do I have the willingness to accept another's theological perspective. I have eyes to see for myself and can draw my own conclusions.

JC: You are implying that my past lies buried in shadow.

DC: Yes, and shining a light into that shadow is my intention. I can't help but stop and marvel at your accomplishments. You had a transformational effect on people. You inspired your disciples and followers to follow in your footsteps, and they went out and transformed their world in your name. This is no small feat. Without you there is no inspiration and there is no heart to transform the world. How can one man inspire so many to accomplish so great a thing? That is a phenomenal achievement. So my interest in your beginnings is not unreasonable.

JC: No, it is not. If I can use your words, before I could transform the world, I had to transform myself. I was entrenched and misguided by my emotions, thinking, perspectives and prejudices. I was conditioned by my society and my religion. But I was not the only one entrenched and misguided. My society was as well; we were ensnared in a web because of our allegiances, practices, thinking and traditions.

DC: Explain that to me. How did you need to transform? And what occurred in your society?

JC: Let me start with my society. Misery flowed like a river, confusion filled our hearts, hunger gnawed at our bellies and blindness covered our eyes. Our hearts were hard as rocks while our minds festered with cynicism. The world was viewed as hopeless, brutal, godless and irrational, and life itself seemed like a plague. Our politics served the affluent and punished the underprivileged; our religious practices were outdated and the Roman hand pressed down on us firmly.

DC: How did you and your ministry address or alleviate this situation?

JC: My message of love galvanized listeners and my miracles healed the infirm. Cold hearts warmed and cynicism softened. I offered hope to the hopeless, redemption to the downtrodden, wisdom to the seeker and compassion to haters.

DC: We spoke earlier about your personal transformation, and this embodies your missing years. I'd like to circle back and address the content of your missing years. I know what you did in your ministry. Now I want to know how you got there.

JC: Do you think my missing years are more important than my ministry?

DC: Not at all. Your missing years are another side to your humanity and I'm just as interested in your personal story as I am in your ministry!

JC: All right! You said you explored my past and that you peered into it? Explain how you did that.

DC: I collected your sayings and organized them thematically. I looked for small clues, suggestions and patterns, and then catalogued my findings.

JC: What were they?

DC: I found issues involving money and no money, banquets, food and drinking wine. I noticed traveling, sailing, digging trenches, and conversing with the poor and dispossessed. I saw an impassioned anger toward the religious establishment, and I saw connections to horticulture, merchants and farming. Your sayings also discuss robbery and thievery, lost and found, quiet and lonely places, inheritance, arrogance and pride, heartlessness and compassion, and wisdom and stupidity. Separately these bits and pieces do not amount to much, but collectively they paint a vague yet noticeable individual portrait.

JC: Suppose you knew my history. Would that matter? What would you do with that knowledge?

DC: I haven't thought that through, at least not to the end. I might try to introduce my discoveries into society and see if the new portrait I am seeing gains traction.

JC: I have my doubts; a new polished image of an old God? I don't see the point.

DC: You were the one who said, "… seek and you will find; knock and the door will be opened to you." (MT 7:7)

JC: Those words are not about me and they point in several directions – to the Father, the Kingdom of Heaven, and the adventure in living life outside the prescribed rules and beyond the boundary of fears.

DC: One thing I noticed in your sayings is that you were willing to take risks and be adventurous like an entrepreneur.

JC: What do you mean by *entrepreneur?* I don't know the word.

DC: An entrepreneur is a person with a product who fearlessly goes out into the world, marketing and selling that product to customers, and who willingly accepts the risk and responsibilities of that enterprise. I see you as an entrepreneur whose product was the Father, the Kingdom of Heaven, compassion and wisdom.

JC: We had a tradition of such a person but we used *prophet* instead. You mentioned earlier that my ministry reflects my missing years and my missing years reflect my ministry. What did you mean?

DC: My hypothesis is that one thing reflects another; that the big reflects the small and the small reflects the big. The logic works like this. Suppose I see a very large cargo ship on the ocean stacked high with containers. I can't see the harbor to which it is sailing, but I can assume the harbor must be large to accommodate the size of the ship. Conversely, if I was at the large harbor and saw massive cranes, rail cars and trucks, I could safely conclude that all this large equipment is not for a small sailboat or motorboat. In other words, the large harbor was built for a very large ship. Even though I cannot see the other I know it must exist – the scale and complexity of each simply requires the other. In the same manner, your ministry reflects your missing years and your missing years reflect your ministry.

JC: Anything else?

DC: I sensed you were one thing at an early age and something else when you started your ministry. I noticed an arc of transformation like a caterpillar turning into a butterfly. It was then that I realized you deliberately hid your personal story. I would guess a handful of disciples and followers knew, but you leaned toward secrecy. I also believe the New Testament writers hid your past but for different reasons. Why did you do that?

JC: To keep people focused on my actions and words.

DC: You were deliberate and calculating, and felt the need to minimize your history because those facts didn't promote your message or image. You were a man of theater who wanted to grab people's attention and snap them from their stupor and sleep. If the people who followed you and if the men who became your disciples knew you were privileged, arrogant and prideful, your ministry and message might have lost its ring; maybe the magical luster would have tarnished. You wanted to be poor to speak and minister to the poor, the sick and the downcast. You became one of them to bring a new bright light of the divine. They would listen to your message; the privileged as a whole would not. As you say, "It is not the healthy who need a doctor, but the sick." (MK 2:17) You felt their pain. You wanted them to be healed and to be renewed with hope. Sacredness fills life; it has meaning. You knew that.

JC: I was accused by my detractors of being a glutton and a drunkard who spent time with sinners and tax collectors. To conduct my ministry effectively I had to separate myself from my family and from others who wanted me to be something I was not.

DC: You were also the type of man who enjoyed trouble.

JC: I poked fun at and challenged certain ideas and traditions while directly testing other expectations. I did what was necessary and I did not confine myself to one prescribed method.

DC: At the same time, it was necessary to distinguish yourself from all the other self-prescribed messiahs. Please don't get me wrong. I'm not judging or condemning you for what you did or how you did it. Far from it!

JC: I knew my message was hard to fathom and digest. I created a variety of tools and used them appropriately and accordingly to jolt people's attention.

DC: We've stepped into a territory I want to save for a later discussion. For now, I want to circle back and mention that I recognized my story in your stories. Some of our experiences overlap, and once I understood this I could see you more clearly.

JC: How so?

DC: I was raised during an economic boom. My father was a licensed contractor and developer who capitalized on the real estate market. I listened to stories about money and investment. I was educated. I spent time with my parents' friends who were like-minded. We had gatherings at our home. We belonged to a club. I had a heart for God. I found myself searching for my place in the world and I felt I had to search for God even though I had a heart for him. I attended church – your church. I turned away and looked elsewhere. I saw the ills of society, I traveled in search of the sacred, and I learned a craft and built things with my hands.

JC: What did you build?

DC: Houses, furniture, cabinets, movie props and sculptures.

JC: Your library does not reflect your last comments. Now I'm curious. I'd like to know if you had a teacher or if you had a community that taught you.

DC: I went to school and college and had numerous teachers, but there was neither a single person nor a single group who taught me. Many men and women entered my life and provided me with unique perspectives, new insights and wisdom.

JC: Books were not your only source.

DC: That is correct, but enough about me. I want to know about you. Let's talk about the influence your Jewish culture and heritage had on you.

JC: They were like leaven and yeast, and once mixed they could not be separated. I experienced the world as a Jew. I lived in Galilee and grew up in Nazareth. My people as a whole lived according to Jewish customs and law, and were filled with Jewish hopes and expectations. You must remember I was born in a time of Roman occupation. This was a perpetual thorn in our side. One couldn't look the other way and say it wasn't a problem. It was and it affected everyone in some manner.

DC: Tell me about the Messianic hope during the first century. How prevalent was it?

JC: It was in the air. It was on everyone's mind and stirred in everyone's heart. One couldn't help but wonder how circumstances would unfold.

DC: From my research, aspects of the Jewish religion were questioned. Other religious or philosophical ideas circulated, different views of the afterlife gained traction and a new identity definition emerged.

JC: That's true. Communities sprung up in the wilderness. Revolts broke out. People questioned the efficacy of the Temple order. Identification of our father, Abraham, waned in light of the new inner community. It was a dynamic period. To say otherwise would be an understatement.

DC: How did your family react? Actually, let's discuss your family first and get to their response later. To the Jewish culture, family is a central value. The gospels are narrowly specific in regard to your family. They tend to minimize your family and I believe that is intentional. With that, I have several questions regarding your upbringing and family and we can dovetail them together. Generally, what can you tell me?

JC: We were devout and adhered to the dietary and purity conventions. We celebrated the various festivals and Holy Days, and frequently traveled to Jerusalem for Passover. We were observant, believed in our history and heritage, and frankly we couldn't see ourselves differently.

DC: The Hellenistic world view of the Greeks and Romans didn't affect you?

JC: That depends on what you mean by *affect*. Everyone was affected. If you became a more devout Jew you were affected because you wanted deeper roots into Judaism rather than foreign influences. If you allowed Hellenism into your heart and gave it room you were affected by it; one was half in and the other half out. One couldn't ignore it or look the other way. It was pervasive.

DC: There is more to the saying "No one can serve two masters," (MT 6:24) and to the "house divided" analogy. (MK 3:25) I surmise one couldn't be part Jewish either.

JC: Again the implication of these sayings had teeth. Many people were perplexed and baffled by the steady changes occurring in our society. Many questions were raised and the Roman occupation and influence exacerbated the problems.

DC: This interview explores some of these changes, but I'd like to set that aside for now and talk about your family. Would you consider yourself, or your family for that matter, progressive or conservative?

JC: I'd say traditional, but that is not to say we didn't have doubts about the Romans, our royal lineage, and a concern or two about the priests and temple practices. When I began my ministry, the family had to evaluate their traditional position, especially in light of my message of the Father.

DC: Did you question your religious roots?

JC: Uncertainty crept into my mind.

DC: At what point did it creep into your mind?

JC: Before I went to John the Baptist. I embraced my roots at first, but my experience of the Father left profound insights and affected me in a manner I did not initially appreciate.

DC: Questioning your roots and successfully navigating the transition from your Jewish traditions to the understanding of the Father was no small matter. It was a sizable shift.

JC: And necessary.

DC: I just thought of this. I can now appreciate a saying in the Gospel of Thomas attributed to you: "If you bring forth what is within you, what you have will save you." (THOM 70)

JC: In this context, the saying speaks for itself. As you mentioned earlier one must do, move, try and be free of debilitating doubt and fear in order to achieve.

DC: You said, "If you have faith as small as a mustard seed, you can say to this mountain, 'Move from here to there' and it will move." (MT 17:20)

JC: You see life is present in action. Faith resides in the action which is tied to purpose. Recognize the wisdom of that. Faith and action are two sides of the same coin.

DC: One must have faith and be willing to act in order to bring forth what is inside oneself.

JC: Otherwise that truth, whatever it may be, will putrefy in its dormancy.

DC: You used the analogy of a man building "a house on the ground without a foundation. The moment the torrent struck that house, it collapsed and its destruction was complete." (LK 6:49)

JC: Yes, I did. It points to a fundamental truth I understood.

DC: That truth, faith, purpose, compassion and mercy are tied together in relationship, as similarly as a family is tied together between siblings, parents, cousins, aunts and uncles. It is not transactional like buying an animal for ritual sacrifice.

JC: I came to know that the former was more important and truthful than the latter.

DC: Your father Joseph is mentioned briefly in the Gospels of Matthew and Luke, but after you turned twelve he is not mentioned again. Neither the Gospel of Mark nor the Gospel of John speaks of him. I can't help but believe he influenced you. Tell me about him. What was he like? What was his character? What did he believe?

JC: He was complex, principled and conservative, with a strong religious, moral and ethical ground. He was guided by the wisdom and teachings of the Torah. At the same time, he was sharp and shrewd with money. He had a gift of seeing opportunities where others could not. He knew when and how to seize the moment to take action and was not afraid to act. Calculating opportunity and understanding risk was his wisdom. There was another quality I admired about my father. He was charitable, although he was in the habit of announcing his charity.

DC: What did you do at night? Did you tell stories? Did Joseph? I ask this because you are an excellent orator and it makes me believe you were encouraged to speak your mind at an early age.

JC: Joseph told stories at night. Sometimes he captivated us with stories concerning his travels to Egypt, his business deals, and the stories and wisdom contained within the Torah. He obtained a scroll from the Jewish elders because of his influence with them. At times, I told the stories because I was eloquent and captivating!

DC: You were good at it. Sounds like you were a bit of a showman.

JC: I liked words, ideas and religious concepts, and I spoke about my favorite theme, which was the God of our forefathers.

DC: Did you go to synagogue?

JC: Regularly.

DC: Tell me about your mother, Mary. I get the impression she had a dignity about her that was diplomatic, genuine and sensitive. I also believe she was a good mother, and that she was astute and loyal.

JC: She was even-tempered and cared for her family passionately. Her aptitude for cooking was exceptional; no one ever complained about her meals.

DC: Did they put a smile on your face?

JC: Not only mine but, at times, on our neighbors' as well.

DC: Is there anything else you can tell me about her?

JC: She was insightful with an inner strength, she too told stories because she was wise, and she had an ability to experience the supernatural.

DC: Meaning the Archangel Gabriel?

JC: That wasn't the only supernatural encounter.

DC: Maybe your family was mystically or intuitively inclined.

JC: That thread ran in my family. It ran in me. I was gifted in that respect. Most of my family, though, was devout and observant, firmly rooted in the here and now.

DC: Can you elaborate on your mother's brand of storytelling?

JC: She had rhythm, cadence, tone and inflection. Many characters filled her stories and she was notorious for surprise endings.

DC: Can you recall any?

JC: Not offhand, but when I shaped a parable I often thought of her characters and endings. I added exaggeration. Oh yes, I remember a story she was fond of telling. It was of my birth and of the star of Bethlehem.

DC: Did you feel she was capable and competent, maybe as a teacher?

JC: Yes. Had she been given the chance she would have been a good teacher, but at the time women were not allowed to teach.

DC: You wanted to change that custom?

JC: I addressed it in my ministry. That's why I had women disciples.

DC: Did you encourage Mary to teach?

JC: I wanted her to develop her voice, but she was not allowed a strong one; my father frowned upon my encouragements and didn't think it was right or appropriate. We didn't see eye to eye on that. A whisper was all right, but not a loud voice. At the same time, it was not in Mary's character to lead. Instead, she encouraged and supported me in my pursuits.

DC: I wonder if Mary recognized something in you that was different from your siblings.

JC: Of course, she loved all my brothers and sisters equally. Occasionally, she took me aside and told me that I possessed a certain light that my brothers and sisters did not. When she told stories about me, particularly about my birth, my siblings became jealous and a rivalry developed. They thought I was more special and gifted and received more of Mother's attention.

DC: Did you play it down?

JC: No.

DC: I'm reminded of the story of Jacob and Joseph. Joseph's siblings were jealous over Jacob's favor to him.

JC: Jacob's favoritism and the multicolored-coat gift aggravated and upset his brothers. That is why they sold him into slavery. I can appreciate Joseph's experience.

DC: In one instance, your brothers teased or goaded you to go to Judea saying, "'Leave Galilee and go to Judea, so that your disciples there may see the works you do. No one who wants to become a public figure acts in secret. Since you are doing these things, show yourself to the world.' For even his own brothers did not believe him." (JN 7:3–5) They also said, "He is out of his mind." (MK 3:21)

JC: It took a long time before they acknowledged or recognized my ministry.

DC: Ecclesiastical history portrays Mary as the Mother of God. Would you agree with that? Is that how you saw her?

JC: As I mentioned, she was generous and loving, good-natured and sensitive, and a loyal and devout mother. So the answer to that question is no! None of my family would have accepted or agreed with that title. As a family, we disagreed and feuded, but none of us would ever accept that kind of statement.

DC: Again, ecclesiastical history portrays her as a perpetual virgin.

JC: That is very peculiar, isn't it? It fits into their theology more than it does in history. It's difficult to fathom how they drew that conclusion. A simple question resolves the issue: "How could she be a virgin and have me at the same time?" The truth of the matter is that she was a young girl when I was born, not a virgin.

DC: They call it the Immaculate Conception. In the story, God comes to Mary, who was innocent, pure and virginal. He impregnates her and she later gives birth to the divine child – namely you. At the opposite end of this story is the account of the pure and innocent Sacrificial Lamb who takes away the dark sins of mankind. Of course, the innocent lamb is also you. I can't help but be reminded of other virgins – the Roman Vestal Virgins – who perpetually kept the sacred fire of Rome burning in the Roman forum. Virginity, it seems, is a consistent theme from two different cultures.

JC: Ecclesiastical history is in the habit of portraying my family inaccurately.

DC: Your brothers and sisters were turned into stepbrothers and stepsisters.

JC: By way of implication, my father Joseph was previously married?

DC: That is the implication. Another detail was added – he was much older than Mary.

JC: I didn't have an extended family, nor did I have half brothers or sisters.

DC: I find this part of your family rather intriguing because the Mother of God – the Virgin Mother – motif plays a key role in the Christian religion. I don't accept the premise or its reality, but it conforms to other mythic accounts recorded in history. Numerous male infants were born to women impregnated by a God, and all the boys grew to become men of distinction. The common denominator among them is that they were remarkable and extraordinary, and they affected human history and its direction. Offhand I can think of Hercules, Alexander the Great, Dionysus and Pythagoras. Rebecca, Isaac's wife, bore the twins Jacob and Esau. And then there's you, Jesus. From the East we have Buddha, Lao Tzu and Confucius. You made the list.

JC: This is curious. When I started my ministry, I didn't view myself as remarkable or extraordinary, just devoted.

DC: Were you aware of any incidents or stories regarding the divine or other worldly beings impregnating human females?

JC: I recall two stories from Genesis: "the sons of God went to the daughters of humans and had children by them." (Gen 6:4) The other, as you previously mentioned, Isaac's wife, Rebecca, was beyond child-bearing years but miraculously gave birth to twins nevertheless. (Gen 25:20–22) So yes, this idea was not without scriptural precedence.

DC: A celestial event revolves around your birth.

JC: You are speaking of the star of Bethlehem.

DC: I am. The star of Bethlehem dovetails into another prophecy known at the time as the Star Prophecy, which had Messianic significance. The fact that your parents gave you your name Jesus, which means *savior*, does not seem coincidental. Rather it appears calculated and possibly influenced by political and religious events during the time of your birth.

JC: You don't agree with the supernatural occurrences surrounding my conception and birth? You don't think they are accurate?

DC: The star of Bethlehem is an episode referenced in the Gospel of Luke. The Archangel Gabriel appears to Mary and tells her she is carrying the divine child and that he is to be named Jesus. (LK 1:31, 2:21) The Gospel of Matthew tells a slightly different version. Could your name have been inspired differently? I wonder. Mary and Joseph may have thought the name Jesus appropriate because of that visible celestial object shooting across the sky, or maybe they were inspired by the revolt occurring at the same time. Or maybe they were inspired by both. Are any of these plausible assumptions?

JC: A shining star, which all could see because of its brightness, flew over our land about the time the revolt started. The Pharisee Judas the Galilean and his followers set out on a terrible and vicious campaign of murdering people, burning houses to the ground, slaughtering farm animals and destroying Galilean villages and towns. It was an ugly and hostile affair.

DC: If you don't mind, I'd like to talk about this revolt shortly. But before we do, we were discussing your name.

JC: What do you suppose is in a name?

DC: I think a lot. I believe the names of your brothers lend credence to this idea. You and your brothers are named after historical, important and recognizable Hebrew men. This is significant. I can peek into the minds of your parents and see with whom they identify.

JC: My parents were proud of their Jewish heritage and embraced their history passionately. They couldn't separate themselves from it, for Joseph "was faithful to the law." (MT 1:19)

DC: Your brothers are James, Joseph, Simon and Judas. (MT 13:55) Who were they named after?

JC: James is actually Jacob in Hebrew.

DC: The name went through Latin and Greek translations and by the time it was translated into English, Jacob became James.

JC: And Jacob is the son of Isaac, the patriarch, and the name also honors my grandfather of the same name. Joseph is named after my father, who in turn is named after the son of Jacob, another patriarch. Simon and Judas are names of heroes from the Jewish Maccabean war.

DC: The names Simon and Judas also evoke political and religious nationalists.

JC: The names evoke heritage, imply freedom, and suggest adherence to God's will and following that will.

DC: Your mother, Mary, is a derivative of Mariamme. For those who do not know Mariamme, she was the granddaughter of Hyrcanus II who was the wife of Herod the Great and Queen of the Jews. Your entire family is named after powerful and influential men or women, while you are named after a person who embodies nationalist hope.

JC: I am.

DC: Maybe I am drawing conclusions that are not present, but I find this fact important because it gives me an insight into the way your parents saw themselves and what they subconsciously passed on to you. Your names were drawn and identified from patriarchs, national leaders and a Messianic savior/leader. Your names alone suggest you were out to embody and transform Israel.

JC: Don't get ahead of yourself; each one of us identified with a particular facet of our Jewish heritage. The family as a whole embraced our heritage in light of the Roman occupation and Greco-Roman influence. Factious sentiments developed along many lines.

DC: Now I'd like to discuss Judas the Galilean. There is a passage from the Book of Acts I'd like to quote: "Judas the Galilean appeared in the days of the census and led a band of people in revolt. He too was killed, and all his followers were scattered." (Acts 5:37) As we noted earlier, Judas' revolt occurred sometime around your birth.

JC: The revolt and its aftermath were kept alive in the memory of the Jews, especially among those living in and around Galilee.

DC: I presume in the Romans' as well. I'd like to explore this revolt in more detail. This passage doesn't fully capture or convey the extent, the intense feelings or the reasons for its outbreak. The passage from Acts glosses over and minimizes, which is characteristic of the author.

JC: Judas was a learned and persuasive rabbi who inspired many followers to revolt.

DC: Can you explain?

JC: The insurrection had two faces. One was the outrage over the Roman census, taxation and occupation; the other was the overt and covert Jewish acquiescence to Rome.

DC: What happened?

JC: Upon the death of Herod the Great, his son Archelaus became king. Unfortunately, he was inept and mismanaged the country. Rome sent Coponius as procurator and endowed him with full Roman authority, but Judas the Galilean objected and stirred people into revolt. He cried out, stating people would be cowards if they submitted to Rome and allowed themselves to be taxed. As a Pharisee, he understood people should serve God alone and not become slaves to Rome.

DC: Aside from his viciousness and ruthlessness was there something else that was disturbing?

JC: Instead of attacking Romans he attacked Jews, considering them enemies for submitting to Rome. He treated them as such.

DC: What did he do?

JC: You have to understand that we fought a hard and bitter campaign to rid ourselves of foreign invaders during the Maccabean War. Our victory granted us political and religious freedom – we were not bound to anyone. Judas was not willing to relinquish his freedom to any foreigner, and he deemed anyone who acquiesced to Roman rule as unworthy and guilty of infidelity. To him, normal Jewish people were hostile to Judea, like the Romans. He committed atrocities; he was barbaric, he was gratuitous in his killing and destruction, and he was merciless.

DC: He judged these people unfit to live as true and righteous Jews.

JC: As I mentioned earlier, he and his followers looted property, rounded up cattle and set dwellings on fire. He meted out just rewards, like the avenging angel of death, to anyone who accepted Roman slavery.

DC: Which cities did he attack?

JC: Sepphoris, which is near Galilee where I grew up, along with many other towns and villages.

DC: There is mention he attacked Emmaus as well. Emmaus is a village "about seven miles from Jerusalem." (LK 24:13) I find this village curious. I don't know what to make of it. It is the spot you appeared after your crucifixion to two unsuspecting men – Cleopas and another unnamed man. (LK 24:13-35) I sense that Emmaus had some historical significance that the New Testament writers felt compelled to remember, and they used a post-resurrection appearance as a point of healing for a town that was scarred from the revolt.

JC: I heard whispers Emmaus was attacked. When I entered towns and villages I saw the remnants of Judas' violence – scars remained even after many years. Damage to property was visible. What was not as obvious was the pain that lingered in the hearts of the older people.

DC: Can you tell us what happened to the revolt?

JC: The Roman garrison crushed it and Judas and his followers became martyrs.

DC: Did Judas' revolt make an impression on you and your family?

JC: Judas' treachery was not easily forgotten, as I just mentioned. This episode was stunning and left an indelible imprint on the entire Galilee. It was difficult to accept that Jews killed other Jews en masse.

DC: I can see a perplexing dilemma. After the shock, I imagine people were confused and later became angry. How did the people view this uprising? Did they accept it as punishment from God for accepting Roman rule and taxation?

JC: Many felt shame that Judas perpetrated atrocities and that we were not autonomous from the Romans. I was too young to appreciate the full consequences of this revolt and of Roman occupation, but my time came later.

DC: Several questions gnaw at me concerning your birth story. The revolt occurred sometime around your birth, either slightly before or shortly after. One, was the revolt the cause of your parents' travel to Bethlehem or the reason your family moved to Egypt? Judas the Galilean's ruthlessness would have been a good reason to leave. After all, he and his followers were slaughtering Jews who accepted the census and subsequent Roman tax. According to the Gospel of Luke, your parents traveled from Nazareth to Bethlehem for the Roman census. Two, was the relationship between the Roman census and the Star Prophecy or the star of Bethlehem contrived for theological reasons? Three, and this is not a question but a point of contention that involves Herod the Great, the Gospels of Matthew and Luke state that Herod sent henchmen throughout Israel to kill all the newborn sons in the hopes of destroying you. No historical facts, however, support the gospels' claim of this event. Rather, Herod is known for and is guilty of killing his wife, sons, brother-in-law and father-in-law because in his mind they threatened him and his throne. It should be noted that Herod's son Antipas had John the Baptist beheaded and he questioned you during your trial. When you refused to show him a miracle he got angry and handed you over to Pontius Pilate for execution. I'm not dismissing the Herod's genuine concern that their throne was threatened; I am questioning the manner in which they handled it and how it was portrayed in the gospels. The latter two stories, John's beheading and Antipas' handling of you during your trial, ring true, while the former, Herod the Great's infant massacre, does not. Not all of the above stories can be historical or factual, but somewhere in these stories lays the truth. When I examine your birth story I can accept the truth that your family was on the move; what I cannot believe are the generally accepted Christian reasons for their journey.

JC: To reiterate, I had a family; I had brothers, sisters, a mother and a father. I was Jewish. I entered this world as an infant and left it as an enlightened man. I lived a life. I had many experiences, and near the end of my life I became a living sacrifice to the Father. I walked, sat, ate, drank, slept, wept and bled. I faced my fears and my external challenges. I knew pain and anguish as well as delight and joy. I was not and my life was not a theological construction, metaphor or symbol. I merely followed my heart, I followed the Father, and I spoke and embodied the wisdom of the Father.

DC: I see in your birth story a Jewish storytelling technique called *Midrash*. What can you tell me about Midrash? Please explain its purpose and meaning.

JC: Midrash is the Jewish method of interpreting texts within the Torah. It involves the study of and the inquiry into the law and religious practice on one hand, while discovering and understanding deeper or hidden meaning of a text on the other. Each approach endeavored to clarify or resolve either an inherent problem or a seeming contradiction and they both addressed specific questions.

DC: I was taught that the Bible is the Word of God and that all the stories in it are historically accurate. Now I'm trying to get my hands around Midrash in light of the accuracy of historical events. I'm a bit confused.

JC: What confuses you?

DC: What is the scriptural relationship between actual history and history as a form of storytelling?

JC: David, please be more specific and elaborate on your dilemma.

DC: I was raised and educated in the West and I have a Western mindset. This way of thinking harkens back to the ancient Greco-Roman world. The Greek ideal of history was to recount people, events and circumstances in actual place and time to reveal motives, consequences and outcomes as they actually occurred. It is based on fact, logical sequence and cause and effect – this leads to that, which leads to that over there, which in turns leads to where I stand now. This is what I was taught. But the Jews were storytellers who saw the light of truth and history differently. If I can summarize it and as I understand it now, the Jews were more interested in the truth of an idea, principal or ethical and moral position than they were in actual history. For them history merely set the stage for a story to be told and a deeper truth to be revealed.

JC: My Jewish heritage is the birth of a nation, the Promised Land, paradise, the patriarchs, the Fall, sin, religious law and practice, and the revelation of God as recorded in the text of the Torah. In regards to the Torah the Jewish mind sought and inquired intently into the texts. The sages and religious leaders believed the Torah and history were open to interpretation to understand God more completely. They also believed that time, whether present, past or future was connected.

DC: You recognized continuity in time from the sacred past to the venerated present to the hidden future.

JC: We recognized that the truth of God is eternal and not fixed to or in time. Space and time is the point of intersection between God's revelation and action. Regardless of where one stands, the ripples of God's truth can be seen and known in every generation throughout time.

DC: Explain that to me in more detail.

JC: History is a stage of competing and interacting forces. It is between forces of right and wrong, of good and evil, and of proponents who maintain God's precepts and those who do not. It is between making a choice – right or wrong – and watching the effects and consequences of that choice throughout time. The outcome of justice versus injustice, truth versus falsehood, or faith versus unfaithfulness tells a greater moral story. Something is shown in light of the other. History contains a lesson; it shows God in action or silent in non-action. The point was to discover and understand the hidden wisdom. One had to find the connection and apply the moral truth of the story. The Midrash interpretive technique assisted one to understand history in relation to and in light of the law, the prophets and patriarchs, the temple and the Torah.

DC: The New Testament writers were aware of Midrash. In fact, the gospels were the subsequent response to their Midrash textual inquiry and interpretation.

JC: The writers were well aware of the Midrash tradition.

DC: By exploring the texts of the Torah for hidden passages the New Testament writers discovered the long-awaited Jewish Messiah. In essence, you became their textual Midrash findings, and through their textual insight and their creativity they fashioned new laws, new religious practices, new homilies and new scripture. The sacred past finally revealed itself in the venerated present. You were transmuted into the Word and the truth, and you became the one to seek and the one to be discovered. They replaced the text from the Torah with you. I want to reiterate: you were turned into the new text to be interpreted and understood.

JC: The writers were creative.

DC: Curiously, this raises a side issue. How were the seekers and inquirers affected by this discovery of you within the Torah? Creativity is an element of Midrash, as is deep contemplation. I would imagine they were thrilled to find you in many passages of the Torah.

JC: How do *you* feel? You are engaged in Midrash. Don't you see it? You are seeking intently to discover something new about me because you are troubled, and you are seeking to understand me more completely through my sayings. Are you not? After all, my sayings are words in scripture.

DC: I see that now.

JC: What was it like for you to glimpse into the shadow of my life and discover another side to me?

DC: I was awestruck and my enthusiasm kept me up at night; I couldn't sleep and my creativity raced to new heights. My discoveries led me to conduct this interview.

JC: The effects on the New Testament writers were no different.

DC: If they created new scriptures based on their findings, then I ask what I can accurately know about you in light of their textual interpretation. Which parts of your story are historically real? Who is the real Jesus?

JC: A portion of me is present in them.

DC: Then the point is to separate the chaff from the wheat.

JC: Isn't this the reason for the interview?

DC: At least one of them. We were speaking of your family and the names of your brothers before we detoured into Midrash. I suspect their names had something to do with the rebellion and that their names allude to this event.

JC: Instead of seeing it specifically in that manner I'd rather say that my family felt deeply about our traditions. The Jewish family is central to being a Jew and it is central to our religion. Family is an embodiment and expression of the sacred and it is life.

DC: I can envision the structural logic in this way: A devout family translates into a devout community, and a devout community translates into a devout nation. The small reflects the large and the large reflects the small.

JC: One cannot exist without the other and one truth exposes the truth in the other.

DC: We spoke earlier of your sibling rivalry, that your mother recounted your birth, which was an irritant, and that you possessed a special light. But I suspect other reasons exist for your sibling rivalry. Your *house divided* aphorism makes me think it encompasses more than the general "conflicts within your society" interpretation. That is the first and foremost way of understanding it, but I also see two fingers pointing in other directions.

JC: What do you mean?

DC: I see both your family and you as a *house divided*. Your statement reflects an unconscious turmoil inside of your family and inside of you.

JC: That is a sharp allegation. I was not in turmoil. I was clear when I conducted my ministry, but please don't dismiss the fact that our society was splitting apart, or that lines were drawn and differences accentuated.

DC: I'm not discounting or dismissing your society's problems. But I happen to believe your *house divided* aphorism also includes your family and, to a lesser extent, you. A number of your sayings suggest festering problems and concerns between you and your family.

JC: For instance?

DC: I'd like to talk about your family first. You say, "Who are my mother and my brothers?" (MK 3:33) Your family said, "He is out of his mind." (MK 3:21) In the Prodigal Son parable, the son demands his inheritance and leaves. (LK 15:11–13) "Still another said, 'I will follow you, Lord; but first let me go back and say good-bye to my family.' To which you replied, 'No one who puts a hand to the plough and looks back is fit for the service in the Kingdom of God.'" (LK 9:61-62) Your brothers goad you to perform miracles in Judea saying, "No one who wants to become a public figure acts in secret. Since you are doing these things, show yourself to the world." (JN 7:3–4) Your mother and Mary Magdalene are present at your crucifixion but your brothers and sisters are not; James accepts your ministry after your death, becoming the leader of the Jerusalem Church; and your father is never mentioned again after you are twelve. I see family tension in all of this.

JC: When I started my ministry, I was committed to the very end and I didn't look back. Everything I knew I gave up – family, home, friends and work – to follow a divine calling which, by the way, pressed in my heart and roared in my mind.

DC: How did your family respond when you left on your ministry? Did they feel you turned your back on them?

JC: Yes and their feelings were justified. I did turn my back on them because my ministry took on a life of its own, becoming very important. They couldn't appreciate or understand its significance in spite of my discussions prior to and during it.

DC: You didn't just wake up one morning and say, "So long everybody, I'm starting a ministry today. Oh, and by the way, I doubt I'll be back." And I seriously doubt they replied, "What a fantastic idea. We give you our blessing and wish you all the best. Before you leave can we have a group hug?"

JC: No. The conversation was fiery and tense. My decision had consequences for the entire family. But why do you suppose the *house divided* saying concerns me?

DC: I see an internal conflict simmering within you. The conflict might not have been fully active during your ministry, but an underlying current is there nonetheless; I surmise you resolved it but I don't know when that occurred. I see traces of this conflict in your Our Father prayer; I see it your desert temptations, particularly in the story when Satan offers you to be ruler of the world; and I see it in your resolve and grit to conduct your ministry, which I see as over-compensation and your need for acknowledgement and visibility. You could not live an ordinary life. An identity crisis and a genuine concern over your life's purpose and direction seem to be at the heart of this. As a teenager or young man you felt the need to accomplish something momentous, to do something incredible and to become ruler of the world. But this didn't occur. Instead, you worked with your hands as a carpenter or builder. I have to wonder if you had questions and doubts. I believe your ministry was the next best thing to soothe your restlessness; it was the necessary outlet for you to be fulfilled, and it provided your life with meaning and purpose. I think this is when you made your peace with God; before that you fought him.

JC: God cannot be seen, touched or heard with our human senses. It is believed and acted upon as real that God exists beyond the edge of our normal perceptions and outside of creation. Rarely is God known intimately unless his light or presence shines in one's heart or mind. That light is present in the beginning of one's life and continues straight through to the end. One might be aware of God's presence at the outset or one might become aware of it later; I was aware of God's presence very early in my life. What changed for me was that I finally recognized that his presence is everywhere – it is in all things at all times. I then knew I was a living temple to God, and that recognition became an intimate living reality for me. Before that, my ambitions, desires and interests had guided me, but that changed. When my will, hopes and desires became the Father's and when I fully embraced that truth my internal conflict ceased.

DC: Transitioning from "your will be done" to "the Father's will be done" is no small feat.

JC: No, it is not. It is agonizing, tumultuous and disturbing. Silencing the ego must become as natural as a flower blooming in the sun.

DC: I'd like to explore this episode of your life in more detail later, especially in relation to your experiences with John the Baptist. But for now, I'd like to make a right-hand turn and continue our discussion on your family.

JC: By all means.

DC: Historical suggestions indicate that your brothers were older, but the Gospel of Luke contradicts this understanding: "Joseph and Mary took him [Jesus] to Jerusalem to present him to the Lord (as it is written in the law of the Lord, 'Every firstborn male is to be consecrated to the Lord.'" [Exodus 13:2–12] (LK 2:22–23) Are you the first-born male?

JC: What is this line of questioning? What do you want to know?

DC: I'm trying to understand the dynamic between your personal history and your family's. I believe it is woven into your ministry. The fact that you are older places a nuance on your brother James and the role he played in your ministry or the lack of it, and it places a spotlight on your father Joseph. I see a few missing pieces to an unsolved puzzle. For instance, how did your family react when you started your ministry? Did your wisdom of the divine and your subsequent ministry cause a division in your family? And then there is this intriguing question: did James take over the family business after you left to conduct your ministry?

JC: Someone had to oversee the family affairs when I left.

DC: Your father Joseph is not referenced again in the New Testament after you were twelve. From one of your sayings I surmise he died sometime near the start of your ministry or shortly afterward. His death, in all likelihood, upset your family and threw it into turmoil and confusion.

JC: How did you arrive at that conclusion?

DC: You tell a man to follow you and he replies, "Lord, first let me go and bury my father," to which you answer, "[L]et the dead bury their own dead." (MT 8:22, LK 9:59-60) It appears this is fresh in your mind. If it is the case that your father died sometime a little before or a little after the start of your ministry, then I surmise your family was grieving and mourning, making your decision to minister at such a dreadful time all the more unconscionable.

JC: As I said previously, my decision had consequences – some unavoidable, others predictable.

DC: There is mention in some metaphysical circles that the absence of your father refers to the Widow's Son or the Son of a Widow symbol which, incidentally, was metaphorically and philosophically included in other Mediterranean religions. For example, the Egyptian falcon-headed god Horus is considered a Widow's Son. He was born from the union of Isis and Osiris and his father, Osiris, was murdered by his brother Set; hence the Widow's Son.

JC: There is also a Hebrew tradition that refers to Hiram Abiff, the chief master craftsman involved in the construction of Solomon's Temple, "whose mother was a widow from the tribe of Naphtali and whose father was from Tyre and a skilled craftsman in bronze." (1 KINGS 7:14)

DC: Each of these references has underlying mythological implications pointing to the need for a master craftsman of great skill in many disciplines, capable of applying his divine skill and insight into the construction of a temple for God. This story is masked in the New Testament gospels. From their perspective you are a carpenter, the master craftsman who, through your ministry, builds a metaphorical temple rather than a physical one.

JC: The Widow's Son also implies a mother facing her future alone in anguish, pain and fear.

DC: If my suggestion a moment ago is accurate, then this statement reminds me of your mother, Mary, who must have been grieving about your father's death. I can imagine she would follow you to ease her suffering. Maybe she wanted to leave her home and her memories behind, and when she did, she found relief and satisfaction in your ministry.

JC: I can't deny that, but remember – my ministry was challenging. Like all of us she encountered people's hostility toward and appreciation of my message. Like all of us she faced the fear of the unknown – from the villages, towns and unfamiliar roads to the new faces, Jewish authorities and Roman soldiers. Every day we experienced something new or unsettling. Nothing was always the same. Nothing was predictable, but she felt more comfortable and satisfied while on ministry than suffering at home without her husband.

DC: I'd like to add another meaning to the Widow's Son before we move on. Abstractly, the Widow's Son also symbolizes the separation between the material and the spiritual world. After the Fall, our connection to the divine was severed and our bondage to this fallen world began. We became like the Widow's Son who wants to re-establish his relationship to his father but instead must become the master craftsman in order to build the temple of God. This is mythologically driven and points to each person's responsibility and initiative to become a master craftsman to build their own personal temple and thus reconnect to the father.

JC: Very good. You have eyes to see.

DC: Before we move on I'd like to say that I adopted a particular approach to this interview, one aspect of which is to explore inherent symbolism as it relates to you. Simply, when I see a symbol I question it in order to seek an alternative answer or to find a deeper buried truth. It is not my intention to dismiss or reject every symbol. Rather, I intend and hope to discover something new, and I have a few questions for you in this regard.

JC: What are they?

DC: Did you see yourself following in the footsteps of these spiritual traditions? Is this how you would characterize your life at this point? Should I see you as a symbolic character in a symbolic context, or did you really have a history as I would understand it?

JC: To imagine that my life is symbolic is to whitewash and minimize my life's content. I lived a life. I made decisions. I had feelings. I learned from my mistakes. I taught, healed and shared my wisdom. I knew the Father. I died because of my convictions and actions. My aptitudes, my inspirations and my decisions had meaning. They had consequences; not only did they affect me, they also affected those around me, my family, my followers and disciples, my listeners, those I healed, my society –

DC: – and to a larger extent the world in general. The effects ripple through time. People's hearts and minds were stirred then, as they are today and, in all probability, as they will be tomorrow. This illustrates the truth that a man of conviction and action can make lasting change.

JC: If my life captivated a person or a group to understand my deeds, my words and my actions, either symbolically or metaphorically, I have nothing to say. I cannot control how others want to perceive or understand me. I cannot moderate how another speaks of me or writes about me. People will see what they want to see. They will hear what they want to hear. They will do what they want to do.

DC: It is no different today except for the speed at which information travels. What occurs on our planet is known in seconds, minutes or hours. It's incredible.

JC: Word traveled fast but not that fast. But back to the point: I knew what I had to do and I did it – plain and simple. The rest was out of my hands.

DC: Thank you for clarifying that. I'd like to return again to your decision to leave and conduct your ministry. I suspect leaving your family had other ramifications.

JC: What do you suspect?

DC: If you were, as I assume, the oldest son, you would be responsible for the family and its business affairs, should anything tragic befall your father. If you leave and conduct your ministry, then logically James assumes the role of head of the family because he is the next oldest son behind you. I say this for this reason: when the gospels mention your siblings, he is at the top of the list, suggesting he was the next oldest. It then becomes incumbent upon him to step in and become the family patriarch. If this is accurate, James could have been consumed either by anger or bitterness. Maybe he found the situation and your ministry loathsome. Maybe he didn't want to be the family patriarch. If this is true and is coupled with his jealousy over Mary's favoritism toward you, then it is reasonable to suggest that your ministry created another point of contention and grievance for him.

JC: He was upset. But there is another current to James' frustration that runs deeper.

DC: How so?

JC: I told a story more convincingly and succinctly. I could captivate my audience; he could not. That wasn't his strongest talent. People didn't enjoy listening to him as they did with me. Also, my understanding of the divine was more robust, and my ability to grasp complex ideas and make intuitive connections was a talent he lacked.

DC: Did he feel God short-changed him?

JC: When he compared himself to me. We had different personalities. I took chances, he would not. I tried new things, he would not. I liked trouble, he did not. I discovered things on my own, he had to read about them or listen to the elders. He was pragmatic and conservative rather than innovative and revolutionary.

DC: The latter part is your strongest suit. Did James have a mind for the God of your forefathers?

JC: Yes, but his wisdom differed from mine. He was inclined with other proclivities. James' heart was large and his loyalties unshakable when he was convinced of the truth of a matter. He couldn't be moved.

DC: I believe the writer of the epistle James is your brother James, but some scholars are not as convinced. In any event, I'd like to quote from his epistle. "You adulterous people, don't you know that friendship with the world means enmity against God? Therefore, anyone who chooses to be a friend of the world becomes an enemy of God." (James 4:4) It's difficult for me to reconcile this statement with your wisdom. Would you agree with this conclusion?

JC: I do not agree with his intention or conclusion.

DC: Can you tell me how he arrived at his conclusion? Was it a sentiment expressed in your family that he embodied? Was it an idea consistent within your society which he embraced? Or did James adopt Christianity's inherent disdain, disapproval and hatred for the world, the flesh and the devil?

JC: I'd like to speak for a moment about my family. We did not shy away from our burdens or responsibilities. We were taught to face them and we were taught to live our convictions according to God. If our convictions included doing something in the world to change it, move it, teach it in some manner, or set it on some new path that seemed correct to our belief, then we were not discouraged. But we were not taught to instigate insurrection or revolt.

DC: Even though the gospels state tension and rivalry between your ambitions and your family's?

JC: Yes, my convictions unsettled each of them and my ministry appeared ludicrous until they realized I wasn't coming back home. Then they finally accepted my convictions, actions and ministry.

DC: Was there anything about your message or actions that encouraged or inspired James to think that friendship "with the world is hatred toward God"? (James 4:4)

JC: No! This was not my message.

DC: Tell me about that.

JC: To believe that the world is intrinsically flawed or evil was not my message. Rather, our society dismissed and discounted an entire group of people God saw as his own and whom he loved. Economically and spiritually, this group of people of whom I speak were disavowed and not allowed to participate in our society to their fullest capacity. Life was a crushing and deadly burden; a load too heavy to carry on one's back.

DC: James' statement is devoid of joy.

JC: His words sadden me and they mean more than they say. He grieved and was angered by my death. It had a lasting effect.

DC: The concept he espouses is devoid of the pleasure one should experience in work, family, children or friends, in making or growing things, in learning, or in relating to the divine. It embodies a grueling militaristic, hostile environment that suggests us against the world. For James, the world is bleak; it offers only intolerable struggles with no end in sight and is the source of perpetual pain and suffering. It implies that the only hope one can have is for God to return to the world, to judge it, to condemn it, to rid it of its twisted evils – including people – and to grant a believer eternal life in heaven.

JC: Careful. Don't disparage James; after all, he is my brother.

DC: My apologies. Please don't get me wrong.

JC: I experienced the world differently than James. I found joy in the Father. I found life in him. I found a wellspring of love in him. When I looked out on my world I saw people moving here and there, doing this and that, seeking this and that, satisfying cravings through material things, satisfying appetites for food and clothing, satisfying anger and hostility through violence, and satisfying complacency by looking the other way or by judging and condemning. And then I saw another group of people as outcasts without hope and in need.

DC: You knew there was more to know and experience in relation to the divine. I am reminded of your saying, "The coming of the Kingdom of God is not something that can be observed, nor will people say, 'Here it is,' or 'There it is,' because the Kingdom of God is within you." (LK 17:21) This statement continues to ring in my mind.

JC: This message was difficult to grasp and understand.

DC: I found that it cannot be known intellectually. It must be known experientially; its simplicity, what it points to, is easily overlooked and dismissed.

JC: To know "The Kingdom of God is within you" (LK 17:21) is to experience it. One can't read about it and then know it in the rational sense. The words point to the truth as a finger points to the moon. It says, "Look there!" It is within each person to know it. I'm pointing to it.

DC: I also believe it is known in the heart. Let's refocus on James; I sense he fell back upon – I hate to suggest this – an unresolved anger or conflict he had with you. He misinterpreted you in several ways, yet he felt compelled to accept your ministry posthumously by becoming the father of the Jerusalem Church. He took on your mission.

JC: He honored my name and was like a rock in that sense.

DC: From an early age you had a special gift for God.

JC: I did. It was innate. I knew things about the "God of our fathers" that not only astonished me but my family and the elders. I was precocious in that manner.

DC: Was your ambition to become a rabbi?

JC: That was in my heart. In Jewish culture, a religious life had social privileges and I wouldn't be completely honest if I said that didn't appeal to me. Status and privilege appealed to me when I was young but waned as I grew older.

DC: I'd like to talk about food. Jewish festivals were celebrated with a variety of foods while food and banquets were important components in your sayings and ministry. For instance, you eat with a variety of people. You miraculously feed people. Food appears in one of your desert temptations, in the Our Father prayer, in several parables and in the Last Supper. Can you explain this? Also, was your family in the habit of having banquets?

JC: Not regularly, but it was not foreign either. We were a big family with a large appetite. Food was plentiful and we never went without. At times, we were invited to our neighbors to share a meal. I enjoyed food. I liked everything about it – tastes, textures, flavors and fragrances.

DC: Is there some kind of food you preferred over another?

JC: I enjoyed wine.

DC: That's surprising.

JC: It's true. I liked wine.

DC: It just doesn't fit your image and conjures thoughts of heathens, Greeks and Romans. For a man who is supposed to be of God, well, I think I'll leave it at that.

JC: Don't brush this aside. I fought with the religious establishment and the devout over this issue. People were in the habit of judging and condemning. If one stepped outside prescribed conventions, then one felt the wrath of family, community or elders.

DC: After two thousand years nothing has changed. *Hypocrite* is thrown around all the time.

JC: You prove my point. One walks a fine line between living an inspired life, offending customs and challenging social prejudices and expectations.

DC: I could use a small break and get some water. When we return I'd like to delve into the religious conditions and the political atmosphere of your time.

JC: When I traveled with my disciples and followers from village to village and town to town, we took many breaks. Our feet ached and small pebbles or rocks wedged in our sandals. We stopped to sweep them out. We also needed to laugh, or eat and drink.

DC: What else occurred during these breaks?

JC: Someone told a story, another asked for clarification of a saying or parable, or we talked about the experiences we had from the last village or town. Sometimes silence found us and we listened to the wind rustling through the leaves or birds chirping and crying. Some would quietly think about the next village or town and thought, "What is in store for us?" That crossed our minds. And at times I mulled over the details for a new saying or parable.

DC: I surmise these small moments brought you together.

JC: Like a family.

DC: I also surmise you walked during the daylight hours and camped at night.

JC: We were always on the move. At the end of the day if we hadn't reached a town or village we had to find a particular spot to camp; if we couldn't find one we moved on until we did. We didn't stay in any one place too long. Now I could use another glass of water, please.

CHAPTER 2

AWAKENING

DC: Before the break, we discussed your family, briefly reviewed social conditions, and spoke about Judas the Galilean. I'd like to examine the political and religious conditions of your time in more detail. Can you describe these conditions and the prevailing sentiments? What was going on? Was there a gap between the affected and the unaffected?

JC: No one was insulated. Everyone was affected in one way or another.

DC: How so?

JC: Every Jew struggled with their heritage and with the traditions of our ancestors. Should we continue with them or should we modify them? People were divided. We thrashed in consternation over the half-Jewish, non-royal Hasmoneans who the Romans placed in charge to rule the Promised Land. We anguished over the Western ideals and practices that Alexander the Great brought to us and that continued with the Romans. We squirmed with the daily sacrifices the temple priests made to Rome and Caesar, and we despaired with Rome for dipping their hands into the sacred temple treasury and taking what they wanted.

DC: That is the *Corban*, a gift devoted to God. (MK 7:11)

JC: *Corban* had a central meaning. It was an offering, whether blood or bloodless, money or charity. It could be the tithe to the temple, or a gift I give to you that was dedicated to God, but it could not be appropriated for any other use. The *Corban* had a particular meaning but different methods of application.

DC: It would appear Jewish society was monolithic; that it was set; that it knew what it was, who it was, and how to function in the world; but that is not necessarily the case. Jewish society was comprised of many factions and groups, and at times, those groups competed and fought against one another. The common bond that held these groups together was the Jewish religion. It even seemed Jewish religious literature was under duress, questioned and re-examined. Is it a coincidence that the Christian religion emerged during this time? I would imagine Roman occupation accentuated the tension between each faction and forced Judaism to change or adapt.

JC: It did. Greco-Roman influence was powerful and spread in many directions.

DC: How so?

JC: There were the Roman political and religious appointments, Roman taxation and Hellenism. There were also the collusion and corruption between the Romans, Hasmoneans, the wealthy, and the temple priests who worked in concert toward common ends.

DC: This combination must have frustrated and angered many, making it more difficult to ignore.

JC: I wish I could say otherwise.

DC: Taxation is troublesome for anybody in any society. The American independence movement from British rule and my country's formation involved taxation. Earlier we discussed Judas the Galilean's opposition to the Roman census and taxation. He seemed to know something ominous was about to transpire. What taxes did the Romans levy? And what can you tell me about taxes in Israel?

JC: The Romans instituted a head tax. Imagine a tax simply for being alive. On the Sea of Galilee there was a custom fee for the boat, a permit fee to go on the lake, and when a load of fish was brought back to shore, the haul was levied. To exacerbate the problem, the Romans hired Jews to collect their taxes.

DC: People must have been furious.

JC: Yes, discontent reached a fevered pitch, and the fact that Jews collected taxes for the Romans made matters worse.

DC: From my research, I know that the Romans allowed tax privatization. A wealthy Roman individual or group could pay the estimated tax up front in one large sum for a particular province, and then be free to collect the tax indiscriminately throughout the year. In the case of the Jewish province, the Herod dynasty was the strong arm of the tax collector. I want to sidestep for a moment and present another practice that doesn't get much attention but I believe occurred and had serious side effects.

JC: What was that?

DC: There was a Roman custom called *patron–client*. It probably wasn't obvious but one could see it if one looked hard. It involves the benefits the Roman Governor received by his appointment and I can only imagine it had an insidious effect. The Romans weren't draconian or oppressive in relation to the upper class. The Romans included the upper class of all occupied territories in Roman society. In practice, the Romans needed them to maintain peace, taxation, stability and everyday normalcy.

JC: You'll have to explain the patron–client relationship to me.

DC: The patron–client is the relationship between individuals. The patron, a wealthy Roman, is on one side while the client, a person seeking more prestige, power, status and opportunity in relation with the patron, is on the other. I believe the Romans introduced this practice into Judea. In this case, the patron is the Roman Governor, while a selection of Jewish elite are the clients.

JC: What does it entail?

DC: The Governor received a percentage of the client's wealth and business transactions; in other words, he skimmed riches off the top from the client. One would think this benefited the patron only, but that's not the case. Instead of squeezing and crushing each client, like a heavy tax burden, the patron would introduce the client to other merchants, other sources, or other markets to expand the client's business opportunities. It was a win-win situation for each party and mutually beneficial. The Governor became wealthier while the client also got wealthier because of new opportunities that otherwise would not have been available. Those who didn't participate didn't get the business, the opportunities or the protection from the Governor.

JC: I felt something amiss and suspected secret agreements and arrangements. I noticed certain people's wealth continued to grow while the wealth of most others shrank. It baffled me considerably.

DC: Smaller merchants found themselves on the other side of the fence. Certain markets were open to the favored but closed to outsiders. The playing field was uneven and favored an ever-increasing narrow segment of the population.

JC: Extreme wealth placed undue stress upon the poor. Wealth was disproportionate, as were economic opportunities, education and food. This created imbalance, discontent and misery, and I felt it was an injustice and not of God.

DC: This condition affected your ministry and I assume it inspired your advocacy for the poor and dispossessed.

JC: It did.

DC: You addressed this problem through a new vision of God. You brought divine riches and favor to them. After your death, your followers initiated a practice of wealth redistribution to combat the growing economic problem.

JC: I had immense compassion for these people and I wanted to bring them something that our society could not or did not provide.

DC: I'd like to shift focus again and speak about the political situation. Tell me more about this. Was the country divided into jurisdictions?

JC: At the time the area was divided into four sections: Judah, Samaria, Galilee and Iturea, each governed by a Roman appointment. Judea was under direct Roman rule while Herod's family ruled the Galilee and the surrounding territory.

DC: Was the Galilee peaceful? Was it economically depressed? Was it under direct Roman duress?

JC: During my life, the Galilee tended to be peaceful, the exception being Judas the Galilean's revolt. His actions affected us in a way we didn't want repeated. We didn't want to experience his atrocities again. Regarding wealth, as a rule cities were centers of markets, trade, and the exchange of goods and services. The larger the city, the wealthier it was and the more it flourished. The Galilee was more pastoral and rural. It centered on communities invested in family-owned farms, orchards, fishing and construction.

DC: What were some of the agricultural products?

JC: Fruit trees, fig trees, olive trees, palm trees. The soil was rich in the Galilee. Trees and plants grew abundantly; one had to work to get the most out of the ground, but one didn't have to labor and toil until exhausted or become a slave to the ground.

DC: What about the Romans? Did they leave the Galilee alone?

JC: Mostly, except for the taxes and the appointment of Herod the Great. On principal, his rule was a source of irritation because he was not legitimate.

DC: Herod the Great was Arab and of Edomite descent. His ancestors converted to Judaism. He was partially Jewish, not a full blood and not of the Davidic throne. He was married to Mariamme, a Hasmonean princess and granddaughter of the Jewish High Priest Hyrcanus II, to soften his illegitimacy.

JC: Herod's dynasty was neither liked nor recognized. He had ten wives, he was ruthless, and he had blood on his hands for killing his two eldest sons, his brother-in-law, father-in-law, and his favorite wife, Mariamme, whom he falsely accused of being unfaithful and an adulteress.

DC: After reading his biography, I got the distinct impression he was obsessively insecure. In addition, I get the sense that his insecurity, his actions and his large family fueled a portion of Jewish angst and unrest. Something rather peculiar transpired in the Galilee that seemed wrong or disjointed. Across the board people were frustrated and angry with his dynasty, which may account for the several resistance movements beginning in his region.

JC: What are you saying? Elaborate on this.

DC: You came from this region, as did John the Baptist and Judas the Galilean. Each of you saw something wrong and wanted to make changes. Your ministry focused on creating a new man and a new community, as did John the Baptist. Judas the Galilean, on the other hand, focused on a community dedicated to violence and opposition against the Jewish people. Later, in 66 CE, a Galilean military force rose to defeat the Roman Legion stationed in the area. I cannot overlook this pattern. It is glaring and obvious.

JC: The Galilee was known for its men of courage and passion. We were tough, proud and physical. When I started my ministry, I did not include violence as a tool and neither did John the Baptist. I learned from Judas the Galilean in that respect. I wanted an interior change through love, compassion and wisdom. Others wanted an exterior change through power and violence.

DC: You wanted a change of the heart.

JC: Yes. I felt an open, pliable heart for the divine was more effective than a heart swayed by force, power, self or violence. I felt that if enough people had an interior change of compassion it would affect the exterior landscape. Apparently others didn't agree with my understanding and acted otherwise.

DC: When I read first-century Roman and Jewish history and examined that against your sayings, I began to wonder if as a teenager or young man you questioned or had misgivings about the direction in which your society was heading. I sense a gap widened between your privileges and knowledge and that of the impoverished and poor.

JC: Explain what you mean.

DC: Were you and your family insulated from the ravages of Roman rule and the various revolts or uprisings? Did you and your family have advantaged that others did not? Did those less fortunate suffer more at the hands of the Romans or Judas the Galilean than you? There must have been talk or concern within your family. Do you have anything to say?

JC: No one was insulated. Everyone was affected in one way or another.

DC: How was everyone affected?

JC: The Hasmoneans were corrupt, the Romans and temple priests taxed us, and protesters and agitators were brutally mistreated, tortured or killed. At the same time, unjust burdens and hardships were customary.

DC: Tell me how you were burdened by the Jewish temple.

JC: There was an obligatory temple tax, and the priestly tithe collectors demanded payment. At times, their collection methods were brutally harsh. It should be known that the temple was not just a religious center. It was involved with the exchange of money; it produced and sold incense, purified oil, sacrificial animals and meat from the sacrifice. It was the place of worship, and symbolically it was the center of the Jewish identity.

DC: When I examine the social landscape, I can't help but imagine that the poor and underprivileged struggled to survive. The structure of society was stacked against them.

JC: The situation continued spiraling downward. The privileged benefited from the labor and productivity of the working people.

DC: I can understand and accept that, but there must have been some reprieve due to the building boom during Herod the Great's dynasty. That must have helped. Can you describe Herod's building projects and how they benefited your society?

JC: Herod's building projects were substantial and widespread. Some even continued after his death. Herod constructed the city of Tiberius and the port city of Caesarea Maritima, which became the center for maritime trade. The port city housed a large hippodrome for chariot races, a gymnasium for wrestling and a large Roman-style palace for him and his family. This palace later became the residence of the Roman Procurator. Herod erected and commemorated temples to Rome; one such temple was built in Capernaum not far from the house I used during my ministry. The five cities west of the Galilee expanded, as did the Jerusalem temple, a forty-six year remodeling project. He also built his fortress at Masada and his mausoleum. Herod was a tireless and relentless builder.

DC: He was also shrewd and sly. With one hand he pleased and honored his Roman benefactors, with the other he tried to appease the Jews.

JC: He could not balance them simultaneously, and this practice pulled him in two directions. He constantly looked over his shoulder wondering who would replace him. Would it be the Romans, someone within his own family, or some other Jewish faction? Some thought I would ascend and usurp the Hasmonean throne. He didn't take chances. That is why he murdered his wife and sons and his brother-in-law and father-in-law. He was afraid of them and their popularity. Eventually he went mad, became hated by his subjects and died a horrible death. Rumors circulated that worms crawled out of his stomach. The entire affair was unfortunate and unsustainable.

DC: I can see the need for an honorable king – one who righteously guides his people.

JC: That was the hope.

DC: Continuing with the building boom, I'd like to know what ramifications it had on you specifically and on your society generally.

JC: I benefited from the boom, had work and applied my building skills. Generally, tradesmen, merchants and craftsmen throughout the Roman Empire and surrounding area came into the Galilee, Judea, and Samaria.

DC: I can see a ripple effect in this scenario. As their numbers swelled, demand on everything grew.

JC: It did.

DC: And the economy expanded. There was a greater demand for meat, vegetables, fruit, wine, clothing and textiles. I assume the production from the local farms, orchards and vineyards increased to meet this new demand.

JC: That's not all. Trade in construction tools, materials and supplies expanded, as did trade in olive oil, salt, wheat, spices, incense, perfumes and fragrances. Merchants and farmers flourished.

DC: How was your family affected by the building boom?

JC: My father positioned himself well and capitalized on the new economy. Financially we were fortunate, but we couldn't escape the burden of taxation or the religious tithes. We grumbled, were upset and voiced our discontent. This intensified when the building boom came to an end.

DC: What do you mean?

JC: The building boom created a new class of people in the construction, merchant and farming trades, and this affected the greater region throughout the Roman Empire and in the East. People prospered and incurred debt to expand their businesses, thinking the success and prosperity would continue. They did not, and when the boom collapsed people lost fortunes and many workers were not paid for their labor.

DC: I'm reminded of your parable concerning just this situation, "The ground of a certain rich man yielded an abundant harvest. He thought to himself, 'What shall I do? I have no place to store my crops.' "Then he said, 'This is what I'll do. I will tear down my barns and build bigger ones, and there I will store my surplus grain. And I'll say to myself, 'You have plenty of grain laid up for many years. Take life easy; eat, drink be merry.'" "But God said to him, 'You fool! This very night your life will be demanded from you. Then who will get what you have prepared for yourself?' "This is how it will be with whoever stores up things for themselves but is not rich toward God." (LK 12:16-21) In this parable you chastise the man and make him an example; somehow his poor misguided decision is arrogant because he allowed himself to be motivated by real circumstances. This is the logical thing to do when one is involved in a capital enterprise. Why wouldn't he do it?

JC: Many were seduced by the circumstances. I addressed materialism in my ministry because I knew people who were entangled in it and suffered greatly. I also knew others who were swept away in the wake of the building boom. I felt this reliance on the economy was false and that the real truth was in the Father.

DC: Other changes occurred in your society besides the collapse of the economy. As mentioned earlier, you and your countrymen were discontented and faced growing political, social and religious problems.

JC: It was as if the ground beneath our feet shifted. The situation destabilized, became untenable and, as a whole, we felt under siege. The Jewish national identity and our foundational roots changed with the weight of Roman occupation and Hellenism. Things we took for granted could no longer be counted on. Life, circumstances and our religious values were changing.

DC: Such as?

JC: The use of property. Ancestral land designed for small family farms or local communities was not sustainable. Either the land was sold or it was taken over and converted into larger farms. To compound the problem, Greek and Roman culture eroded our traditional identity. Our traditional heritage and methods could not thwart the change, despite one's best effort. One either became complacent and downcast, more religiously devout and radicalized, or adopted the ways of the gentiles.

DC: I'd like to explore one issue of this cultural change in relation to the body. According to Jewish religious custom and understanding, the human body was considered unclean.

JC: We constantly purified ourselves, ate pure food and used clean utensils. Yahweh demanded righteousness and holiness, and that filtered throughout our society. In our religion, one's heart and mind were susceptible to sin, and the body was the means for sin to enter and spread. Thus, our rites, rituals and practices staved off sin or counter-balanced it, while the priest sacrificed unblemished animals to atone for our sins. This picture sets the stage for what I'm about to say. The Greeks and Romans, in contrast, introduced the glorification of the human body, the pleasure of the senses, sex, sport, gymnasium, philosophical rationality, and idolatry. They erected statues of their gods and of Caesar, and they believed man was the measure of all things, not God. These ideals were diametrically opposed to our understanding, our way of life and our concept of the divine.

DC: It's difficult to imagine the effects this had on your people.

JC: It was as appalling and stressful as it was difficult to appreciate all the consequences. We found ourselves ensnared in a vicious landscape of economic uncertainty and Greco-Roman culture, taxes, politics and religion. The unifying power of the Jewish nation was splitting apart. People sought solace and reprieve from the confusion and demands placed on them by the changing environment. The Romans were one thing, but another crisis ate at our heart.

DC: What was that?

JC: Jewish religious identity. Theological certitude, resurrection, observance, purity rites, land stewardship and the Messiah were heated topics of discussion and debate. It was yet another point of contention. As the priests continued their animal sacrifices to Rome, the Essenes adhered strictly to purity laws and customs out in the desert. They believed they were the true Jews whom God has blessed, and they maintained they were the rightful heirs of the High Priest because their ancestry stretches back to the Sons of Zadok. They thought a war between the Son of Light and the Sons of Darkness was on the other edge of the horizon and drawing near. Meanwhile, a Zealot sentiment flourished, becoming revolutionary and militaristic. Revolt circulated in the air.

DC: The Sacarii developed later in the mid–first century. They were ideologically driven assassins who resented all authority and governance that was not purely prescribed by ancient Judaism. They wanted strict observance of the law and were willing to enforce it with extreme prejudice.

JC: Extreme prejudice! I appreciate your meaning.

DC: It is one of our terms. Can you briefly summarize the content of your time in relation to the revolt sentiment?

JC: The gap between the privileged and the poor sharpened, the peace of God was absent, and his voice appeared silent. John the Baptist offered hope of a new kingdom; I offered love, compassion and wisdom. Others offered an armed confrontation, the Essenes offered a secluded community, the Pharisees offered traditional teaching and the priests offered animal sacrifices.

DC: Animal sacrifice was a traditional practice from your distant past.

JC: People hoped for the Messiah to solve all their problems, but unfortunately there was neither one person nor one appropriate solution. Each position and each solution to any problem was flawed. The tools at hand, unfortunately, were either ineffective or exacerbated the problem when employed. Few understood the interplay between all the forces, and the solution to all the problems became singular. One thing inherently didn't address another, which in turn didn't address something else.

DC: At what point did this become a problem for you, and what was your reaction?

JC: I have more to say about our condition. As I grew in age I began seeing the discrepancy. My eyes opened to the prevailing religious hypocrisy. I recognized that the plight of the poor and the sick were ignored. Even though they were Jews, they were looked upon differently – as outcasts. People were divided and upset with one another. Positions entrenched and hardened. Our hearts grew weary with each other and our dignity frayed. We were at war with each other and with the Romans. My family acquiesced to this condition; I mean, what could we do? I complained at first. It wasn't loud, whispers and a few questions, but I wanted to do something. I thought our family could do something. We had the means to give money, to invite the poor to a meal, to be more inclusive, or be concerned with the plight of the dispossessed. We didn't do anything.

DC: I sense you were an impassioned idealist. I also notice your intelligence. Did your idealism and sharp mind agitate people?

JC: It was a concern. When I was a young man I provoked and pestered my family and the religious elders until everyone finally grew weary and had enough. I was restless, motivated and strong-willed, and I liked trouble; at that time I was also immature. This was a lethal mixture. I lacked the necessary wisdom to address the problem. I equated actions with godliness and expected the religious establishment to confront the developing rift, but they didn't know what to do either, except to maintain the status quo. Silence, fear, looking the other way and disregard became the course of action. They threw up their hands, expecting God to fix it miraculously. That stance upset and frustrated me.

DC: I had an epiphany that changed my understanding of you and it gave me new eyes to see into your ministry and teachings.

JC: I'm all ears. Tell me about it.

DC: I recognized personal elements in your parables and sayings. Your wisdom is a double-edged sword. One edge of the blade is universal and transcends culture and time, while the other edge is autobiographical. Your history is hidden in your words.

JC: What is hidden and what do you see?

DC: As a young man, you left home and your family in search of yourself and your place in society. Unfortunately, you encountered a series of debilitating disasters that forced you to return home to heal and regroup. Along the way, you were struck by a transformational experience that changed the content and direction of your life. This profound experience gave you the insight of the Father and inspiration to conduct your ministry. That is what I see.

JC: You don't think you are reading into my sayings?

DC: No! I'm confident of my assessment.

JC: That is a remarkable insight.

DC: It was a remarkable revelation. Your personal experiences are the source material for your sayings.

JC: You don't think they were inspired by the Father?

DC: I'm not discounting the content of the Father. What I am saying is that you drew from your personal history. Once I understood that truth I looked carefully for small reoccurring details and themes. Later, I felt I could identify your character traits, personality and history. We have a discipline called psychology; it posits that one's personality and inner realities are revealed through words and actions.

JC: I wouldn't agree completely with the first part of your statement. You conclude I drew upon my personal history as source material for my sayings.

DC: You didn't?

JC: I didn't say that. The truth is multi-faceted. Everyone has life experiences. I read, studied and memorized the Torah. I sat and walked with learned men. I had keen observant eyes. I was curious and precocious. I could put things together and I was imaginative. I also did things, went places, saw things, put tools in my hands and built things.

DC: You had a quick, sharp and witty mind and you used that penchant for God.

JC: I knew things intuitively and practically, and crafted my sayings like a carpenter shaping a piece of wood. I thought about them. I developed characters and placed those characters in settings and situations to illustrate a truth. I wanted people to see what I saw and know what I knew. I wanted people to think about a truth and incorporate that truth into their life. I was in the habit of teaching through parable but responding to confrontation through short, to-the-point sayings.

DC: Whatever came to your mind?

JC: When I spoke and taught, I removed the *me* and *I* from my parables, substituting the personal pronoun with the third person singular – a man, a woman, a young ruler, an owner, a manager. My teachings are layered. They are part autobiographical, part situational, part historical and part imaginative. I didn't want my personal experiences to be the focal point of my message because it was not about me. I didn't want that distraction, but I couldn't help but use my life experiences as material. I must add that not every saying references my life. I did not want people to say, "I see Jesus' past in that saying." If that happened, then the impact would have been lost. I was not the message; I was the messenger. As my ministry and events unfolded I did not need to use my history for source material. I was inspired by developing situations. I could do that.

DC: When I read the New Testament gospels, I see a man motivated and inspired in many ways. But when I thematically cataloged your sayings, I discovered your primary subject was money, treasure, wealth, riches, the pearl, and treasure in heaven. Tell me about that.

JC: Riches, money, wealth and treasure are important subjects. People chase after wealth while many are without it. Some enjoyed the success and delight of it only to feel the misery and sting of losing it. Money consumes like the plague. Those with it burned for more, while those without it sank deeper into misery and drudgery. My words on this subject simply reflect the landscape I encountered daily. I wanted to speak of riches and wealth of another kind because many people were poor. They needed encouragement and inspiration.

DC: I want to switch focus and look at money from another perspective, and it concerns you. The gospels portray you as poor, but I have my doubts.

JC: I emptied myself of material possession. Why is that hard to believe?

DC: I'm speaking of something different. I know when you ministered you relied on the generosity of others. I can't help but believe another truth lies at the heart of the matter.

JC: I sense something nags you like a splinter you can't pull out of your finger. You have a question.

DC: I'm not disputing the characterization that you were a poor itinerant teacher.

JC: You're not?

DC: I'm saying that your family was relatively wealthy compared to those in your surrounding community. You had privileges others did not. That is what I've come to understand by reading your sayings. Your knowledge about finance, money, wealth and business does not stem from being poor, astute, or observant. That is incongruent. You have an intimacy with the subject. It seems to me that you were around it and of it, rather than an observer who looked at it from the outside. If I were a betting man I would wager you came from money. I would also wager that something happened to you that changed your status and made you experience life without it, or at least you didn't have it like you once had.

JC: You draw that conclusion from my sayings?

DC: Yes, I do. I can't see it any other way. Money is your number one subject.

JC: I want to point out that wealth is relative. Caesar was wealthy. Herod was wealthy. The High Priest was wealthy. My family certainly did not have that wealth. I recognized two types of riches; one was material and the other was spiritual.

DC: That may be the case, but I don't see you subsisting. You had access to a lifestyle – to education, travel and positions – that others did not. You didn't go without. You and your family frequently traveled to Jerusalem for Passover. The Gospel of Luke states it was every year. (LK 2:41) The round trip took approximately three to four weeks. Poor people couldn't afford to make that trip as often as you did. It was too expensive.

JC: I agree Passover in Jerusalem was expensive.

DC: I had to think long and hard about your relationship to money and wealth. You experienced it first hand and from two points of view. You knew it as one who had it and as one without it. You knew the realities and effects of both. This seemed more obvious when I systematically and thematically cataloged your money sayings and compared them to your other sayings. You speak twice as much about money as you do of the Father. Your money sayings spring from an informed and authoritative position. You tell stories of capital investment, capital gain and capital return on investment, collection of debt, lending at interest, inheritance, establishing wages, labor, labor disputes, and good and bad management. These concepts are difficult to appreciate unless you know the mechanics of money. You know the business of farming, you have the mind of a merchant and you speak of trade effortlessly. You know what money does to one's mind and what it does for good and ill. You know it shapes one's world view. You know that people are viewed and judged through its lens, and you know that the divine is moved to the side because of it. Each of these made me ponder your history and your family. Of all the truly gifted and spiritual men throughout history, and of all the spiritual and mystical literature I have read, you are unique. You are the only one I know who equates money with the divine. Yet you are not a materialist. You are for and against it simultaneously, but this is not the end of it. Two other money dynamics exist in relation to you.

JC: What are they?

DC: You talk of inheritance. It is not earned but freely given. In a parable, a wealthy, privileged person gives money to different people who are then tasked with investing it. Some invest it wisely and earn a return while one buries it in the sand and makes no return. Additionally, before your ministry you earned a wage as a builder or carpenter. You worked with your hands. It is hard to square the circle of a poor man who knows so much about money unless he came from money.

JC: You think these sayings relate to me and reflect my status rather than my wisdom?

DC: I see both. I believe you came from money and were nimble and astute, equating money and business with spirituality. You knew the pitfalls of money, but you also knew the mechanics of making money and incorporated that knowledge into your ministry.

JC: Money has positive and negative values. I saw many things dualistically and addressed each accordingly. As a young man, I was inspired by money and treasure. I picked the apple from the tree, bit into it and devoured the entire fruit. With that, I lost sight of the divine and my mind became clouded and perverted. I watched others lose their identity as well. But when I started my ministry, my mind was clear and I knew I could craft parables from the knowledge I gained from money. So I created a new spiritual insight that involved investing.

DC: Your business was the Father, compassion and healing. You understood the relationship between risk and reward; you substituted material wealth for spiritual treasures; and you gave away that knowledge for free or for a small donation, or exchanged it for food. If people accepted your wisdom and followed you, if they invested in your concepts, they received the same rewards from heaven as you did.

JC: That's not so hard to understand. You mentioned earlier that your epiphany gave you insight into my past through my sayings.

DC: Yes.

JC: Was there a particular saying or parable that struck you as the most autobiographical?

DC: Two jumped out at me – the parables of Prodigal Son and the Good Samaritan.

JC: Those two! What struck you about those parables? Why them?

DC: These were the last two parables I cataloged during my research. It is hard to describe how both struck me, except that I was hit with a strong intuition. I sensed you were the Prodigal Son who asked his father for his inheritance. In the Good Samaritan parable, I realized you were –

JC: – the Samaritan?

DC: No, the man half dead who the Samaritan helped.

JC: You saw that?

DC: I did. Will you comment on that?

JC: I have ears and I'd like to hear what you think happened to me.

DC: Let's step back. Even though your sayings and ministry reveal certain things about your past, they don't reveal enough to bring you out of the shadows. A true historical chronology with definition is difficult to reconstruct. That said, I wanted to see if I could understand your life in more detail, particularly your missing years, so I asked a number of specific questions. I believe I found bits and pieces that fleshed you out, but this picture is imprecise at best.

JC: Fair enough! What questions did you ask?

DC: Did you leave home? Did you travel? Did you go to the Orient? Were you married? Did you have a child? Were you an Essene? Where did you learn your wisdom? Did you have a mentor or teacher? What do you mean by "the Father"? How did you arrive at the knowledge of the Father? Is the Father the same as Yahweh? How did you develop a compassionate heart? When did you learn the structure of Greek rhetorical argument? Did you accept and believe in eschatology, which is the term we use today to describe the End Times? How could you have learned and accomplished so much in so little time?

JC: My mind was sharp and I was eager and curious to know God and the world.

DC: I'd like to explore your personality in more detail and connect it with the various ideas we previously mentioned.

JC: How do you see me?

DC: I would characterize you as a precocious, intelligent, tough-minded, arrogant and prideful person who, as a young man, spoke his mind often. I sense you were aggressive, fearless, privileged, and someone who praised or exalted himself. You were charismatic, a storyteller with an aura surrounding you, and I'd say you were a genius. You had an immense capacity for the divine, which expressed itself one way at first and then changed into something different later. Things bothered you greatly, enough that you were willing to do something about it. You didn't sit back, watch and complain. Maybe you did at first, but eventually you rolled up your sleeves and got to work with your ministry.

JC: There you go again with your metaphors.

DC: You also liked metaphor. Regardless of how I say things, I have to take your ministry into account, start there and work backwards. I also have to understand why you conducted and trained for it, and how you acquired the vast knowledge for it. I believe the two parables I mentioned above hold the key.

JC: Keep going.

DC: All right. The Prodigal Son is a unique parable for its orientation toward family, individuals in that family – the father, son and brother – their relationship toward money, commitment toward family and the son's wayward exploits. I'd like to know what inspired this parable and whether it is universal or autobiographical in nature.

JC: I was in the habit of deliberating and searching for double meanings; wisdom that pointed in several directions. Wisdom can point outward, which is the most obvious, and you say, "It is about that." Wisdom, however, is deeper than the most obvious and it could point inward, as you recognized. Wisdom is like a vast pool and the further I swam in it the richer, more meaningful and more textured the world became. Ironically, wisdom is not about one thing. It is about many things simultaneously and, like a living puzzle and delicacy, wisdom is mysterious and it is a guide. I blended my history with metaphor, like leaven and yeast. It was a literary device I used.

DC: Wisdom aside, did you receive an inheritance?

JC: My ancestors received an inheritance from Yahweh which I accepted. I was the recipient of that heritage; it was in my soul and I lived within its traditions. As a young man, I felt my religion ineffectual and my inheritance wanting. Later, as I re-examined my ancestral stories, I recognized God's presence and open arms to anyone wanting to find Him and receive His embrace. At this time, I understood God differently than my ancestors and I called Him the Father.

DC: Given this broad definition, I see inheritance differently than what you described in your Prodigal Son parable. It appears inheritance is more particular than general – the father gives the son money, which he squanders. Should I understand this parable figuratively or literally?

JC: You claim my history is present in my sayings.

DC: Yes, but I also sense you conveyed a deeper Midrash truth in many. If I accept the figurative nature of the Prodigal Son parable I find myself puzzled by the metaphor of leaving home.

JC: Why?

DC: The son asks his father for his inheritance in the parable and leaves with it. If this represents your Jewish heritage, then I question where the son went with his inheritance. Tens of thousands of Jews lived in the Promised Land and were committed to ancient Jewish rites, practices, stories and festivals. Did they squander their inheritance? Does the son represent the Lost Tribes of Israel? I doubt it. I can't imagine the Jewish heritage fully bankrupt, nor can I imagine the parable foreshadowing the Church as the Christians claim. The story revolves around lost and returned love, of forgiveness and restoration, which are important themes to you. The son returns, differences mended, and the father–son relationship restored. For this reason, I believe the parable speaks about you and sheds light on your actual father and brother, rather than the metaphorical restoration of Jews and God. Maybe you felt your relationship with God was like a son returning home, or that it was like Israel returning to God as Isaiah and Ezekiel suggest. But when taken literally, I would venture to say that your family dynamics reached a critical point and, as a young man, you threw up your hands, asked for your inheritance and left. Do you have anything to say about leaving home in this regard?

JC: One grows older and leaves childhood behind to step into the shoes of an adult. Hopefully, one has a rite of passage. Mine occurred after I left home.

DC: By reading your sayings, I got the impression you wanted to find your way and discover your voice.

JC: Fire burned in my heart that couldn't be quenched, so I pursued it because it needed a place to grow. I was restless, hardheaded, ambitious and, I admit, prideful.

DC: I want to add that you were bold, brave and courageous; you were a troublemaker and enjoyed rocking the boat. You possessed an entrepreneurial mind that could see opportunities others could not.

JC: You can see all that in my sayings and my ministry?

DC: I believe I can. I want to add one more trait; you had the ability to see the Field.

JC: What do you mean by the Field?

DC: You knew who you were; you understood the political, social and religious environment, appreciated human and divine natures, and recognized the power of good and evil. You saw the suffering of the dispossessed, treated it like a doctor and applied your wisdom in the world. You had a comprehensive knowledge of the self, your audience, your world and the Father. That is what I mean by the Field.

JC: Now I understand and I like your assessment. Do you have anything else to say?

DC: You challenged authority, cultivated silence and sought quiet places. You were discerning, understood divine mechanics, and promoted compassion when compassion was scarce.

JC: Yes I did.

DC: Once I absorbed the autobiographical nature of your sayings, I looked for more details that would reveal more about you and your history. Maybe my insights and conclusions are projections and misinterpretations, or maybe I'm seeing what I want to see, but I believe you were compelled to leave your family for several reasons. You saw the problems your society faced. You saw what vexed and infuriated your family and that understanding perplexed and frustrated you, which, possibly, made you angry.

JC: With whom would I be angry?

DC: God? Your family? The Romans? The elders? The priests or Pharisees? That is why you asked for your inheritance and Joseph accepted without much disagreement.

JC: I thought it best to leave and experience the world. Others thought it appropriate as well.

DC: Did you agonize over the decision? Or was it an emotional response? Did you give your future much thought? Or were you certain?

JC: I left the familiar behind – family, friends, customs and God – and set out with purpose.

DC: You were conflicted with competing desires.

JC: What do you mean?

DC: You were allured by the world, its treasure and fruit and you wanted to make a name for yourself. On the other hand, you had an innate love for God. According to the Gospel of Luke, you had a precocious knowledge of God at the age of twelve. I think both these tendencies beat in your heart in equal measure, but you made a fateful decision to side with the world and left God and your family behind. What can you say about that?

JC: My decision was not easy and my heart was pulled and tugged on.

DC: When I faced the unknown, I was both thrilled and staggered. Little is known, anticipation is high and everything is new. I had to feel my way through during such times.

JC: I know what you mean. Also, one doesn't know what one doesn't know. Nor can one appreciate the challenges that lie ahead, appreciate the dangers and pitfalls, or understand the subtle interplay between the desires of the world and the needs of the individual. Without experience, one doesn't know what to look for. One can't comprehend the beneficial from the perilous, or determine friend from foe.

DC: I want to add another point. When I entered unknown territory I brought with me the tools of my upbringing and education, and I carried my parent's mantles. Painfully, those tools were neither appropriate nor helpful. The world was different than I was led to believe and I was not prepared for it.

JC: Explain that to me.

DC: The knowledge I learned in my youth, did not help me with the challenges I faced as an adult. I failed when I met particular challenges; not because they were challenges, but because the tools in my toolbox were inappropriate to the situation at hand. They proved inadequate and resulted in devastating consequences. I learned hard lessons and they took years to sort out. This is a crude analogy but one can't use a sledgehammer to drain a pool and still keep the pool intact without destroying it.

JC: Your analogy is humorous. The point is to create a set of tools and then know which tool is right for the job. Making and using the tools correctly takes wisdom.

DC: Yes. I need a pump, not a sledgehammer, to drain the pool.

JC: That appears obvious, but for the blind the obvious cannot be seen.

DC: You had a mind filled with wisdom and a heart filled with compassion, and they worked in concert with each other.

JC: I balanced and integrated them. That is the trick.

DC: This is why you said, "Be shrewd as snakes and as innocent as doves." (MT 10:16) The heart and mind are not independent of each other.

JC: Far from it.

DC: Two paths are walked; the interior path leads to self-knowledge and the exterior path leads to worldly experiences and wisdom.

JC: Life is a teacher as much as an open heart and quiet mind.

DC: I'd like to talk about a few more personal issues. You were charismatic, which proved beneficial to your ministry.

JC: I was. I was not shy and I enjoyed being with people as they did with me. I met people easily and spent time with merchants, traders, outcasts, the underprivileged, slaves, hired hands, the shrewd and ignorant, and people of wealth. I did not turn away from people with different religious understanding, nor did I turn my back on philosophical or religious discussions.

DC: In Pompeii, on the wall in a wealthy Roman's house, reads an inscription, "Pleasure is the greatest treasure." Would this have been acceptable to you?

JC: (*smiling*) Hellenism was in the world.

DC: Many conflicting and contradictory accounts exist concerning your missing years. One says you traveled to England with your Uncle Joseph of Arimathea, another recounts your travels to India, another that you were in Egypt studying the Mystery Religions, and still another places you with the Essenes. There is even an account that you were in Ethiopia.

JC: I traveled; I moved from place to place. My feet were blistered from long walks. I rocked back and forth on a boat while on the sea. I know the scent of the sea, the sound of flapping sails and the groans of the boat under full sail. I bounced up and down on the backs of animals. I know their smell. I know the fragrance of cooking meat and the delicate sweet smell of spice and perfume. I know the heat of the sun beating down on me and the welcome cool breeze blowing against my skin. I've been mesmerized by the light of the sun glistening off the water, and overwhelmed by the bold colors of the sunrise and sunset. Whatever is written about me is merely a record. One lives a life rather than records a life.

DC: If I were to recount my life's story I'd first have to ask which parts are important and which are inconsequential, which are worth retelling and which are not, and which had positive effects and which had negative effects. I would also have to mention my mentors and teachers, and I would have to redevelop my historical context and a chronological timeline. That is a tall order.

JC: You'd have to edit and make choices. You would have to decide what to tell and what not to tell.

DC: In the end it would be incomplete. What is important to me might not be important to the reader or vice versa.

JC: In the end, your story would be more a shadow of substance than substance.

DC: We see this in your case. Anyway, back to your missing years, I surmise you left and went somewhere. I can't be sure because you don't mention anything about other places, cultures or people. I find this is peculiar. When I read the accounts of the Apostle Paul he is eager to write about his past, but you don't talk about yourself and you never mention a far-off place; those details are absent in every gospel. If I can glean anything from your missing years I have to examine your sayings and identify concepts that are not Jewish. I developed three hypothesizes.

JC: Which are?

DC: First, your spiritual ideas are substantial and reflective. The Father, the Kingdom of Heaven sayings, the lilies of the field proverb, and the parable of the woman on the road whose jar is full of meal but pours out along the road and becomes empty are not consistent themes within the Hebrew tradition. Your ministry is a sacrifice of the ego to the Father in order for him to be more prevalent. The loss of ego, emptiness, the Father, and the Kingdom of Heaven sayings are Eastern. It seems plausible you traveled to the Orient and studied with a teacher.

JC: The Father also derives from the Greek philosopher Pythagoras, who states that the Father is One.

DC: Yes, I'm aware of Pythagoras and his understanding of the One. Second, you express religious ideas about your ancestry, particularly of the Levite and Essene traditions, and you use Greek rhetorical structure and style when speaking your aphorisms. Again, it seems plausible that you studied with the Essenes and with the Levites.

JC: And the third possible hypothesis?

DC: You told your back story in your sayings; put the pieces back together in the right order and your history comes to the surface.

JC: Give me an example.

DC: If I join the Prodigal Son and Good Samaritan parables together with the parable of the man who died after building his barn and storehouses –

JC: – I didn't die.

DC: Not literally, but an underlying catastrophe weaves through each story. After the Prodigal Son indulges his cravings and appetites for the world, a personal catastrophe occurs that causes him to reach rock bottom and he is forced to travel back home. A man half dead lies in the street when the Good Samaritan arrives to nurse him back to health, while the man who built the larger barn and a series of storehouses dies unexpectedly. What can I make of this? I see that each story is plausibly connected to you since they feel inspired by actual events in your life. Your stories are not abstractions; rather, they involve identifiable characters in recognizable settings and situations. The challenge is to sort out the people and events and build a timeline.

JC: Why is that a challenge?

DC: One needs to have time for a "Prodigal Son" and "Lose Everything One Built" experience. One needs to have time to walk a spiritual path, to be transformed by it and to gain the spiritual wisdom from it. I have to wonder how you managed to accomplish and experience so much in such a short period. It doesn't seem possible to experience all that you did in so short a time.

JC: Why not?

DC: Some of your spiritual wisdom contains Essene, Levite, Greek and oriental religious philosophy. Some of your parables involve themes of catastrophe, disaster and lost and found, while others include carpentry, farming, pleasure, merchandise, and buying, selling and investing. It's hard to reconcile these ideas and it is just as hard to believe you were involved with each. Yet, it is equally hard to believe your quick mind and imagination envisioned each without actually living or experiencing them. Were you that observant? I know that is one of your strong traits but was it that strong? One thing I learned about you is that you were intimate and passionate about your knowledge and wisdom and that you knew things from the inside. So how could you know all that you speak about? Somewhere in this mix is the truth.

JC: You mentioned before that my story reflects your story. I would like to know more about that.

DC: As a young man I welcomed and embraced the future and anticipated what it would bring. I was brazen, proud and mildly arrogant. I believed wealth would follow me throughout my life, but Fate dealt a different hand. I received a small inheritance and invested in myself to make something of myself, but the results were limited. I believe we have a few other things in common.

JC: Such as?

DC: You are a poet; I am a visual artist. I had mystical experiences and so did you. I travelled and sailed and so did you. I built houses and so did you. If left home for college, and I believe you left home to experience the world. I thought I would be somebody when I grew up and I believe you did too.

JC: Why would you think that?

DC: During your ministry, you believed you could change society and people's beliefs. You wouldn't have felt that way if it wasn't already inside of you, implying you felt that way before your ministry. Your temptation in the desert to be ruler of the world suggests this secret desire. Is this something you carried with you from an early age?

JC: I felt I was destined for something great but I didn't fully appreciate how that would happen.

DC: Before your ministry did you ever find your stride? Did you reach a point when you felt you were on the right path and that you made it? Were you comfortable with the course and direction of your life? Were you right with the world?

JC: Do you think I found my stride or place in the world?

DC: Your ministry is revealing on this point. Your missing years prepared you for it but I don't think you found your place until you found the Father and embarked on your ministry. I also believe that for you to accomplish your ministry, you drew upon and were motivated by two traditions.

JC: Which two?

DC: The first was the Greek tradition, particularly Alexander the Great. By the age of thirty he conquered the Persian Empire and became the ruler of the known world. Alexander set the bar very high and I imagine his achievement was in the back of your mind because you started your ministry at the age of thirty. The second involves your Jewish tradition, particularly the patriarchal tradition of Noah, Abraham, Jacob, Joseph, Moses, Joshua, David and Solomon. Each man accomplished great things in the name of God.

JC: Alexander the Great's accomplishments were known and I was raised on the stories of our patriarchs and prophets. But to say that I emulated Alexander is misleading. In Hebrew society, one could be a teacher at the age of thirty.

DC: I believe other missing-year experiences contributed to preparing you for your ministry. Much is contained in those years and I can't see it any other way.

JC: What other experiences?

DC: Humility. Loss. A supernatural experience. Forgiveness. Love. May I tell you one part of my story that helps me understand your past?

JC: I have ears.

DC: I traveled a long path filled with steep mountains and deep valleys. A crisis set me on the path and some fiery compulsion kept me on it. I sought the Wisdom of Solomon and received wisdom in an unexpected manner. An event changed me. After many years, with a snap of a finger, my mind opened and I could see eternity.

JC: Stop right there! What do you mean your mind opened? What happened?

DC: It's hard to describe except to say that my mind simply opened.

JC: Tell me as much as you can.

DC: At the time, I was remodeling my house and the project was nearly complete. In quick succession, two close friends, my grandmother and my sister died. I grieved and mourned for months. I read Buddhist scripture, the Gospel of Thomas and Sufi literature to help manage my misery and console my sorrow. One day, as I was reading the Gospel of Thomas, confused and bewildered by the sayings, the inexpressible suddenly occurred. For months I felt a glow: my eyes felt glassy, my step was a little lighter and my intuition was more crisp and clear. I had experienced this glow before, so I wasn't distracted or annoyed by it. I knew something was brewing and I was curious about what it could be.

JC: I sense you are struggling. Let me ask you a few questions to make this easier.

DC: That's a good idea.

JC: We'll start from the beginning. Where did this experience occur?

DC: In La Canada, California.

JC: Were you alone or with somebody?

DC: Alone.

JC: When did it happen? Morning, afternoon or night?

DC: In the morning. I don't remember the exact date, but it was the first week in January of 2012. I had driven from Tucson, Arizona, in late December to spend Christmas and the New Year with family and friends.

JC: Can you characterize the experience?

DC: I entered a trance while sitting in a chair contemplating the sayings in the Gospel of Thomas. It was a deeper and more profound trance than I had ever experienced before. Metaphysical experiences occur often to me, so I was not alarmed. As I mentioned earlier I felt a glow around me, but I knew something was coming so I waited. The air around me seemed electric and alive and something inside of me was happening. Then instantly it happened. Not as a bolt of lightning, or thunder or a loud voice. I was not transported to heaven, nor was I transfigured like you – Jesus – on the mountain. I didn't travel anywhere or have an out-of-body experience.

JC: What was it?

DC: It was quiet and subtle, almost faint like a whisper, yet I could not miss it. My mind opened slowly, surely, steadily like a delicate flower blooming to greet the sun. That is the best I can describe it and it was all so very natural. There was no violent birth. No bloodletting. No emotional earthquake. No climbing the mountaintop. No sailing the vast ocean. No grueling initiation rite. No vision quest. No great sacrifice of time, money or heart. Some of these had happened earlier in my life. Possibly I had prepared the ground for what happened to me.

JC: Most likely.

DC: I think so, too. In this instance my mind simply opened and I received the light of revelation. My mind's eye, my intuitions and my body were hyperactive, like thousands of miniature sensors. Impressions, feelings and emotions filled me. I felt immersed in the divine. I experienced it as … emptiness! I experienced it as … nothingness! I experienced it as … absolute blackness and absolute silence. Curiously, I was not aghast or shocked by its magnitude. I was not pounded into submission by its horror. It was ordinary, normal and natural even. I was relaxed, at ease and awed.

JC: Many believe God is the Supreme Being and that he is supremely greater than any other sentient being in substance, form, quality, energy, intelligence, love and consciousness, whether angelic or demonic or anything else. Consistent with this belief is the fact that He is the Creator of "all of creation."

DC: Who resides in heaven and as such is outside the boundary of creation. In a flash my experience informed me of something quite different.

JC: What did it show you?

DC: That God is not a being. The divine is not a being. There is no being with substance, and the divine is not a "thing" because it is formless. It is closer to emptiness and nothingness than a sentient being.

JC: How did this experience change your perception of the divine? Was it swift and indelible? Did you have one notion of God before and then another afterward?

DC: As a young man I imagined I would go to heaven when I died. I assumed I would be able to ask God a series of questions and receive a series of answers. After this experience, however, I knew that would not be the case. Oddly, I was not disappointed. I knew I would not swagger up to God with an attitude, whether sheepish or brazen, and fire away because I realized there was not anyone to receive the question, nor was there anyone to answer it. Yet, in spite of nothingness, everything was there. It is the One, the singularity of reality, that which is without distinction, without separation and without duality. It is nothing and everything simultaneously, being and nonbeing, existence and nonexistence. It was all very clear, all very simple and all very normal. I am in God. God is in me and we are both one and the same. I am not outside of the divine looking in. Rather I am in the divine, I am of the divine, and I am the divine experiencing the divine. It is like the dream within the dream.

JC: I know from experience that wisdom contains wisdom which contains even more wisdom. Wisdom is tied together like links in a chain. In light of that, was this the only revelation for you? Or was there more?

DC: There was more! Instantly and intimately the mystical core of every major religion was laid bare for my eyes to see and for my heart to feel. The particular details of each were not as important as the essence. In the snap of a finger, I understood the deepest concepts and heart of the mystical traditions of mankind. After this baptism I saw clearly and understood plainly the inexplicable sayings in the Gospel of Thomas. They are not babbling or incoherent words; rather they are rarefied gems of wisdom. The Sufi wisdom tradition of divine reflection was not a curious musing but a tangible reality. I grasped both the Gospel of Thomas sayings and the essence of the Sufi wisdom tradition. But something else occurred that was just as astonishing.

JC: Which was?

DC: I realized that my experience was universal. Many people throughout the ages experienced the same thing, or something similar, and many strive for it. The religious and mystical literature stretching from the East to the West – Hinduism, Buddhism, Gnosticism, Sufism, Greek metaphysical philosophy, the Cabala, and Christian mysticism – speak of this unifying presence. After the proverbial dust settled, I was impressed by something altogether different. It involved the nature of the particular. Universality is one thing; the particular is something else. My experience left me with an exacting fullness of myself. It spoke directly to and affected my personality, my mind and my nature in a manner consistent with the grain of my soul. It is as if I became fully me, and with this came an understanding of the divine workings that spoke directly to my individuality and to my deepest self.

JC: This puts a smile on my face.

DC: My personality and nature are comprised of many elements. I have a pound of spirituality, a dash of engineering, a splash of hands-on building and a strong measure of creativity and curiosity. My enlightenment spoke to each and affected each equally and proportionally. Through this hyper-lens I witnessed the divine in operation. Daily I watch its awesome flow. The divine continuously informs, provides the ground of being, and gives life to all processes, activities, energies, knowledge and experiences. It is pure potential in action; it is everything and nothing intimately woven together. It is the matrix of consciousness, energy and form moving as a partner with the infinite. It is creation continuously expressing itself anew and strangely awesome. It is life expressing itself, knowing itself and experiencing itself as it truly is – divine. Nothing exists outside of it. It dances with itself and we are its partner. Without music, a floor, dancers and movement there is no revelation of dance. It cannot be known. The dance has to be danced. Regardless of our awareness, whether conscious or unconscious, everyone and everything of the dance is a divine act expressing the divine nature, and the nature of the divine is divine.

JC: And therein lies the mystery.

DC: Enough of me and my experiences. Let's continue with you. Is that all right?

JC: Your explanation of emptiness and nothingness are not dissimilar to my experience of the Father.

DC: Would you say one must awakened to the Father?

JC: The Father is hidden while the Kingdom of Heaven is in all and is everywhere. In the Father's wake is the Kingdom of Heaven. One must be open for both. To know the Father one must be committed to the process of transformation and accept the necessary steps. When the awakening comes, it comes swiftly and unexpectedly. One has to be ready and willing to receive the information this brings, and one has to be willing to carry and share that information with others and not discard or bury it.

DC: You say in the Gospel of Thomas that the Father is not born of a woman. That saying made me realize you understood – something in effect or close to – the One, the Mystery, emptiness and nothingness. You introduced a new concept of the divine into your society and called it the Father.

JC: That is correct.

DC: I'd like to discuss the Father in more detail later in this interview, but for now I'd like to circle back and talk about your missing years and several episodes from this period.

JC: Before, you mentioned humility, loss and a supernatural experience, and that these incidents prepared me for my ministry.

DC: I also mentioned forgiveness and love. I've narrowed the possible episodes to three. One, you were fully immersed in a spiritual education and your ministry is a logical extension of that education. Two, you lived a life that had nothing to do with spirituality or religion, but you had some kind of conversion experience that completely turned you around and pointed you in the direction of your ministry. I say this because both the gospels and your sayings describe "quick turnaround events." I coined that term to describe the speed at which life spins in another direction. For example, the sick or infirmed are suddenly healed; the hungry crowd is miraculously fed; servants receive money to invest and have to make a choice about investing; the shrewd manager is fired; hired workers who are delighted at the start of the day are seized with anger at the end of the day; and the rich person who dreamed of investing his money died that very night. This is what I mean when I refer to quick directional changes. The last possibility involves the combination of a religious education, a life of pleasure, a business venture gone terribly wrong, and a profound conversion.

JC: Explore the third possibility. What would that have looked like?

DC: After you left with your inheritance, Israel and your family became a distant memory. You merged with the Jewish Diaspora, leaving the God of your fathers in the land of your ancestors. You forgot God and the problems facing your people. You enjoyed yourself. You were restless and yearned for more. Your father's influence, however, motivated you to be a success, and you felt an obligation to invest your inheritance. You might have bought a small farm and employed hired hands and a manager. In the beginning, your endeavor was successful. You built barns to store the excess of produce. You were prosperous and it was at this moment that you felt the most comfortable with life. I can hear you say, "I am on the right path," but you noticed you were not a good manager and owner. The details and requirements for running an estate didn't interest you and you lacked the heart and mind for it. You were a poet, not an owner. You were not suited for running an estate and you missed your mark. You were neglectful and mismanaged the entire affair. To make matters worse, your manager was not as honest or skilled as he had led you to believe. You were more interested in the pursuit of wealth and its fruit than in managing it. You lived extravagantly. You were indiscriminate with your money and you mistreated your workers. Your eye clouded and the light within your body and in your soul turned to darkness. You became "blinded by the pursuit of food, clothing, and possessions." (Q53) You got into debt, owed money, and were taken to court and lost. Your situation turned from bad to worse and your worldly pursuits ran their course. You lost everything.

JC: You expanded upon the Prodigal Son parable.

DC: Yes, I have, because I believe this parable was inspired by actual events in your life. You don't explicitly say it and neither do the gospel writers. It is, therefore, purely conjecture on my part, but I suspect it's true nonetheless.

JC: In the parable, the Prodigal Son returns home and is enthusiastically welcomed by his father. This can be Israel returning to God.

DC: Or it is the lost sheep returning back to God through the Church! Why not? That is the Christian perspective. Let me summarize two prevailing positions before we explore my theory: One, Israel gets wise through Job-like calamities and returns back to the Father after reaching rock bottom. Does this refer to the three Jewish Wars with Rome between 66 CE and 135 CE? Is this your message? Because I see it differently. You brought new wine and new wineskins, and this metaphor and your ministry do not comport with the son leaving home and returning. Two, the parable is prophetic in that it points to the creation of the Church and dovetails into the Apostle Paul's theory that the Jews are the first of the Covenant and all the promises come to and move through them. After they reject you, and after your crucifixion and ascension, God creates a new paradigm and a new covenant with the gentiles. The blessings intended for the Jews are temporarily suspended and given to the gentiles, but they will be restored after a probationary period when Jesus Christ, the Son of God, returns wrathfully to earth and restores Israel to its rightful position. Is this the meaning of the son's return? I have my doubts.

JC: Why?

DC: Paul creates a complicated theology in relation to the Second Adam, Salvation theory, Jesus' return, and God's blessings to the Church, which after an unspecified time reverts back to Israel. My issue with Paul is his pride and arrogance for believing he can read and know the mind of God. He is convinced that he alone comprehends the mind and actions of God. But isn't this the very moral dilemma of Job? "Where were you when I laid the earth's foundation? Tell me, if you understand. Who marked off its dimensions? Surely you know! Who stretched a measuring line across it?" (Job 38:4–5) The same idea threads itself through several passages in Isaiah: "We are the clay, you are the potter" (Isaiah 64:8); "neither are your ways my ways" (Isaiah 55:8); "Who has understood the Spirit of the Lord?" (Isaiah 40:13)

JC: Paul is not alone in his hubris.

DC: Will you tell me the remainder of the Prodigal Son story? After all it is your story.

JC: Where do you want me to begin?

DC: Begin after the son "squandered his property by living extravagantly." (LK 15:13)

JC: The son's financial situation declined rapidly and it ended in a catastrophic famine. He was too proud to beg and felt too old to dig trenches. He had to do something and was forced to do the unthinkable – he begged and dug ditches and then hired himself out to a pig farmer. The irony is too hard to contemplate.

DC: The son was a menial laborer?

JC: Yes. He tended pigs, my ancestors' unclean animal. It was his fall from grace and it couldn't have gotten worse, or so he thought. It was a humiliating and shameful experience. He went from wealth to poverty in an instant. He couldn't borrow money and his situation became desperate; he nearly starved to death. He ate carob pods, which the pigs ate. Nobody helped him. It was a very dark time in his life and he lost hope. When he got hold of his senses he traveled back to his family where his father welcomed him with open arms.

DC: It is my contention that this intimate parable details and explains your back story prior to your ministry.

JC: I'm ready to walk the labyrinth now.

DC: I see it's raining.

CHAPTER 3

THE FATHER

David and Jesus stand outside, in the rain, adjacent the labyrinth.

JC: The fragrance in the air reminds me of the Sea of Galilee.

DC: That's the creosote and it sends an ocean-like smell into the air when it rains.

JC: Which way do we go?

DC: Follow me down the left path. You'll notice we are walking in a clockwise direction.

JC: I notice this path circles the labyrinth.

DC: Yes.

JC: I see a cross, four corner angles, and four points made from black volcanic rock and white rock that form the serpentine pathways.

DC: I laid out the east, west, north and south cardinal points with the black rocks and the remainder of the labyrinth with white rock. The entrance is in the southern position over there.

JC: Tell me more about your labyrinth.

DC: It is a classic seven-ring labyrinth. My original intent was to use the thirteen-ring labyrinth in the medieval cathedral in Chartres France.

JC: What happened?

DC: I wanted the path to be twenty-four inches wide, and had I used the thirteen-ring design the outer edge would have been over there in the driveway.

JC: It was too big and you didn't have enough room.

DC: Not for thirteen rings.

JC: Your labyrinth is a blend of beauty, artistry and intelligence.

DC: I appreciate your comments.

JC: Why did you create it?

DC: I felt the property needed a spiritual design. I don't have a rational answer. I just felt it needed one. During construction some incredible things occurred.

JC: Oh?

DC: A black and orange king snake slithered from the south cardinal stone to the center stone and coiled up. Later, a morning blue jay flew from that tree over there and landed on the west cardinal rock there, inspected my work, then flew to the north cardinal rock, inspected it, and then proceeded to the next two cardinal points. I was amazed that the blue jay did the inspection clockwise. A mother deer and her two fawns ate the fruit from that barrel cactus there, and either a bobcat or mountain lion grooms its claws on the agave over there.

JC: Show me.

DC: You see this leaf?

JC: It's shredded like string, and so is that one over there.

DC: Along with that one.

JC: Is this the entrance to the labyrinth?

DC: It is. I'll let you lead the way.

JC: I feel peace. Tell me about the significance of the labyrinth.

DC: I will tell it through metaphor. It's a bit like life.

JC: How so?

DC: At the beginning, the initiate starts at the edge and is fully immersed in the material world. With time, the initiate slowly winds through the labyrinth step by step, weaving in and out, up and down, and snaking around toward the center. With each step the density of the material world dissolves and the truth and power of spirit, which is immaterial and formless, awakens and fully comes alive at the center of the labyrinth. Unfortunately, one cannot stay planted at the center but must travel back to the material world where the journey began. Only this time, a transformation has occurred and the initiate knows the difference between the world of matter and the world of spirit and knows the difference between truth and illusion.

JC: The heart of reality is then known. I prefer the terms *Father* and the *Kingdom of God*. Either way, it is wisdom.

DC: Do you equate mystery with the Father?

JC: They are woven together and any difference is practically nonexistent.

DC: The Christians believe in the divine relationship between Father, Son and Holy Spirit. In the fourth century, this was formalized into the Trinity. Father, Son and Holy Spirit are mentioned at the end of the Gospel of Matthew, but the Trinity concept was set in Catholic stone in the fourth century. You seem to prefer the Father to Yahweh or Adonai, and you mention the Holy Spirit occasionally.

JC: Is there a question?

DC: There is an insight rather than a question. As I came to understand your *Kingdom of Heaven* sayings, I realized you were not talking about the Jewish Creator–Creation concept. Nor were you inspired by Elohim, Yahweh, Adonai and Ancient of Days, Lord of Lord or Lord of Hosts. The character and meaning of the Father and the Kingdom of Heaven are woven together and neither are expansions or continuations of your ancestral Hebrew heritage. The Kingdom of Heaven and the Father are radically new and I want to talk about the importance of this.

JC: What do you want to know?

DC: I wonder what the Father means to you and how you arrived at that concept. The ancient Greek philosopher Pythagoras coined the term and used it to refer to the One, the origin of the all and the source of all. From the One comes the multitude which then creates more multitudes, and so on. Reality is a geometric progression. From one comes two; this is the first cause, and once this occurs everything is set in motion – from two comes four, from four comes sixteen. This analogy is a multiplication sequence, but it illustrates the point.

JC: Once something gets started it grows into a multitude. I used the metaphor of the mustard seed explain this concept. The small mustard seed eventually becomes a vast living plant for the birds of the air to nest in.

DC: We are coming up on a barrel cactus. Careful. You have to watch out for them. The cacti in and around the labyrinth have sharp pointed spikes.

JC: You called it a barrel cactus. I've never seen one and now I want to touch it.

DC: You feel everything, don't you? You have to touch, hear, taste, smell and see because your senses are alive.

JC: They are.

DC: You also knew that wisdom and knowledge springs from the senses.

JC: These thorns are sharp. (*A pause as Jesus caresses the cactus with his finger.*) It is not only through our senses that we know. Mind knows mind. The infinite mind and the finite mind know and experience each other because at the root they are the same; maybe not in scale but in essence. Shall we continue?

DC: I'm in no rush.

JC: You are not? I say otherwise.

DC: Hang on! I've come to enjoy a slower pace. Because of it, I've learned to be silent and aware. I've awakened to being alive and I like the way it feels. I'd say, right now, we are caught up in the flow of our thoughts.

JC: We are walking the labyrinth. As you said, it snakes around, up and down, inside and out. We are doing just that. Let's continue to the center. Maybe we'll discover something.

DC: I hope so. I want to compare your concept of the Father to the Eastern view.

JC: What intrigues you?

DC: The Buddhists prefer the term *nothingness* to the *Father* and *everything* to mean form, potential, process, consciousness, energy and the like.

JC: Regardless of words the One remains the same. Words are inadequate in describing the ineffable. Words point to it but that is the best they can do. I found metaphor, analogy and parable effective in this regard.

DC: The oriental view is characteristically aloof and abstract and lacks a personal relationship. You are aware of this abstraction, but the Father was not a mere abstraction for you. It was a living principle.

JC: It wasn't a principle. The Father is alive and is real. He is life. The Father animates all things and we are intimately connected with him but most fail to recognize this truth.

DC: Why did you use the term *Father*?

JC: I could not sidestep my background or disconnect my life from my culture. One way to know and understand God was through relationship.

DC: Which involved a covenant or contract, a marriage of sorts, where each side had defined obligations and duties.

JC: Yes. I shifted the understanding to include a side-to-side and up-and-down relationship – a relationship with each other and one with the Father. I introduced the family as an analogy with the Father at the head. This was one reason I used the Father concept.

DC: You bridged two distinct ideas and relationships with a familiar, all-encompassing term.

JC: Had I used the term *The One* or *The Mystery* as the Greeks did, I would have lost my audience and they would not have connected to me. I had to address them specifically by offering something recognizable. At the same time, I had to push them further into unknown territory without them knowing it. Otherwise they would have reacted differently and dismissed me and my message.

DC: Even so, those in authority remained committed to killing you because you challenged them and their religious conventions.

JC: Regardless, I masked the true meaning of the Father in a familiar tongue. If one spent time with it, thought about it and acted on it, one would arrive at a similar understanding as I did and as you have.

DC: The Father is not a rational concept. It is not a logical argument that is systematically moved through. One cannot walk up to it and say, "Here it is" or "There it is." It is everywhere and, at the heart of it, resides an inexplicable mystery. The gap between the rational argument of the Father and the reality of the Father can only be bridged intuitively, mystically or experientially.

JC: You described earlier your "opening of the mind" experience. You read many books and had numerous life experiences before it occurred.

DC: I did. I'm also prone to epiphanies, intuitions, dreams, gut feelings and visions. This is normal for me and if I don't have them frequently, I feel disjointed and out of balance.

JC: Do any stand out? Is there one more profound than another?

DC: Four are head and shoulders above the others. Each was specifically potent and unique; each turned my life around or upside down or inside out, and each provided me with new and unexpected insights. Of the four, one was terrifying and startling.

JC: Tell me about them. Are you comfortable doing that?

DC: I've kept them close to my chest and revealed them only to a handful of people. The first came as a lucid dream when I was four. The second occurred when I was a young man and on the verge of stepping into my adult life; I experienced what St. John of the Cross describes as the "dark night of the soul." The third happened a few years after my "dark night of the soul" experience, when you appeared to me in a series of visions. The fourth was my enlightenment experience, which occurred a few years ago – the one I described before we came out to the labyrinth. I'd like to go out on a limb here. When I contemplate my mystical experiences and the effects they had on me, and when I compare them with you and your ministry, I can't help but believe you had a series of mystical experiences prior to your ministry.

JC: Why do you draw that conclusion?

DC: Initially this was difficult to see. Neither the New Testament nor any other first-century writing reference or cite it.

JC: But you say I had one?

DC: I have several reasons. Mystical experiences were common with your disciples, Paul and Old Testament prophets. Your disciples saw the resurrected Lord, Thomas touched your wounds, the disciples received the Holy Spirit at Pentecost, the Apostle Paul was knocked off his horse and blinded on the road to Damascus, while Abraham heard the voice of God, Moses saw the burning bush and Isaiah's lips were seared with a hot coal. These are but a few examples recorded in the Bible. When reading further, the point to notice is that the mystical encounter transformed and left an immediate and indelible impression on each person. It is also noteworthy to add that the divine was understood one way before the encounter but differently afterward, and that each person did one thing before but something very different afterward.

JC: Yes, after their encounter each moved into a greater and deeper relationship with God.

DC: This pattern makes me think something happened to you and I would wager that a mystical experience is the manner by which you came to know the Father and the reason behind your ministry.

JC: Are the examples above your only examples?

DC: No, I have others. You say you were a prophet and prophets tend to have a special relationship with the divine.

JC: They do. Go on.

DC: This is a side issue, but important nonetheless; all your mystical experiences recorded in the New Testament occurred at the beginning of, during or after your ministry. For example, after your baptism, when the dove descended upon you, God spoke to you; after your desert temptations the angels attended you; you were transfigured on Mount Hermon, resurrected from the dead and later ascended into heaven. None of these accounts testify to a mystical event before your ministry.

JC: No they don't.

DC: I have two pieces of circumstantial evidence.

JC: What do you mean?

DC: It is apparent to me your wisdom is celestial or otherworldly and does not derive from study alone but is motivated and inspired supernaturally. Something happened to you; afterward, you had access to divine wisdom.

JC: And the second piece of evidence?

DC: You conducted your ministry with an unnatural fiery zeal that seems inconsistent with the requirements and insights necessary to aggressively conduct your ministry. A gentle whisper doesn't seem enough to sweep you through the rigors and troubles of your ministry, nor does it seem sufficient to carry you through the ordeal of your trial, false accusations, flogging and crucifixion.

JC: When I started my ministry, I was filled with the Spirit of God; during my ministry I was transfigured and while I ministered I continuously felt attuned to and led by the Father.

DC: I'm not disagreeing with or questioning that. I believe that kind of mysticism and intuition were real for you and your ministry but they don't address the type of mystical experience I feel was necessary for you to begin your ministry. Again, I'm going out on a limb. The mystical experience to which I refer cannot be known by reading literature because it is not literary, and my assessment is that the type of experience to which I refer is neither gradual nor cumulative. You didn't have a series of small mystical experiences that added up to something big. Rather, something dramatic transformed the constitution of your heart and mind and, whatever it was, it propelled you forward to conduct your ministry in a manner similar to that of the Apostle Paul, your disciples and Old Testament prophets. I would venture to say it was as extraordinary as the burning bush was to Moses, the fiery wheels were to Ezekiel, or the angel with the red-hot coal was to Isaiah.

JC: I want to say that I was mystically inclined.

DC: You are being dodgy. I know you were mystically inclined. I assume someone in your family, like your mother Mary, was mystically inclined and this ability ran counter to your other family members who were inclined to be righteous or zealots.

JC: I like being dodgy and I want to test your conviction before I address your theory. What kind of mystical experience do you think I had?

DC: Of all known and possible mystical experiences recorded in the world's spiritual traditions that I know, I believe I've narrowed it down to one. I do not believe you had an angelic encounter; I do not believe you had a vision or a dream; I do not believe your mind was altered through hallucinogens; I do not believe you arrived at the Father through the study of scripture or other writings; nor I do believe you had a series of cumulative nonverbal experiences.

JC: Why does this part of my story interest you?

DC: I'm interested in motive and purpose. Something happened to you before you went to John the Baptist and it provided you with a direct connection with Father. It filled your heart with love and compassion, and it inspired you, like a muse, to compose your sayings. You didn't learn this knowledge from scrolls, scripture or basic life experiences. It was different.

JC: I smile at this.

DC: Why?

JC: We've reached the center of the labyrinth. Let's stand here and enjoy the moment.

DC: The rain is coming down in buckets.

JC: You don't mind, do you? I like the drops hitting my head and landing on my body. I like the feel of water. It reminds me of my baptism. Open your mouth and catch the rain.

DC: I haven't done this since I was a child.

JC: Then act like one. Children know how to have fun and live in the moment. The world is a magical place for them. Adults forget these joys and tend to be too serious.

The rain pours down and it is received happily and playfully. Finally, the moment breaks.

JC: What do you believe is the mystical experience in question?

DC: Pardon me?

JC: You believe I had a particular mystical experience before I went to John the Baptist. Of all the types of mystical experiences one can have, which one do you suppose I had? What is your conclusion?

DC: An NDE.

JC: Say that again.

DC: An NDE - short for near-death experience.

JC: Describe that to me.

DC: A person is clinically dead for a short period of time. The heart stops beating, the brain shuts down, and the soul leaves the body and enters the realm beyond the physical world. It is called either heaven or the afterlife. In any event, the person experiences life after death, but they are faced with a question, "Do you want to stay or do you want to go on?" If one wishes to stay, one may. If one wishes to return to the world, one may and live out the remainder of one's life. I believe this happened to you. You made a choice to come back and apply the knowledge you learned. Your NDE was the inspiration of the Father and the impetus for your ministry.

JC: What makes you think this happened to me?

DC: Your ministry is characterized by the Father, by compassion, by wisdom, and by physical endurance. You know the mystery of existence and you have an open heart. You are fearless in confronting the political and religious authorities, you have little regard for the needs of your body, you disregard pain and discomfort, you dismiss and shed criticism, and you became egoless. I think the NDE is the reason behind these traits.

JC: You've dug deep.

DC: In the Gospel of Thomas you say, "When you see one who was not born of a woman, bow down and worship. That is your Father." (THOM 15) You experienced or saw the Father. Tell me what happened.

JC: Rarely did I speak of this. I spoke only to a few. I was on the road from Jericho to Ein Gedi. The sun hung low on the horizon and the day was nearly over. I was perplexed and troubled when I stopped for the night. As I pondered why all the bad things had happened to me in my life and what I was going to do, I failed to recognize that I had reached a particular area on this road notorious for its danger. As I settled in I was attacked by a group of highwaymen.

DC: Outlaws?

JC: The other term for them was bandits, and they were particularly unruly and nasty. In any event, they suddenly appeared, wanting my possessions and money. But mainly they wanted to prey on me. They liked the power it gave them.

DC: What did you have that they wanted?

JC: A blanket, tunic, several coins, pieces of food and my water skin. Of course, I didn't want any trouble and I let them know that, but it didn't matter. They chided and taunted me, and as they made their demands known, they surrounded me. I unsuccessfully tried to humor them, but I was surrounded, outnumbered and at their mercy.

DC: You must have been petrified.

JC: I was. I feared for my life. Then I realized I had to do something, otherwise I would be assaulted and possibly tied up.

DC: Did you run?

JC: I was hemmed in.

DC: You fought them?

JC: I didn't want them to take everything I owned without a fight. I am a proud, dignified Galilean who didn't want to be pushed around.

DC: What happened?

JC: The leader stepped forward and attacked first, hitting me hard in the face with a quick swing. I staggered back, gained my footing and took a swing at him, hitting him on the mouth. This stunned him. His shock turned to anger and then to rage. He was consumed with a frenzy of hate and fury I had never seen before. Then he and the others jumped and assaulted me. I was overwhelmed by the hits from all directions. Their arms swung with clasped fists, their teeth clenched and their eyes burned cold. Blows fell on my face, blows fell on my stomach, and blows fell on my back. Suddenly a series of images flashed across my mind. I had an eerie sensation I was about to die and past memories flooded my mind. I recalled Passover feasts, my family, my brother James, my mother's smile and the kisses she pressed on my forehead. I remembered the neighborhood where I grew up, the eyes of my friends, and the clothes we wore. I recalled reading the Torah and listening to the rabbis in the synagogue. I recalled the scent of my home, the smell of pressed olive oil and the taste of figs. Then I remember crashing to the ground and crumpling into a protective fetal position. The sting of each hit, the blow after blow, and the kick after kick were unbearable. Slowly my life slipped away, fading toward death. Oddly, I felt serene. I had never felt this serenity before.

DC: What do you mean? Can you describe it?

JC: Before I continue let me mention the prevailing ideas of the afterlife and the heart of the Jewish religion. There was little regard for the afterlife. The revelation of the law, the Promised Land, God's husbandry of the Jewish people from nomadic tribe to nation, and his continued presence in the temple were divine gifts and all we could expect. On the surface these seemed satisfying enough, but a perplexing and disturbing issue stirred and captivated the Jewish mind. We couldn't completely make sense of life's tragedies. They seemed incongruent with divine mercy and justice.

DC: That was ground zero, so to speak.

JC: It was a philosophic and religious concern.

DC: Understanding and interpreting life's tragedies were expressed in your stories: the temptation and Fall of Adam and Eve in the Garden of Eden, Noah and the flood, the plagues and sufferings of Job, the destruction of the Temple of Solomon, and the laments in the Psalms.

JC: Our interest revolved around life in the here and now and interpreting life's tragedy and inherent evil. The consensus regarding the afterlife, however, was something akin to sheol – eerily dark and smoldering in a half-awake, half-asleep trash heap.

DC: As I understand it, sheol was the grave, located at the center of Earth.

JC: It was shadowy, dusty and beyond the scope of God. "Death and Destruction are never satisfied," says Proverbs. (Proverbs 27:20)

DC: It always laid in wait. "Therefore Death expands its jaws, opening wide its mouth." (Isaiah 5:14)

JC: It was a bottomless pit without escape.

DC: A one-way journey.

JC: I don't know what you mean.

DC: One didn't enter and then exit; it's one directional. Once you were in, you were in forever and couldn't come out.

JC: Yes, and there was no reward either. The idea evolved during the Jewish exile into Babylon. We once believed that if we left the Promised Land behind, God would not be with us, just as in sheol. We discovered otherwise and our wisdom literature reflects this change.

DC: This paradigm shift accelerated during the Seleucid persecutions following the death of Alexander the Great. The Seleucids wanted to eradicate your religion, which the Jews steadfastly resisted. People were cruelly tortured and brutally murdered for practicing the Torah.

JC: They were, and that is when ideas of the afterlife circulated. The question about the afterlife revolved around a question: how could a just and merciful God allow the torture and persecution of the faithful, especially when that person adhered to and abided by the law, commandments, and prophets? The conclusion drawn from that question was that a just and merciful God rewarded one's unwavering conviction with immortality. Some believed in a glorious heaven, others advocated an imperishable soul, another believed in the End Time wrath of God, while another group believed in the resurrection of the body.

DC: Resurrection is an Egyptian concept.

JC: In any event, before the end of my beating my spirit left my body. I experienced something entirely new.

DC: Can you describe it?

JC: I rose above my body, stopped and looked down, drifting. My awareness expanded and heightened. I could see my open wounds, the blood seeping from them, the ground receiving my blood and the men kicking me until I lay motionless. After they ransacked my clothes, stripped off my tunic and took all that I had, they left me for dead. I experienced a vividness I had never experienced before. I realized my body was inert, but I was alive, more alive than I had ever been. I gazed at my body, not the body lying on the ground, but this transparent body (*tapping on his chest*). I didn't have a physical body; strangely I had this uncanny notion that I was still me, and I was filled with a divine white light. I was peaceful and the atmosphere was pleasant. My recent concerns and worries vanished in a twinkle. They didn't matter and I didn't care.

DC: The near-death experience is not willed or practiced in meditation; neither is it a trance or a lucid dream.

JC: This is what you believe occurred to me before I went to John the Baptist?

DC: Yes, and it is the factor behind the Father and your ministry of love and compassion.

JC: Then we understand each other and speak the same language.

DC: Did anything happen after this?

JC: I saw a long silvery, pulsating cord about the width of three fingers extending out through my shirt to my transparent light body. As I recognized the cord another very bright, luminescent and vibrant white light appeared, and I found myself inside it; it was vast and seemingly infinite. I noticed another umbilical cord or some kind of tube, I can't remember, and I wondered what it might be. In my mind, I thought I should investigate, and with a sudden rush I was swept into that opening moving at great speed. I was in a current traveling faster and faster. I thought this very exciting. Then I stopped and stepped into paradise. I can't describe it any other way. I'm at a loss for words. Paradise was filled with intense love and compassion where I basked and bathed in both. I experienced infinite warmth and an indescribable, almost intolerable joy. I have never known such love or tenderness. An angel emerged from a mist, and he came up to me, placed his hands on my head, and caressed it. I hadn't thought about it but I sustained head injuries during my beating that needed healing. He then placed his hand on my heart and spoke to me without words, yet I knew everything he was thinking and saying. He showed me my past actions, or I became aware of them. It was strange. Many of my deeds and actions caused pain and unhappiness. A feeling of sadness and anguish rushed through me. I realized I gave birth to suffering and sorrow that at times was intentional and at other times was unintentional. I didn't like these feelings. Then the angel showed me the power of words and how they create and how they destroy. I was shown the destructive nature of my words, and the pain and suffering they caused. I couldn't bear this revelation either. I was a destroyer of hearts and I selfishly crushed people with my intellect. I used my mind antagonistically with a closed heart. Now I felt a depth of shame and guilt, as if I were in a deep sea of it. Not only did I suffer from the shame and guilt of my recent failure, but I was now suffering shame and guilt through the realization that I afflicted others. I was living in a collective heart of anguish; all the people I hurt became one heart, and with each beat of the heart I felt a wave of pain.

DC: I know this is tangent from what you are saying, but when I was a young boy I massacred an army of black ants that invaded my bathroom. Afterward I understood implicitly I had killed colony of living creatures God created. Not long afterward a profound sense of remorse and guilt swept over me and I knew I had done something terribly wrong. I was a destroyer of worlds and that practice flowed against the grain of my soul. I vowed right then and there I would not act that callous again. I did not want to be nor did I want to act like an avenging angel. I wanted to create not destroy.

JC: I understand you exactly. Strangely, this revelation wasn't a judgment. I want to emphasize that. The angel didn't condemn or judge me; he illuminated and opened my heart to feel for the first time. My shame, guilt, wounds and anguish burned away as quickly as a red-hot coal burns flesh. All those feelings vanished! Gone! Next I was seared with love. My heart expanded in unconditional love. I realized anger, hate, greed and misery pulled and lulled one to sleep. Acting in such a way blocked and countered the divine. At that moment, I knew I could never hate again, nor could I say words of judgment or condemnation, about me or anyone else. Everything is alive and in a state of grace. The divine is all around and in all. The sensation filled me with peace and tranquility, so much so that I didn't want to step away. The sensation and knowledge were beautiful.

DC: Did the angel leave you?

JC: He did not. He knew all along I had questions to ask, ones I wanted to ask for a long time, but for which I hadn't been able to find the answers. He spoke to me in my mind; he was not speaking, yet I was hearing his words. And he said, "I know you have many questions. You will have time to ask them."

Then the angel directed me to a black dot. I looked at him skeptically, yet I was allured. The black dot appeared as if it were the pupil of God's eye. And I heard, "Go!" And with an intentional thought I was at the black dot with an extended finger and I touched it.

DC: Incredible! What happened next?

JC: Darkness breathed into me, absorbing me. I was turned inside out.

DC: Darkness as in the darkness of evil?

JC: No! No! There is nothing evil associated with this darkness, nothing at all! I can't emphasize that enough. It's not unlike the void or a womb, for that matter. I entered a profound realm, as if walking into a room in a mansion, a mansion with many rooms never known before. I was completely absorbed in the darkness. Then, like before, I moved very swiftly in some sort of deep current; I soared like a bird above our planet, then to the sun and out past Mercury, Venus, Earth, Mars, Jupiter, Saturn, Uranus and Neptune. I saw the heavens and then in a flash I raced beyond our galaxy.

DC: If you don't mind I'd like to say something and tell you of the dream I had when I was four. It's uncanny how close my dream is to your experience.

JC: Tell me.

DC: Remember I was a four-year-old boy having a dream.

JC: As you said.

DC: In my dream I was an old sage with long flowing white hair and a long white beard to match. I wore a magician's coat, like Merlin the Magician and I sat riding on the back of a large muscular white horse. The colors of the forest around me were extremely vivid and vibrant, like a hyper-realist painting. The ground underneath my horse's hooves wasn't brown or dense as expected. Rather it was translucent and consisted of many colors. Pulsating below the surface was a river of sparkling white light that nourished every plant, tree and blade of grass. Every animate and inanimate thing was fused with divine light that radiated a halo. As I rode my horse I held three crystal spheres in my open left palm; the spheres were the size of a softball or a bit larger. The voice of God called to me; well, it was more that I could hear the words but they were never spoken – they were inside my mind. In any event the voice directed me to enter a sphere. It didn't matter which one. I was commissioned to go into one. All three were mine. I agreed. Instantly my body transformed and dematerialized into divine particles of light that streamed into one of the spheres. I was now inside the sphere, deposited at the extreme edge of the universe, which was black. Like you,

I zoomed at great speed through the universe, past clusters of super-galaxies, into our Milky Way galaxy, to the outer edge of our solar system, past each of the planets, and to the planet Earth. I traveled in the opposite direction as you. Then I woke and found myself in my bed.

JC: You came from a place outside the universe to Earth. Let me tell you my experience and reveal what I learned. The most pressing question on my mind was "What is the void? What did God hover over?" I was thinking of the first words in Genesis.

DC: Did you get an answer?

JC: More than that! Moments before I was lying on the road dead and now I was in this place I cannot describe. Time didn't seem real. Time is all time or it is no time; past, present and future don't exist and yet they exist together as one. This is a troubling conclusion and it is a profound mystery. As I traveled at great speed through the heavens my mind continued to expand. Then something odd transpired. I was not traveling. It seemed it was, but that was not the case. I was not moving. Instead, my mind stretched out to absorb the cosmos – the all, everything. Then the movement stopped and I entered another realm of darkness, one of absolute silence, stillness and blackness. It was like an unbounded womb. Everything became infinitely large and infinitely small simultaneously. I was filled with incredible amazement and wonder.

DC: Did you feel anything?

JC: I did not panic and I was not alarmed. Rather, I was at peace. This was the place of all potential – where existence and nonexistence touch, where being and non-being slip past one another, the place before creation. I even got the impression it was the eye of God. It was here that I glimpsed that narrow slice of the Father. That is the best I can do, since words cannot describe this realm. They fall short, very short. They point to it but they cannot touch or illuminate it. In this realm, which is possibly our concept of the void, was a waiting.

DC: What was it waiting for?

JC: The voice of God, but it was more than that – a boom or bang, or the sound of a drum hit by a stick, a vibration, or the initial movement from nothing to everything. At this moment I had a profound revelation that really affected me. I realized I am in this space at the same time I am the potential of this space and, this was strange, I am the space. In addition, I knew at the deepest level of my being that I am it and it is me and that I am me and I'm not me simultaneously. I exist and don't exist at the same time. I wasn't expecting this revelation and insight.

DC: There is no spatial relation and no "I," no ego and yet "I am."

JC: It is and isn't. Instantly, like a seed impregnating the darkness of the womb, the light of the divine is everywhere, expanding, creating and knowing itself.

DC: Experiencing itself through creation.

JC: Yes. The Father knows and experiences Himself as Creator and creation.

DC: We are that.

JC: Yes.

DC: I suspect at this moment the angel was not guiding you in this revelation.

JC: That is correct. I was filled with awareness and needed no guidance.

DC: What did you do after this enlightenment?

JC: I was in a state of bliss and didn't want to leave. Yet I felt I couldn't stay there. I didn't hear the voice of God, nor did an angel encourage me to return. I knew I had to live out the remainder of my life. With these experiences, I knew life continues and cycles through time. Death is not the end, just another beginning, another odyssey in the divine.

DC: So you didn't want to leave?

JC: No, but that was my choice.

DC: Can you describe the return to your body?

JC: At the point of decision I was a translucent body of light. I have no words to describe it. I was a soul, awake, alert, aware and alive. Instantly the void turned inside out again; it went from absolute blackness and silence to infinite light. For a moment, I was immersed in this bright light, and then it dissipated like an early morning fog. The intensity subsided, receding into normal daylight. During the change, I floated above my body. I could see the horizon in all directions and I spotted a man approaching me. As he neared I felt his alarm. He hurried to me. An overwhelming compassion filled his heart, which I felt. He knelt over my body to offer his assistance and it is then that I slipped back into my body. I felt heavy and dense, my body racked with pain. I was back in this world with the divine knowledge – elated to be alive, though barely.

DC: This is incredible. I need a few moments to gather my thoughts. Let's wind our way out the labyrinth, dry off and change these wet clothes.

JC: May I borrow some of your clothes?

DC: Of course. I think I have something that will fit you. I could use a cup of hot coffee. I know a place we can go.

JC: Take me there.

CHAPTER 4

HOMECOMING

JC: What are these clothes you gave me to wear?

DC: Black cowboy boots, my old faded blue jeans with tears and holes, and a black, long-sleeved shirt with a Celtic interlaced design running down the length of the arms.

JC: These pants are frayed with loose dangling fabric strings hanging from each tear.

DC: People pay a lot of money for those types of pants.

JC: Did you?

DC: No. I wore them out and they are the only pair I have that fit you. You look like a contemporary rocker.

JC: A rocker?

DC: Yes, a lead singer of a rock-and-roll band. Hop in.

JC: What is this?

DC: My pick-up truck. We'll drive to the café.

JC: Oh.

Jesus settles in the front seat and the truck speeds away from the house. Silence fills the cab until Jesus breaks it.

JC: Your truck goes fast; I haven't experienced anything so fast.

DC: I want to share a fact with you. On July 20, 1969, the Apollo 11 Lunar Lander touched down at Tranquility Base. An American astronaut named Neil Armstrong exited the spacecraft, climbed down the ladder and set his foot on the surface of the moon. He was the first man to do that and I watched the entire black and white episode on television.

JC: An American man walked on the moon?

DC: Not just one but twelve American men walked on the moon during the Apollo missions. What I find curious is that you are closer in age to Neil Armstrong and the moon landing than you are to the first Egyptian King.

JC: When did he reign?

DC: The Scorpion King reigned roughly 3,500 years before your birth. You lived closer in time to the moon landing than you did to the first Egyptian king.

JC: You are fascinated by many things.

DC: I am. We're here.

JC: This is the café?

DC: Are you hungry?

JC: I am.

DC: They have sandwiches.

Jesus and David enter the coffeehouse. Customers at tables and couches read newspapers, talk with friends, or work on laptops. Flickering dodgy stares assail them as they cross to the order counter. Jesus seems strangely familiar, but no one nods a greeting until a sobbing woman tucked in the corner looks up and eyes him. Tears streak down her red curved cheeks. Jesus, compassionately, strides up to her as David follows close behind.

JC: Hello! May I interrupt? Why are you crying?

SOBBING WOMAN: Who are you?

JC: I am Jesus.

SOBBING WOMAN: Jesus? In that outfit? You're teasing me and I don't appreciate it.

JC: My robe was soaked from the rain and I'm wearing David's clothes while it dries.

SOBBING WOMAN: You look like a country singer.

JC: Will you tell me what's wrong?

SOBBING WOMAN: There's something about your eyes that I can trust but I don't want to burden you.

JC: Please tell me.

SOBBING WOMAN: I buried my sister yesterday.

JC: How did she die?

SOBBING WOMAN: She had pancreatic cancer.

JC: Were you with her?

SOBBING WOMAN: I was. I'm haunted by the fear I saw in her eyes before she died and now I'm overwhelmed with sorrow. The pain won't stop. It keeps flooding me.

Jesus moves closer, stands beside her and offers his hand. The woman's bewilderment disappears and she takes his hand and rises to meet him. Jesus tenderly embraces her. Every person holds a bated breath; keen, intent eyes focus on him as he whispers into her ear. Grief shakes her and tears stream down her cheek. Again, Jesus whispers into her ear and suddenly she stops crying.

SOBBING WOMAN: You are very kind.

JC: God feels your anguish and cries with you. He loves you a thousand times more than you can imagine.

Jesus releases the woman from his arms.

SOBBING WOMAN: Thank you. Thank you for your words. I feel a little better.

She slumps back into the chair with a sad smile. Jesus turns to the customers and addresses them.

JC: One compassionate heart knows the sadness of another; one heart knows another; one heart feels and accepts another and allows it to be. God loves each of you with great passion. Know this and embrace it. Know and embrace each other. God is with you and you and you – he is with all of us. Do not be afraid to express your love for each other. We are all sons and daughters of God and his love continually shines as the sun shines. Love each other. Find peace in love.

People are astonished and react with hushed uncertainty. Jesus turns to David.

JC: I'm ready for my sandwich and coffee.

DC: Let's order.

JC: I received the same response when I spoke on the mountain, in the villages and in the synagogue.

DC: The Sermon on the Mount?

JC: Why are you surprised? This is the reaction I received most of the time. At least your neighbors don't want to kill me.

The owner greets Jesus and David at the order counter.

OWNER: *(eyeing Jesus intently)* Quite a speech. What will you have?

DC: *(to Jesus)* What would you like?

JC: I'll have what you have.

DC: *(to the owner)* Two medium lattes with whole milk and those two egg and cheese sandwiches. Put a little raw sugar in each latte.

OWNER: You want that for here or to go?

DC: *(to Jesus)* Do you want to stay here or go back to the house?

JC: I want to stay here.

DC: *(to the owner)* For here.

OWNER: That will be $18.53. Have a seat and I'll bring it to you.

David pays the owner as Jesus finds a table with a view of the mountains. Now David takes the open seat beside him. Customers' cold stares pierce them like darts. Jesus responds with a kind smile and gracious nod.

JC: Let's not speak about the woman or the words I said to her.

DC: That's between you.

JC: Thank you. I enjoy watching the rain fall and lightning strike.

DC: I lived near the ocean and experienced its moods and temper. I must admit I'm still drawn to it, but I couldn't fully appreciate the desert until I moved here. It's vibrant, stark and raw, with an unfiltered exchange between sky and ground. I like the drama.

JC: The desert is unencumbered by the demands of culture and free of man's language. The desert is in my bones.

DC: Civilization beats to its own definition and rhythm; its dominating voice and strong hand shapes and nourishes a person. It did for me. I doubt I'd survive if I tried to live "off the grid" or in the wilderness like my ancestors. I need the city.

JC: Balancing the social and the natural order is complex.

DC: Balancing solitude and silence while living in the city is complex. I had to tune out the noise in my head and the noise in the world.

JC: When cultivated, the divine can be heard and known.

DC: I found the voice of God in silence.

JC: I also found the voice of God in the "all that there is."

DC: When did you come to know that truth and the truth of silence and solitude?

JC: I was open to many new realities after my near-death experience.

DC: Elaborate on that point.

JC: My senses were acute. My heart was on fire, my mind could see far into the distance. I was alive. I knew it. I was observant. I felt I was on a journey of self-discovery. My life unfolded in unforeseen ways. It ebbed and flowed with high and low moments. Every day ushered in something brand new – a feeling, a thought, a fragrance or an experience. I enjoyed my new sense of time and being in the moment. I enjoyed watching my life stream where it wanted and opened as it did. I was in the mystery of life and was thrilled by every experience whether significant or superficial. That was a remarkable place to be and I knew it was a gift from the Father.

DC: With my enlightenment my mind opened. I was filled with awe and ecstasy, and wonder and joy. I was hyper-sensitive and I didn't want the sensation to fade which, in the end, it did. But something didn't fade.

JC: I'm sure you found, as I found, that the knowledge and wisdom from the mystical experience didn't diminish over time. The effects of my NDE softened and eventually disappeared, but my mind, intuition and heart opened and became charged.

DC: Was there a particular place you could go to get away from the "demands of the world"?

JC: I made a quiet place in my home. At other times, I went out into the countryside or in the hills to be by myself.

DC: I have a quiet place in my home. I learned to like my solitude. Ironically, I became a hermit and secluded myself from the world.

JC: I didn't do that. I could have but I didn't. Instead, I did the opposite and I went out into the world with my ministry.

DC: I also learned troubling, difficult and painful experiences are woven into life and become teachers. They leave scars, hard lines of definition.

JC: Choices have to be made; either use those experiences positively to gain wisdom or use them to fertilize and nurture anger, discontent, frustration and bitterness. Life becomes hard as a rock and devoid of joy and laughter if the latter is chosen.

DC: It takes time to heal painful wounds.

JC: I'm not addressing time. I'm addressing consequence. What is one supposed to do with uncomfortable, stressful and painful experiences? If not properly channeled they harden the heart and fill the mind with darkness, which then grows and spreads, dimming the light of the divine.

DC: Speaking of which, I'm stunned by your revelation. I'm still trying to wrap my arms around your NDE.

JC: Why does this experience surprise you?

DC: How can it not? I knew something happened to you because I recognized an invisible force propelling you forward like a shot from cannon. There was a military precision to your ministry.

JC: Military precision?

DC: It was intentionally focused and devoid of nonsense. I'd like to talk about the consequences of your NDE and Christian theology.

JC: Christians are definite about the meaning of my life and death.

DC: They are. They believe the Son of God was with the Father from the beginning of time, implying your humanity, personality and wisdom were pre-existent and preformed. They believe that your divinity was infused into your being, and that you were predestined to conduct your ministry and die on the cross for the sins of mankind. In essence, you merely waited until the fullness of time to begin your ministry and then die on the cross.

JC: That is the theological implication.

DC: I see two peculiar idiosyncrasies. First, all the spiritual beings in heaven with God had to hold their collective breath to see whether you would carry out your ministry, fulfill your destiny, and die on the cross.

JC: And the second?

DC: Let me finish my first thought. In this odd assumption, your growth and evolution, as every person experiences, is absent. From this position, you are not in the process of becoming *something* because you exist as "I am." As such, you simply accomplished the set goal before you.

JC: That I fulfilled a preordained destiny to die for the sins of mankind?

DC: Yes, and that is the Apostle Paul's position. That concept is too abstract for me. Now to the second point, which dovetails into the first. If there is no growth or change then there is no journey to become the "fullness-of-Jesus." There is no need for a missing year's back story, no Hero's Journey and no personal transformation. There is no need for a family and there is no need to learn anything because there is no wisdom to seek and gain from life. This premise is simply too difficult a position for me to accept and appears more improbable than probable. Life is diverse and filled with joys and sorrows, triumphs and defeats, exhilaration and heartaches, love and hate, and clarity and uncertainty.

JC: The Christian argument states that I had to be human and to have human experiences to know what it means to be human. Birth, infancy, adolescence, youth and adulthood are part of that process. I had to grow, learn and evolve to understand and overcome human weakness and temptation. But you take issue with that perspective?

DC: I would rather embrace your humanity, than your divinity; otherwise the life you lived, the wisdom you gained and the sacrifices you endured are minimized. Your back story is real, your compassion is genuine, your wisdom is true, and your surrender to the Father is authentic. I don't want to overlook these by accepting your death as the salvation of my soul. Instead, I want to learn about the content of your life, the wisdom you spoke and the actions you took, and allow it to be my witness and guide.

JC: You said we shared similar experiences. I'd like to know if you once lost your faith. Did you?

DC: I did.

JC: Were the effects chilling?

DC: They were. Faith in anything is the unconscious bedrock of one's life, and the normalcy of faith lay hidden until questioned or lost. Then fury, destruction and uncontrollable emotions surface with a vengeance.

JC: What happened to you?

DC: It's a long story to tell at this moment. Suffice to say, I lost faith in myself, life and God.

JC: All at once?

DC: No, in succession and over a short period of time. I lost my compass and felt the ground beneath my feet dissolve into quicksand. Fate's hand forced me to accept bleak and dire circumstances and I flailed around to keep from sinking. Fortunately, my enlightenment stabilized my life, swung it around and set me on more solid ground. I discovered that each person unwittingly walks along an unseen razor-sharp knife edge teetering between faith, hope and goodness, and existential despair, meaninglessness and destruction.

JC: Please tell me how you lost faith in life.

DC: I had a brutal initiation rite at nineteen and it was drastic, profound and unbearable. It instantly turned my life upside down and inside out. Does Solomon's lament mean anything to you, "'Meaningless! Meaningless!' says the Teacher ... What do people gain from all their labors at which they toil under the sun?'" (Ecclesiastes 1:2-3) A Catholic monk, Saint John of the Cross, coined the term "dark night of the soul" and it refers to the loss of faith and to an existential state of despair.

JC: I knew the meaning of Solomon's lament later in my life. Those words have no meaning until the agonizing truth invades one's heart and mind. Then they have meaning.

DC: It's ferocious and extremely destructive. If one survives one belongs in a rare fraternity.

JC: True spirituality requires a direct, immediate and intimate experience and one has to be horrified and awed.

DC: Words fail to explain or illuminate it ...

JC: ... and the wisdom contained within such an experience is for the one experiencing it. To anyone else it is hollow and inconsequential.

DC: At nineteen I was optimistic, fun-loving, hardworking, proud and determined. The divine was the wind in my sail. I anticipated my future but I didn't know what I wanted to do with my life. I pursued a couple of paths but they didn't take me where I wanted to go. Possibly the hand of God was directing me in another direction, but my heart stirred and my mind ached and I was emotionally troubled. One day in the winter of 1979, in a flash, a veil lifted from my eyes and I saw clearly into the dark silence of existence. The image was horrific and terrifying. I saw life as a pointless absurdity, empty, inane and without meaning, and I was hurled into a deep state of despair. I could not point to my achievements for solace and nothing could alleviate the dreadfulness I felt.

JC: I understand how you felt.

DC: Another vision followed the first one and it increased my anxiety and elevated my burden.

JC: The first was not enough?

DC: Apparently not. I saw an image of a toy electric train looping round and round its tracks, passing the little plastic train station, the town, the cars and motionless figures, the railroad posts and crossings, belching acrid white smoke, only to return, traveling nowhere. This insight wasn't a metaphor of my life; it was the reality of it. With this I was paralyzed with despondency. It was as if I were naked, huddling shoulder deep in a cold rain-soaked sinkhole. It didn't matter if I picked myself up by my bootstraps, dusted off, and clawed inch by inch out of that hole. It didn't matter if I soared out with wings, burrowed through a tunnel, climbed out by ladder, walked on water or gazed into the face of God. There was no moving on, and even if I were to move on there was nowhere to go. What I experienced is that all motion, activity, achievements and relationships only postpone the inevitable. Nothing in life is worth the struggle; nothing intrinsically merits the effort or fight; nothing can satisfy the yearning for meaning or purpose. Can you really close your eyes and refuse to see it? We are all going to die. Our destiny is the grave. In the end, all is vanity and pointless. Why not throw up your hands with the gesture, "So what is the point?" Meaninglessness and nothingness punctuate life. Death awaits us all. Nothing could erase this insight from my mind, nor was the hand of God going to miraculously plug the blood streaming from the gaping hole in my heart or fill the blackness in my mind with light. I was forever and hopelessly lost; it was nirvana of the absurd. Afterward I was a hollowed-out shell of a person. I yearned for death. Nothing motivated me, nothing directed me, and nothing convinced me otherwise. I was accused of self-indulgence. I felt anyone surviving that poison pill deserves a Medal of Honor, if for nothing else than for just sticking around.

JC: You were alone in that moment. When the ground beneath your feet crumbles and the ideas that bind your world together unravel, one can only hope the hand of God is near because the silence is overwhelming and the pain and hardship are crushing.

DC: I found the path to God isn't straightforward; yet it is individually unique, as each person is unique. I learned to take this in stride.

JC: One part drudgery and another part ecstasy.

DC: One part darkness and the other part light.

JC: I was unnerved by the divine blanket of silence.

DC: I know what you mean.

JC: Did you have a guide or teacher during this time? Did you receive any advice or comfort?

DC: No!

JC: Coming to terms with that insight without descending back into the abyss is complicated, especially without skill or support.

DC: It would have been easier cutting a six-by-six post to size with a twenty-two–ounce framing hammer.

JC: You were too young for that revelation.

DC: My friends and family did not understand my dark agony, nor was anyone equipped to offer the wisdom or assistance I needed. No one could say with conviction or certainly, "Go here or go there," or "Know this or know that," or "Talk to this person or talk to that person." I was alone wading through that ghastly ordeal. The horror of that revelation and the emotional and intellectual scars from that period remain to this day. I shudder when I am reminded of those memories.

JC: And here you are interviewing me.

DC: My rite of passage catapulted me on a lifelong spiritual odyssey. I wouldn't advise anyone to re-create my experience, but then again, I believe everyone eventually arrives at the same destination. I'd like to piggyback on the theme of losing and renewing one's faith. I believe you, too, lost your faith but your NDE reestablished it and gave new meaning, though I don't believe it gave you direction or purpose as much as it gave you insight. I surmise you once again had to find a reason for your life. Can you tell me how you managed the euphoria, effects and consequences of your NDE?

JC: As you can imagine, I had to assess and process its meaning and implication. I had to assimilate its tricky knowledge and insights, and I had to grapple with my upbringing and education, which did not help me.

DC: I also believe you had to accept you were ill prepared to move forward in any definite manner, that your new knowledge conflicted with your understanding of the divine, and that this new knowledge was inconsistent and incongruent with Hebrew sacred literature.

JC: I was on my own. My family and friends could not appreciate or interpret my NDE effectively or constructively.

DC: I can picture an elder's distress and alarm when you told him. I can hear him say under his breath, "Jesus died and came back from sheol, and he's here telling me about it? I am trained in scripture, not this."

JC: The elder would have known about King Saul and the witch of Endor.

DC: All right. Saul went to a medium to speak with the dead prophet Samuel for advice. Samuel was not resurrected from the dead and he did not physically come back to life when the two spoke.

JC: Remember, talking with a medium was a capital offense. I came back from the dead. How do you think I was received? What do you suppose I experienced?

DC: I imagine you were stigmatized. The whole lot must have been disorientating. I can hear you saying in a whispered tone, "Where is wisdom? Where is my direction? Where is my compass?"

JC: That is not far from truth.

DC: I'd like to add one more detail to this list. Since you were alone in foreign spiritual territory, you dealt with this information and its ramifications through trial and error. At first you selectively shared your NDE experience with others but to your dismay they were skeptical and confused and, possibly, they judged and condemned you. Later, for better or worse, you kept quiet.

JC: When something like an NDE touches your life and your society does not have the means or the wherewithal to deal with it, then questions are asked. "Where do I go?" "What do I do?" More than once I asked, "What am I supposed to do with the knowledge I received as I lay dying?" I was confused.

DC: I'd like to move on to a different subject but stay within the bounds of spiritual experiences.

JC: All right.

DC: I believe spiritual experiences have a similar inner reality but with a different outer face. There is an inner truth that expresses itself according to each individual, in each era and in each culture. If I were in China I would experience the Buddha; if I were in the Middle East – Muhammad; in Israel – Moses or Elijah, or maybe an angel; and in India – Krishna or Vishnu. You experienced an angel of love and the void. References to these existed in your culture. Maybe it is not so out of the ordinary as first believed. Now, I don't believe categorically this is how every spiritual vision or experience occurs, but the percentages are on my side. For instance, I'm not having a spiritual experience of the Buddha in the southwest Sonoran Desert of the United States. I'm having one of you – Jesus – because this is a Western unconscious cultural paradigm, not an oriental one.

The owner delivers the lattes and sandwiches.

OWNER: Here you go, gentlemen. Can I get you anything else?

DC: Thank you. No.

OWNER: *(to Jesus)* Excuse me for asking but you look awfully familiar. Do I know you?

JC: We've never met before but you might have heard of me.

OWNER: What is your name?

JC: Jesus.

OWNER: Of course you are! Excuse me for asking! I don't like it when my leg is pulled.

The owner storms back behind the counter.

DC: Where were we?

JC: We were discussing spiritual experiences.

DC: Do you have anything else to add?

JC: Many spiritual experiences spring from within and are shaped by a specific cultural heritage. Some spiritual experiences are agents for change for that culture, while another kind of spiritual experience, which is rare, transcends the specific culture and expresses a more universal nature or essence. My NDE was universal in love, compassion and in the Father, while Moses' and Isaiah's experiences were specific to Hebrew needs and aspirations.

DC: I noticed this pattern in my research. If I may, I'd like to circle back to the time when you were walking home after you lost everything. I'd like to know your thoughts. What crossed your mind? What worried you? What was in your heart before your robbery?

JC: Thoughts and worries? I'd prefer to forget about that period and leave it behind me.

DC: I can think of a few questions aside from the most obvious – "What reaction can I expect from my family?" and "How will I be treated?"

JC: I grieved over those questions. I squandered my inheritance. The sting of failure left a hard pit in my throat too hard to swallow. I parted with my money and had nothing to show for it. I was sickened to return home. This was a confusing and terrible period, and every step back toward the Galilee was the step of a foolish man. It was a bitter, distasteful and painful march of failure. Shame weighed me down, guilt burdened my heart and dread torched my soul. I didn't want to face my family because I knew what was in store. They were going to see me as a squanderer who committed a grievous and unforgivable mistake. Yet there I was marching home with my head hung low, a defeated man.

DC: I also hear you asking, "What am I going to do once I return?" and "What is my next step in life?" It appears you were committed to a particular direction when you suddenly reached a hard dead end.

JC: I had the opportunity to make a name for myself, a chance few get. I didn't know what I was going to do when I returned home. I knew I had to start over, perhaps work with my father.

DC: Uncertainty pelted you like hard rain? It's hard not to ponder the meaning and purpose of life at a time like that.

JC: Don't be flippant or trivial! I was conflicted. On one hand, I was bathed in a pool of tears; on the other I was exuberant.

DC: Forgive me. That is not my intention.

JC: I had feelings of meaninglessness and was overcome by insignificance. The entire episode felt like an unclean burnt offering roasting over the ritual fire. I didn't like this sacrificial meal. During this period the uncertainty of the future consumed me; the unknown unsettled me and hopelessness ensnared me. When I left home for the first time I regarded my future as bright. Occasionally, I'd stop to consider it. I was a little nervous, but I had some money and a sense of direction to navigate the choppy waters. What I faced on the road home, before I met the highwaymen, was new. I never contemplated the meaning of my life or its direction. That changed in an instant. It was as if I was thrown from one path to another. I was shocked with anguish and gripped with fear.

DC: Fear of what?

JC: Fear of my vulnerability, my invisibility, my powerlessness, and fear that my immediate future depended on my family. I wanted to be my own man but failed. Now I was heading back home.

DC: Your missing years were a defining moment for you. They inspired your ministry, gave you new insights into the divine and provided you material for your wisdom.

JC: This period reverberated throughout my life like the sound from a beating drum. Maybe it is what the Father intended. I was forced to learn and embrace this period. What else could I do? Deny or reject it?

DC: I want to point out that you had a unique ability to convert your joyful and difficult life experiences into poetic sayings. But that is not all that impresses me or that I find remarkable. There is something else.

JC: What is that?

DC: Your sayings are devoid of cynicism, sarcasm, lament, disgust or bitterness. Instead, they are thoughtful, optimistic and rather edgy, and this reflects your character.

JC: I wanted to project optimism in a troubling time. I didn't want people to feel that all was lost or that God had abandoned them. But back to your point concerning my sayings – it is true that crisis and pain were their mother and divine inspiration was their father.

DC: I'd like to address another dimension to your sayings, particularly the ones involving robbery and the strong man.

JC: Why these?

DC: You'll appreciate my interest after I quote them. "If someone slaps you on one cheek, turn to them the other also. If someone takes your coat, do not withhold your shirt from them." (LK 6:29) "How can anyone enter a strong man's house and carry off his possessions unless he first ties up the strong man? Then he can plunder his house." (MT 12:29) "The Kingdom of the Father is like someone who wanted to put a powerful person to death. He drew his sword at home and thrust it into a wall to find out whether his hand would go through. Then he killed the powerful one." (THOM 96) Each saying involves a crime while the "strong man" and the "powerful person" show abuse of power, like that of the robber over his victim. I believe these sayings were inspired by the highwaymen who robbed and beat you nearly to death. Actual events such as these occurred to you and were the source for many of your sayings.

JC: Why is it difficult for you to believe that some content of my sayings stem from my life, my observations and my experiences?

DC: That is what I am saying. I agree with you. Wisdom is born in the womb of life, one lived, explored and filled with defeat, triumph, suffering, joy and ecstasy. These are the ingredients of wisdom.

JC: The robbers actually inspired the manner in which I conducted my ministry, not just my sayings.

DC: What? How so?

JC: As discussed, I turned negatives into positives. I don't agree with what they did or what they stood for, but they were bold, courageous, fearless and determined. They knew what they wanted, they knew what they could do and they knew they could get away with it. Herod conducted himself in a similar manner, as did Pontius Pilate. I admired and embodied that particular attitude and incorporated it in my ministry. I knew I could do the things I wanted to do and I did them without looking over my shoulder for approval.

DC: This might sound macabre, and I don't mean it to be, but your robbery and beating foreshadowed the passion of your crucifixion. You were alone, without friends or family, surrounded by enemies, stripped of your clothes, beaten mercilessly, everything taken, and then you were paraded to Golgotha.

JC: Everything was taken from me: my dignity, pride, self-worth, clothes and money. Prior to my robbery and near-death experience, I lived in a state of darkness that slowly got darker until I reached the bitter lesson of total humiliation.

DC: Is there anything else the robbery inspired?

JC: It inspired the Beatitudes you mentioned, and it inspired the second half of the saying "Whoever does not have, even what they have will be taken from them." (MT 13:12)

DC: The first half, "Whoever has will be given more, and they will have an abundance," (MT 13:12) refers to your relationship with the Father, who continually gave to you as you invested in him. You contrast that relationship with the state you were in prior to the robbery.

JC: It was an agonizing truth. My ministry and sayings were influenced and inspired by many factors. I knew there was life after death. I knew the physical body perishes but another part of us is immortal and continues. I grappled with all the various circumstances and truths confronting me, and then I had to bring all that together into something that stirred people to action. It is difficult to wake one from sleep, from one's habitual routines or from cynicism and preconceptions, and then live life without their influence. I also want to mention something else; I crafted my sayings so as not to sound like a Greek philosopher. I didn't want to be distant or abstract. I wanted my stories to feel as though they were real. I found my voice, learned my craft and shaped my stories to address my Hebrew audience.

DC: Continuing with the influence line of inquiry, the Good Samaritan was a teacher of compassion and one significant pillar of your ministry was compassion. Tell me more about the Samaritan's influence.

JC: Remember, he was a stranger who willingly helped me at my most desperate and vulnerable moment. He did what no one else would do. The significance of his actions and generosity unfortunately didn't make sense to me at the time; I overlooked them. But the fact remains that he left an indelible impression on me. Later, I realized his true importance.

DC: I notice, when I think about it further, that you were like the stranger caring for the half-dead and you applied the same compassion and generosity in your ministry as he did for you.

JC: You have eyes to see that finer detail.

DC: I want go back to the moment when you were half dead, lying on the road before the Good Samaritan arrived. Tell me about that transition. What happened?

JC: I slowly regained my awareness. My eyes fluttered open and I tried to focus. It was then I felt the throbbing pain in my body. My head ached, my mouth was dry and parched and my tormented body was caked in dried blood. I must have frightened everyone who passed by because they purposely avoided me. I could hear mean and vicious words muttered under their breath; others were more vocal in their disgust and hurled louder insults at me.

DC: The Gospel of Luke states, "A priest happened to be going down the same road, and when he saw the man, he passed by on the other side. So too, a Levite, when he came to the place and saw him, passed by on the other side." (LK 10:31-32)

JC: Until the Samaritan arrived, nobody helped. "He took pity on [me]. He went to [me] and bandaged [my] wounds, pouring on olive oil and wine. Then he put [me] on his own donkey, brought [me] to an inn, and took care of [me]. The next day he took out two denarii and gave them to the innkeeper. 'Look after him,' he said, 'and when I return, I will reimburse you for any extra expense you may have.'" (LK 10:33-35) Needless to say, I was indebted to him.

DC: This entire episode – leaving home, losing everything, the robbery, the bloody beating, the near-death experience and the Samaritan's compassion – is the wellspring from which your wisdom and ministry flow. The Father, your Beatitudes, a stanza in your Our Father prayer, your wisdom, love, compassion and your sacrifice also follow in its wake.

JC: My life quickly turned around and I doubt whether I would have conducted my ministry without these experiences. The entire episode had unplanned and long-term consequences.

DC: I have a number of questions about this stage of your life and would like to address a few in more detail. In regards to the aftermath of the angel and the void, your death had a direct connection to the divine and you were shown new worlds and given extraordinary knowledge that transcends normal human perception. Although the robbery was dreadful, it paled in comparison to these insights.

JC: I glimpsed and participated with the divine. Before this, I saw things in one way and after it I saw things another way.

DC: Give me an example or two.

JC: As I looked at my society, I saw problems I could not address. Afterward, I saw challenges I wanted to overcome. I knew death was not an end but a transition. I was not afraid to die, so I set aside doubt and fear and lived courageously.

DC: Did you resent the highwaymen?

JC: Briefly, but that emotion quickly vanished. I could not find anger and hatred in my heart to level against them. I was filled with love and compassion. You are aware that compassion cannot live side by side with hate, anger, resentment or violence. Instead, I lifted my attackers up to the Father, offered a prayer and forgave them.

DC: Compassion and forgiveness are powerful healing agents.

JC: For the victim and perpetrator; both compassion and forgiveness permeate life with sweetness and both have downstream consequences. Had I stayed angry, my Wisdom Sayings would not have rung true and I would not have conducted my ministry. Neither would I have healed or known the depth of the Father's love.

DC: Would you say your robbers and your painful incidents were teachers?

JC: One cannot escape being a student; life is always teaching.

DC: Please elaborate.

JC: There is a dynamic relationship between you and the world. Life does not stand still; it is always in motion. Teachers are not the only teachers. Life is a teacher and circumstance is a teacher, as are events and history. Engaging in a trade, like carpentry, is a teacher, as is traveling. Books are not the only source of knowledge, experience is not the only source of wisdom, insight is not the only guide, and observation is not the only judge. Each works in tandem for a rich vibrant life. My advice: be a student. Be attentive, learn from each situation and manage your emotions. Don't let the fury of unchecked emotions drive you; the end of that road might lead you to a place you don't want to be. Lessons are everywhere. See them, be flexible and don't be afraid of change.

DC: I have a saying: "You are either playing the game or the game is playing you."

JC: That is more concise.

DC: There is an aspect of your NDE I'd like to explore and it involves the relationship between you and the divine. The general assumption is that the Creator is different than the creation. I see it differently and I know it in this manner. I wrote, "I stand at the edge of the ocean and walk into the surf with a bucket in my hand. I scoop up the small wave breaking in front of me and scurry back to shore, excited to see the wave I caught. But when I peek inside the bucket I notice the wave is gone. Confused, I wonder, 'Where is the wave?'"

JC: I smile at this. You didn't capture a wave; you scooped up water and the water in the bucket is exactly the same as the water from the ocean.

DC: I have a smaller portion of the ocean.

JC: Each of us, like the bucket, is filled with the ocean.

DC: The wave is an expression of the ocean and its essence does not change because it is moving; it always remains water.

JC: For me the Father is water and the Kingdom of God is the wave. You are in it as it is in you, and both the Father and the Kingdom of Heaven experiences itself through you, the world and everything.

DC: One way to experience *it* is by having an open heart and an open mind free from distractions.

JC: When I was clear, I could see in all directions and the unconditional love of the Father poured through me like a river flowing to the ocean.

DC: Your clarity inevitably led to choices, which led to action, which led to the creation of new worlds and conditions.

JC: My mind had a pair of new eyes, my belly ignited with fire and my heart filled with compassion. The world was wonderful and life was filled with meaning, purpose and direction. I wanted to know something and do something, and I did it with passion fueled by faith.

DC: I imagine, when you conducted your ministry, you saw life as potential and your society as the ground for transformation. Compassion and wisdom were the divine seeds; you became the sower and you sowed the ground.

JC: I was filled with divine power. Not egotistical power but the power to love, to see, to heal, to be courageous and fearless, and to overcome the needs and demands of the body. I was not directed by vanity, food, position, clothes, desire, lust or ego. When I realized that words and actions are instruments of creation, I created. There is a cause and effect in that relationship. Possibility is all around.

DC: You knew the world was the ground of potential.

JC: Faith the size of a small mustard seed can move mountains. I knew the divine was at the heart of every person. One has to awake to that reality, nurture it and, when it becomes large enough, act upon it. I learned the nature of investing as a form of application. I chose to invest in unity, love, compassion and wisdom. My gift was treasures from heaven.

DC: The divine light is everywhere and always on.

JC: The light of the divine cannot diminish, but we have a choice whether it shines bright, soft and dim or not at all. We create our destiny and future through our emotions, thoughts and actions. A large boat sailing across the sea is guided by a small rudder; likewise the manner we emote our thoughts and feelings guides us just like the rudder.

DC: I know this is off topic, but did you tell anyone of your near-death experience?

JC: For many it fell on deaf ears and suspicious eyes. Others listened while a few accepted it. It forced me to learn when to be quiet and when to be bold and outspoken about it.

DC: I surmise you told a handful of your disciples and followers about your NDE and I also imagine your disciples then went on to tell their followers. I say this because when I read the New Testament I get the impression that the Christian writers were aware of your NDE experience, but when they retold your story they chose to insert it at the end of your ministry instead of the beginning.

JC: It is difficult to believe a story about a person dying and coming back to life. It's hard to think that I didn't die, but instead was greeted by an angel who unconditionally loved and healed me, that I was swept into the void and that I returned into my lifeless body. One is hard pressed to accept or appreciate this story whether it occurred before or after my ministry.

DC: In any event, you returned from this occurrence with knowledge and wisdom too profound for words or metaphors.

JC: Even though this story was difficult to accept, not all of it was rejected. People responded to my experience with the angel. Most Galileans never saw an angel, but that didn't stop them from believing in them. It was part of their heritage. They appreciated my angelic encounter because it is written in our scripture.

DC: How did you weigh abstraction with need and practicality in your ministry?

JC: I had to choose between love, mercy, forgiveness and compassion or the Father and the Kingdom of Heaven. These two poles were delicately balanced and I emphasized the heart over the Mystery of the Father. Don't get me wrong. The Father is real but I focused on the basic needs of the people. Our society was in a state of crisis where love, mercy and compassion were strangers. For most, the Mystery of the Father was too complex so I did not overtly share it, except to a small group who had ears to hear such wisdom.

DC: Tell me about the time, after your NDE, when you returned to the Galilee. Did your family notice a change in you? Was there something in your demeanor, a glimmer in your eye, or in the words you spoke that made them think you were different?

JC: My physical wounds were obvious, as was my financial situation. I was noticeably a new man – emotionally, intellectually and spiritually. I was not quick to judge. I did not engage in argument like I once had and I was more compassionate, gentle and peaceful. This was mistaken as a contrite heart, a way to atone for my guilt and sin, but I knew better.

DC: I wonder if your near-death experience is the genesis for the born-again concept. Christians emphasize the necessity for this birth and say it turns one away from the world to God. The rite of water baptism dovetails into the new birth idea. What do you say?

JC: A powerful mystical experience would turn anybody away from the world to the divine, and that experience can be construed as a new birth. Baptism, however, is a softer expression of that event and symbolizes a changed heart, a cleansing, a renewal or a new birth. I chose the baptism ritual for its symbolism and its perceived effects rather than its actual effects.

DC: Again, I'm sorry I'm moving in all directions. My mind is racing. I'm connecting this to your Wisdom Sayings and I'm seeing foreshadowed events in your ministry. I'd like to go back to the chronology of this entire episode.

After your Good Samaritan experience, there was another person and event in your life that was equally important.

JC: I believe you are referring to the father and his response to his son's return in the Prodigal Son parable.

DC: I am. Remember we spoke earlier about the connection of this parable to your life. (*Jesus nods*) Will you elaborate on the moment when you finally made it back home?

JC: Try to imagine the sight of me: I have open wounds, scabs and bruises across my head and body; my clothes are tattered and grimy; and I'm malnourished, dirty, disheveled and thirsty.

DC: In other words, you looked terrible.

JC: I approach my father's field with my head low. I had left home without my father's blessing.

DC: That is a very serious matter.

JC: Yes, it is. I'm ashamed and humiliated, my inheritance is gone and I assume my family remains angry with me. Also, I don't know what I'm going to do with my life. Everything is gone; I'm penniless and I'm confronted with many new challenges. That is the mood and situation of my homecoming.

DC: Then the incredible happens and it must have been startling.

JC: My father recognizes me from afar and ran out to greet me. He threw his arms open and wrapped them around me. He kissed me several times. Tears fell from his eyes and I wept. His heart was relieved and filled with enthusiasm. He welcomed me home. When I told him about my inheritance he waved his hand, brushing it aside. He didn't care. That was inconsequential; it didn't matter. All that mattered was that I was home. That night he threw a feast in my honor, which upset my brother, who was jealous of father's affection. But that is another matter.

DC: I'm getting emotional. This is a very poignant story.

JC: It was for me too. When I relive that moment, I can still feel the love in my father's heart and his silent forgiveness. He did not judge me. I experienced an indescribable peace; my burden lifted and my apprehension vanished. I felt washed and cleansed. It was similar to my encounter with the angel of love.

DC: Not only did you experience divine unconditional love, you experienced the compassion from a stranger and the forgiveness from your father.

JC: I can never forget those moments.

DC: They became pillars of your ministry. How would you describe the period after your return home? Was it a period of assimilation and digestion? What were you thinking and what was happening?

JC: I see the clouds have brought more thunder and lightning. I'd like to watch before we continue. I want to mention this: the importance of this period cannot be overlooked. I equate it as a plowed field and planted seeds. When a farmer plants a seed in his newly plowed field, it appears nothing is happening but that is not true. Things are in motion; the seed is transforming into a sapling. At some point, days or weeks later, the sapling sprouts from the ground and greets the sun. Let's watch the downpour and have another latte.

DC: I'll order two more.

CHAPTER 5

BUILDING THE VESSEL

DC: Coffee.

David sets two lattes on the table, slides back into his seat and sips from his cup.

JC: Few people are capable of having deep conversations.

DC: I know a couple of people who like this kind of discussion.

JC: Shall we continue?

DC: I'd like to go back to your society for a moment and recap before we move on. What unfolded in your society that you were compelled to address? What problems did you see and what did you want to accomplish?

JC: Before I talk about that I first want to mention this – a ministry was not out of the ordinary in those days. I felt I needed to do something because I could not live an ordinary or normal life. If one wanted to have a voice and be heard, then it was common to do one of two things: join a movement and follow the leader, or rise, become a leader and lead. I am known for the latter.

DC: How did you learn about leadership?

JC: Trial and error mostly. I searched, and found things I liked and others I did not. I learned from my mistakes and from my successes. But back to your question – our society was under pressure from many directions: our traditions for one, the stewardship of the land another. Land use was being redefined. People wanted to make money from the land inherited from God. People were stressed to meet growing demands. Trade with other areas of the Roman Empire increased beyond our capacity to meet it. In addition, our hearts and minds unraveled. We didn't know what to do, how to act, or what to believe. People responded differently to these issues.

DC: How so?

JC: One adopted Hellenistic practices, another reverted to ancient and established Hebrew customs, still another sought and put hope in a savior, while another flocked to the "End-of-the-Worlders." That idea permeated the air. Essenes, Pharisees, Sadducees, rabbis, High Priests and Sacarii filled the landscape, sowing confusion and discontent, and promoting rival versions of practice and theology. Each possessed a particular method and ideology and each vied for one's heart and mind. Sectarian struggles ensued between groups. Try to imagine what it was like. There was the question as to the very nature of being a Jew: "What does it mean to be a Jew?" Several versions circulated around depending on the group or individual.

DC: Identity and affiliation drove the question. And I can see a variety of struggles and other points of view: Who is pure who is not? What is right practice what is not? Is there an afterlife? Does the body resurrect after death? All this was going on as well.

JC: There were other issues as well. As I mentioned earlier – and it's worth repeating – the Romans taxed us heavily and established their temples. The Greeks brought their philosophy and competitive culture. They valued the philosophic argument and adored the body, which was an offense to many. The Greeks declared, "Man is the measure of all things." They had their own heroes and ideas about how to become one. The entire lot was a bitter pill to swallow. The Greeks also sold the High Priest to the highest bidder, which the Romans adopted. The Romans recognized the half-blood Hasmoneans who ruled the Davidic Throne. Established bloodlines were disrupted and replaced with outside lineages whose policies and practices were consistent with the desires of our occupiers. Our High Priest made daily animal sacrifices to Rome and Caesar. In addition, the High Priest employed a band of ruthless Temple tithe collectors. The Temple was the financial institution and meat market, exchanging money and selling or trading sacrificial animals, perfumes, incense and oil. Imagine the conflict and discontent of this entire situation. No one knew what to do. Does one offer pure animal sacrifices to a God whose word is in flux and conducted by an impure priestly lineage? What did the sacrifice of one pure animal, one impure priestly lineage, and the voice and practices of God in transition amount to?

DC: You entered the historical dialogue to address perplexing issues. Now that the setting and atmosphere is reestablished your sayings make more sense. "Pay the emperor what belongs to the emperor and God what belongs to God!" (MK 12:17) Or, "A house divided against a house falls." (LK 11:17)

JC: Much had to be done. I tried to right the ship, but there was more than one problem so I had to be creative and imaginative for each burden and conflict.

DC: There was another moral dilemma: paying tax to an unclean or improper agency, namely Rome.

JC: It was ironic. One was obligated to pay a Roman tax to maintain the harshly administered peace and status quo; the whole lot brought trouble, confusion and anger. Our money was not going to our welfare but to someone we believed unclean. Grumbling and discontent were pervasive. That is why I said, "Pay the emperor what belongs to the emperor and God what belongs to God!" (MK 12:17) Then one could be at peace and move on with life instead of being troubled or confused.

DC: It was a matter of conscience.

JC: Correct.

DC: In your mind, there was a lack of direction and leadership, and the individual was lost without hope. How did one cope and survive in such tumultuous times?

JC: It was exasperating. We fed on each other as if in a frenzy. We lost the nature and meaning of stewardship. We lacked justice, mercy and honesty. (Q43) Our thoughts were filled with greed and theft. (Q43) People were worried and blinded by the pursuit of food, clothing and possessions. (Q53) Anyone shedding light on these problems was killed. I was vilified, questioned, spied on, challenged and at times nearly stoned because I advocated love – love for the Father, love for my neighbor, and love for people who desperately needed healing and a miracle or two.

DC: I see the situation summed up in one of your parables. "A man planted a vineyard. He put a wall around it, dug a pit for the winepress and built a watchtower. Then he rented the vineyard to some farmers and moved to another place. At harvest time, he sent a servant to the tenants to collect from them some of the fruit of the vineyard. But they seized him, beat him and sent him away empty-handed. Then he sent another servant to them; they struck this man on the head and treated him shamefully. He sent still another, and that one they killed. He sent many others; some they beat, others they killed. He had one left to send, a son, whom he loved. He sent him last of all, saying, 'They will respect my son.' But the tenants said to one another, 'This is the heir. Come, let's kill him, and the inheritance will be ours.' So, they took him and killed him, and threw him out of the vineyard. 'What then will the owner of the vineyard do? He will come and kill those tenants and give the vineyard to others.'" (MK 12:1-9)

JC: My mind acted quickly and I found inspiration in social conditions and current sentiments. This saying shows how the one who is right, just and fair was treated. Those who wanted to make a lasting difference were resented and not just by rulers and authorities but by the general population. Nothing seemed to be working or making sense. Things were turned upside down. Right was wrong and wrong was right. I encountered perpetual problems that seemed to have no solution.

DC: It couldn't have been that awful. You believed in the goodness of people by sending your disciples two by two into villages and towns knowing they would be received.

JC: They were not always well received.

DC: What did it mean that you were a people of the covenant?

JC: It is an agreement between a people and their God, each party fulfilling and abiding by their agreed-upon part. A covenant is like a contract or agreement – one side does one thing while the other side does something else. In our case, Yahweh would always be our God and the land he gave us would always be ours so that we could be a shining light to a dark world. That was God's side of the bargain. Our side of the bargain required us to keep the revealed law, live according to His rules and mandates, and keep Him in our hearts and minds.

DC: You mean the Ten Commandments, observances, purity laws, calendar days, Temple practices and the like?

JC: There was a fixed element to all of that. It was revealed truth and nothing could change; it was literally written in stone.

DC: Ironically, during your time, new ideas about the word and voice of God arose and put much of that into question.

JC: Various concerns split us and questions were raised. How does the Word of God affect our society today when our society and its conditions are different than the times of Moses or King David? Is there one universal truth for all time? Or is truth fluid because times change and is driven by different personal and cultural needs?

DC: Change was on every front – domestic, personal, political and religious.

JC: The fight between change and tradition was fierce, as were the forces of order and disorder.

DC: I see you focused on the personal front. You brought love, healing and love your neighbor. You addressed fragmentation, the nature of humanity, wholeness and incompleteness, and the relationship with another and with the Father.

JC: That was first and foremost on my mind. The other was the religious or spiritual front: how one could know and experience the Father. Of course, my new perspective challenged our traditional understanding.

DC: You provoked theological confusion.

JC: Inevitably.

DC: It was another form of flipping tables.

JC: I steered clear of politics, yet I knew my ministry would affect people religiously and that it would eventually ripple throughout society and affect the political and religious establishments. A changed person would change institutions, which would change society.

DC: Part of your ministry wanted to eliminate the source of anger and confusion. Yet you say, "I have brought a sword of division." (Q57) This is not particularly inclusive.

JC: One walks a fine line between order and disruption. In any event, people were suspicious, hard, weary, and uncaring. Love, trust, justice, mercy and respect were sacrificed for hostility, callousness, resentment and blind thinking. Some accepted my wisdom and followed me; others were leery and distrustful and did not follow me.

DC: Your words of compassion and forgiveness made people suspicious or distrustful?

JC: Many didn't know what to think because I was not normal. I was rather unusual and I didn't fit within their expectations.

DC: Even your family said, "He is out of his mind." (MK 3:21)

JC: That wasn't the first time. They too didn't know what to think at first. But I had to do what I felt I needed to do. And I addressed particular modes of discontent. Love is a powerful agent. It connects a person to another, and it connects one to the divine. I found the more I loved the greater the capacity to feel, and the greater I could feel the more alive I became, and the more alive I became the greater my awareness of the Father. Then something else occurred: I could never be full of love; the heart and love are boundless. I never reached its end though I tried.

DC: "Whoever has will be given more" (LK 8:18) comes to mind.

JC: The concept is the same. I knew that investing in God was the reward. I felt a tangible closeness to the Father and that increased and became bolder as my ministry progressed.

DC: What did compassion mean to you? And how did it work in your ministry?

JC: Compassion softens the heart. It allows a person to feel another living being – people, animals, lilies of the field. Life is contained within. If a person cared for another – a heart-to-heart exchange as a parent has with a child – the desire to hate, maim, stone or kill would cease to exist.

DC: What other social predicaments did you address?

JC: I wanted people to know the Father and at the same time know each other. Violence and darkness are prevalent in the heart and I witnessed the darkness daily. If darkness begets darkness, then only violence and hate are expressed.

DC: Forgiveness is an active healing agent, particularly to the one who is wronged, and it sees beyond words. Compassion, on the other hand, softens the heart to feel another's sorrow and pain or joy and happiness. Compassion doesn't covet.

JC: It was the antidote to competitiveness, jealousy, hatred and coveting.

DC: You also warn your followers not to condemn or judge.

JC: The practice of condemning and judging was common. One would see or hear something and immediately react either for or against it. They couldn't stop and observe. They had no capacity to look at themselves and recognize they did the very thing they hated and condemned. That is why I was against it. I said, "How can you say to your brother, 'Brother, let me take the speck out of your eye,' when you yourself fail to see the plank in your own eye? You hypocrite, first take the plank out of your eye, and then you will see clearly to remove the speck from your brother's eye." (LK 6:42)

DC: I didn't know I was judging or condemning until I read your words and practiced them. It is hard to overcome that inclination. I can't say I'm completely over it, but I can say that my mind cleared when I wasn't so quick to judge.

JC: The mind clarifies and becomes alert and discerning the more judgment ceases.

DC: Before we switch subjects, I'd like to address a few more issues regarding the relationship to the problems of your society.

JC: Fine.

DC: You have a particular disdain for certain religious practices and you see them as ineffectual and misguided.

JC: Traditional ideas about God did not help and time-honored practices did not work. People believed they could be a good Jew by practicing certain rituals and observing calendar dates. That is fine but it didn't connect one to the Father and couldn't help solve tough problems. The tide rushed in and our society was swept along in the raging torrent. People needed new answers to new problems. The elders and leaders either positioned themselves inside the power struggle or mandated right practice and religious purity. They thought this was effective. "Go back to the old ways," and "Accept our traditions as the only way to God." They couldn't have been more wrong. They looked to the past to solve the problems of the now. The future was upon us and we had to step into it with new tools, new ideas, new hope and a new faith.

DC: What other challenges did you see?

JC: I have to ask you, "How does a Sacarii overcome the violence within his heart?" Practice killing? Kill your enemy? No! That only hardened his heart and made matters worse. It was through love – love your enemy. How do we tear down the walls that separate us from ourselves and from our neighbors? Is it through rites, proper observances and animal sacrifices? No! Those practices had nothing to do with the time. Is drinking from a clean cup important? Is this act getting you closer to understanding yourself or God? No! People who act piously, who act religiously, increase their already inflated egos; they increase their status and comfort; they think of themselves as worthy of something because they do something. Should one go off in the desert thinking they are God's chosen if they strictly follow pious rules they invent? Imagine inventing a set of rules, abiding by them religiously, and expecting a reward or special favor because of it. Should one expect to initiate God's judgment because they think they live in the Last Days? No! Is the world a horrible place to live in? No! The Kingdom of God is not over there or over here. It is right here, and here, and in the heart. Anyone who advocated death, rigid practices, and false piety or hate perpetuated the problem. They were the problem; they were the blind leading the blind.

DC: Everything seemed to tear your society apart – your minds, hearts, traditions, leaders and Romans.

JC: It was hard to watch without wanting to do something about it. I felt the primary issue was not our society but rather a person's fractured heart and unclear mind. That was the plague.

DC: Your concerns dealt with internal rather than external problems?

JC: My concern was with people whose hearts were calloused and bitter and whose minds were filled with cynicism, judgment, fear and hate. These were the issues I wanted to address.

DC: You also knew people could not see the problem correctly. Society was not the problem as much as one's perception of it. The heart merely projects the misery it feels onto the world while the mind perceives its pre-existing biases and prejudices.

JC: I intuitively understood this principal and was confident my ministry could offer a renewed heart and clear mind.

DC: Can you elaborate on this point? How did you address these issues?

JC: By living a life of charity and compassion and by teaching my disciples, followers and listeners about the Father.

DC: You were the Father's emissary.

JC: And charity, compassion and wisdom were his agents. I also knew that the Father is filled with life, not death. I had to show and reveal that truth.

DC: I can appreciate your convictions.

JC: My ministry was a calculated attempt to effectively address the sectarian issues through a compassionate heart and an unbiased and unprejudiced mind. I wanted people healed of sickness and infirmities; I wanted them to live with hope, to be free of fear, and to be refreshed with a new concept of the divine.

DC: I'm reminded of your saying, "Do you bring in a lamp to put it under a bowl or a bed? Instead don't you put it on its stand? For whatever is hidden is meant to be disclosed, and whatever is concealed is meant to be brought out into the open." (MK 4:21-22)

JC: That is correct! No longer could I sit by and idly watch. I had to act. "I have come to bring fire to the earth, and how I wish it were already kindled!" (LK 12:49)

DC: You knew that your experience of the Father and your ministry would usher in a fresh, viable alternative. I enjoy your poetry; you phrase it, "New wine in new wine skin."

JC: Yes, "New wine in new wine skin." As I mentioned before, the past was not our future. Our relationship to one another held the key.

DC: You were forward thinking.

JC: I knew in my heart something had to change. Our political and religious traditions were bankrupt. The alternatives the sectarian groups offered did not serve us and I saw nothing that was useful or beneficial. Replacing one ineffectual system and the traditions that supported it with another was counter-productive and without merit. I envisioned the wisdom of an open heart and the relationship to the Father. These were the agents of change.

DC: We rely on our organizational structures for social order and harmony. What other alternatives do we have to order that which is inherently messy? What viable organizational structure works for tens of thousands of people without descending into authoritarianism? I know the Greeks looked to the Polis as a governing body; it looked to its citizens as a whole to direct politics, government, philosophy, farming, military, trade and religion.

JC: And we adopted the political hierarchy of king and subject. That relationship was the custom of all the empires surrounding us. It was the model and it is one all our tribes adopted when Israel formed our first national government with our first king, King Saul.

DC: You took issue with this model?

JC: I tried to reduce the highest mountains and raise the lowest valleys. I wanted to bore into the root cause of our hardships – the cold calloused heart and the critical and judgmental mind, which was directed and governed by our base nature: lust, greed, ego, fear and callousness. The wealthy and the powerful sneered at the downtrodden and outcast. Our plight was that all of us – the rich, the weak, the powerful and the poor – were against each other.

DC: You inserted yourself into history to change the dynamics. That was a tall order.

JC: It was and I was true to my conviction. That is a lesson in and of itself.

DC: I want to circle back and address your personal development and inspirations.

JC: All right.

DC: The content of your life between your return home and the time you left for the Jordan River to see John the Baptist is pregnant and significant. I characterize it as a time of origins because the ideas and content of your ministry begin in this period.

JC: Such as?

DC: The Father, compassion, love, mercy and justice, sowing, reaping, losing, finding, investing, do not worry, and solitude stem from here. You work with your hands as a carpenter and your relationship with your family deepens. Despite these conditions, this period marks a time of inner turmoil as you faced numerous perplexing issues.

JC: Are you implying that one period is more significant than another?

DC: Some periods are more pregnant than others.

JC: What perplexing issues did I face?

DC: I see a six-point confusion nexus. What to do with your life? How to overcome the shame from losing your inheritance? How to make a living? How to incorporate your insights from the NDE into your life? What to do with the insights from the NDE? And how to share your wisdom?

JC: I want to begin by saying that all spiritual knowledge emanates and flows from within ourselves. It is not outside over there *(He points.)* or over there. It is right here inside. *(He pats his chest.)* That truth has to be discovered.

DC: It coincides with your saying, "The Kingdom of God is within you." (LK 17:21)

JC: That said, I'll start by saying that I encountered a profound silence during my NDE that pressed upon me and affected me in a way I cannot fully describe. I experienced something about myself that was substantially and qualitatively new and things that were otherwise closed were now opened to me.

DC: What do you mean by "opened to"?

JC: Silence, empathy, spiritual wisdom, the Father, unconditional love, compassion, tolerance, peace, joy, prayerful silence, observation, forgiveness, awareness that I injured others, self-examination and personal reflection. I acted and thought in a manner that was not usual for me.

DC: That list is long. Did these insights affect your relationship to your family, neighbors or community?

JC: I'm sure you can guess that.

DC: I'd like to hear it from you.

JC: Of course it did.

DC: How so? Explain it to me in general.

JC: I had to come to grips with being alone. I was very different than most in my community before I left. After my return I sounded mad and acted abnormally, or at least that is what I was accused of. Being different than my neighbors was a blessing and a curse. Oddly, I was able to love and accept them in spite of their apprehension and disdain.

DC: What did you do?

JC: I learned to accept the difference. I learned tolerance. I learned to love. I learned not to condemn or judge. I learned the rhetoric of argument. I learned to be wise in spirit. I learned to quiet the activity of my mind and of my heart. I learned to breathe, to observe my breath and watch the workings of my mind. I learned that silence and motion are two sides of a coin that complement each other. I recognized the divine in each one of us. For most, the divine is not noticed because it is sleeping.

DC: All you faced and had to overcome was daunting, especially in light of your social and cultural norms. Communal religious practice did not provide you the ground to grow. In fact, it was the opposite; it was barren ground. Religious practice and normal religious knowledge offered you very little.

JC: The knowledge from my NDE took time to develop and integrate into my life. It wasn't easy. Since I was always a bit different, a little louder, a little more confrontational, a little more intelligent, and a little more barbed and argumentative than most – which my NDE accentuated – I really had to work extra hard to fit in. Even so, people tended to stay away from me. I also could not go to my elders for advice and direction. I was the odd man out. When I began to share my ideas and knowledge with others I wasn't well received and that became another point of contention.

DC: What happened after you settled back into your life with your family again?

JC: I was safe with a roof over my head. No physical harm fell on me again. I was grateful for that and I healed in relative comfort and safety. It took a while for my physical wounds to heal.

DC: Tell me more about that last part.

JC: I suffered from my wounds and try as I might I couldn't do much about the physical pain I suffered. Every day was a challenge. Slight movements in my legs or arms, a twist in the wrong direction, proved burdensome. Recovering and healing took a long time. I was really beat up.

DC: During your recovery or after it, I surmise you thought about the next step in your life.

JC: I had to rise again, stand on my own two feet and find my way in the world. Also, my robbery and beating had other consequences.

DC: Certain indignity swirled in your heart and mind?

JC: Partially, but not particularly.

DC: No?

JC: No. I experienced unconditional love. That was new and unlike anything I experienced before; it simply was beyond my capacity to imagine or comprehend. I didn't know it existed. Unconditional love slept inside of me, as it does with everyone, and suddenly it awoke and became active and alive.

DC: Because of your NDE?

JC: Unconditional love is not an outside agent acting upon me, it is not out there or over there; rather it was something inside that awoke right here. *(He pats his heart.)* Imagine a seed sprouting from the ground, growing larger, seeking the sun, day by day. The seed and the mature plant are not two different things; they are the same thing but at different stages in the plant's life.

DC: Expand on that.

JC: I felt a boundless, enveloping and expanding love pouring in and through me every day. It was bottomless, without boundaries and without end. I would liken it to an insatiable fire burning inside of me. Nothing contained it nor could anything stop it. Honestly, at times, the sensations were so great that it was hard to manage and I felt I might lose my mind. Every day, at every moment, I experienced its expansive presence.

DC: Was there any particular expression or outlet for this unconditional love?

JC: There was. Hate, anger and violence disappeared from my heart and were replaced by an outpouring of joy and peace. Self-loathing fled away. I never experienced it again. I felt the world imbued with the presence of the divine. I wanted to pass that love on to my assailants and I forgave them. As my own father had forgiven me and allowed me back into the family, I forgave them hoping they would find the Father. I could have allowed anger, bitterness and revenge to fill my heart but I didn't. Actually, I couldn't.

DC: You couldn't?

JC: Those emotions vanished from my life. They were also no longer welcome in my house.

DC: You're speaking figuratively.

JC: I am, but the truth remains. Your heart and mind are your house. If you want those emotions to enter, simply open the door. I recommend you do not. If they storm in, throw them out. They are not welcome. Unfortunately, most houses are inhabited with unruly guests who disturb and destroy. Now it is difficult to get rid of them but not impossible. It takes determined work.

DC: What psychological effects did forgiveness have on you?

JC: It is easy to say, "God, I have forgiven, please reward me." It is not about punishment and reward. The reward is freedom; freedom to continue experiencing and knowing the Father; freedom to love and know compassion; freedom to live without fear, rage and hatred. A mystical umbilical cord exists and one doesn't want to sever it or block it with hatred, anger, cynicism, lust or greed. If it is blocked, the consequences of discontent and dissatisfaction grow and blossom into larger fields of discontent and dissatisfaction. There is a connection, a dance of sorts, between the individual and the community and the community the individual, both influencing the other.

DC: After returning home I surmise your social status changed, as did your religious position. What more can you tell me about that. How did your family treat you?

JC: The response was mixed. Some were aloof and reluctant, some suspicious, and others a bit more accepting. But Joseph and Mary's relief and joy upon my return were real and a breath of fresh air. Over time the entire family's heart softened.

DC: How did the community treat you?

JC: I was eyed suspiciously and with disdain. They knew I was proud and vain. The rumor circulated that I was beaten and robbed. They felt I got what I deserved. I became an outsider in my hometown and it made me slightly uncomfortable, but I learned to set that aside. I could not abide by their expectations, nor did I want to. Then the social problems I recognized before I left turned for the worse.

DC: What did you want to do about it?

JC: Nothing at first. I had to live responsibly, become a man and earn a living.

DC: When did you become a carpenter?

JC: Working with one's hands was encouraged by my father at an early age. As a boy, my father Joseph thought it a good idea to learn a trade even though I expected to become a rabbi. I learned carpentry. It was also a social custom and a Jewish religious tradition. Even the devout and pious Essenes recognized the importance of working with one's hands.

DC: The Apostle Paul worked as a tent maker during his ministry.

JC: That illustrates the Jewish understanding and importance of the relationship between the work of the hand and the work of the mind. The two are opposite but complementary forces. Performing both effortlessly was a sign of maturity.

DC: What was the rationale behind that?

JC: To join two principles into a single person.

DC: Why was it important to integrate two different disciplines? Will you explain that in more detail?

JC: The practice intended to integrate the power of creation with the power of the mind. These two principles represent the image of God; God created *all of this* because He knew and because He spoke. So too one could know God and creation through the practice of "creation," like carpentry, and the practice of "wise speaking," like a rabbi telling a story. If one could do both one could know and participate with the divine more thoroughly.

DC: That is an intriguing relationship.

JC: Once I fully recuperated from my injuries I took up the carpentry trade again. It was therapeutic and helped ease my mind. Carpentry and building are demanding but I didn't have to make a lot of important decisions and that was good. I lived a quiet and ordinary life.

DC: Was it possible for you to live an ordinary life?

JC: At first, but my restlessness and ambition surged back to life. Carpentry was not satisfying and I felt the urge to move away from it.

DC: Did you return to your religion?

JC: Not at first. In one sense, when I left, I turned my back on God, and felt God had turned His back on me. When I returned, I had a different understanding of the divine, but even so I read the Torah.

DC: There is another feature I see in this stage of life "before John the Baptist" and it consists of your Hebrew heritage.

JC: I don't follow you. What do you mean?

DC: When I read the gospels, I get the uncanny sense you had another mystical or intuitive experience that gave you a greater awareness of your ancestry. I would characterize this experience as the second of your profound mystical experiences, the first being your NDE. Am I right in thinking you had an epiphany or mystical experience of your ancestry. Can you talk about this?

JC: I'd like to know how you drew that conclusion.

DC: It is subtle but became more apparent the more I read the gospels. I see several Jewish patriarchs and prophets sitting in the background guiding and inspiring you and whispering in your ear.

JC: Who do you see?

DC: Moses, Enoch, Noah, Elijah, Isaiah, Jonah, King David and Solomon.

JC: You see them by reading the gospels?

DC: I do.

JC: You have a gift.

DC: I got the impression you understood and connected to the men I mentioned. Somehow, they were a woven pattern in your soul. It is one thing to live your life according to them and acknowledge their importance. It is another to find inspiration in them; after all, they shaped Jewish history and set the Jewish nation on a particular course. The Jewish nation would be different without them. They shaped your heritage and introduced something new into Jewish history. You emulated them because you had a heart to heart and a meeting of the mind. You wanted to be a force like them to help redefine the Jewish nation and redirect its destiny. You wanted to reconfigure the Jewish religion and set it on a new religious path. Had the Jewish nation listen to you they could have experienced the divine as you did; they could have integrated your new image and practice, and could have avoided the catastrophe you sensed coming over the horizon. You empathized with your people who you considered lost. I believe you had an epiphany that brought you to this conclusion, which is why I consider it your second mystical experience. The first was the unconditional love and the Father. You could have conducted your ministry in some other country but you didn't. I had to ask myself, "Why did Jesus conduct his ministry in greater Israel, Judea and the Galilee?"

JC: When I conducted my ministry, I thought of myself as a prophet. I even say, "No prophet is accepted in his hometown." (LK 4:24) A Jewish prophet ministers to his people and surrounding neighbors.

DC: Tell me about your mystical experience.

JC: One day as I was reading the Torah an overwhelming sense of my Hebrew heritage flooded over me. One takes one's identity for granted, and I didn't think much about it until this moment. I said to myself, "I am Hebrew. I am really Hebrew." There is something in my soul, heart, mind and blood stemming from this particular lineage. I felt it. I knew it. I couldn't be anything other. Yahweh spoke and guided my people. I was a part of that lineage. I was from an ancient people who were divinely blessed and guided. I knew I had a new understanding of the divine I had to share with my people.

DC: Hence, the reason you chose to minister to Israel.

JC: I saw them enslaved and conflicted on many fronts. Like Moses I wanted to bring them out of that slavery and into a new Promised Land centered on the love and compassion of the Father rather than the law. I saw the law inhibiting and constricting rather than liberating.

DC: You could have taken your message to the people in the north, in Asia Minor or in Egypt. They would have listened.

JC: I probably would have been accepted and not persecuted or mistreated, but I considered my people lost and in desperate need of a shepherd. I had love for them and felt their loss intimately.

DC: God commanded Hosea to marry a prostitute named Gomer. God knew she was promiscuous and would seek other men but Hosea was commanded to love her, have children with her and not throw her out of his house. The point illustrates God's love for Israel even when Israel loves harlotry more than God.

JC: I was familiar with Hosea's predicament and used the principle in my ministry.

DC: I'd like to talk a little further about your Hebrew influences. Your ancestors spoke to you, not literally, and inspired you. I'd like to go through a few. Can you explain the influence and motivation of each?

JC: All right.

DC: Let's start with King David. What can you tell me about him?

JC: David was brazen, unabashed and fearless, and accomplished a great feat at such peril. As a young shepherd boy, he found the courage to confront the Philistine giant Goliath who taunted all of Israel. David was angry that Goliath could be so obnoxious, loathsome and disrespectful. So David stepped onto the battlefield, gathered a few small rocks, placed one in his sling, swung it around and around and then hurled at Goliath. The small missile hit Goliath in the head and dropped him to the ground. David quickly ran over to the giant, drew his sword, cut off his head and held it high for both friend and foe to see. This one act had inconceivable consequences. David became renowned for his courage and caught the eye and good favor of King Saul, who invited him into his court. I identified with David. Even though Israel was not a Philistine, the people acted like one. I saw the people of Israel similar to Goliath; they were a giant with a flair for insolence and impertinence.

DC: How did Elijah influence you?

JC: He was a man of faith, devoted to God, and had the capacity for miracles. His most notorious was the miracle of the cake. In the story, an old noble woman gives Elijah the only food she has, which was a ration barely enough for one day. She had no means to get food for the next day or the day after that. Even so she shared a portion of the cake with him; though the portion was small, the gesture was enormous. It was a selfless and pure gesture. Elijah blessed the cake, thanked God and God, in turn, blessed the cake. The old woman and Elijah had enough food for months. The woman's act was a test of great faith. I took away the act of miracles, that small gestures have huge impacts, and that miracles work on people who have the courage of faith regardless of circumstance.

DC: Isaiah?

JC: An angel appeared to Isaiah and touched his lips with a burning coal. After his encounter, Isaiah fearlessly ministered to the children of Israel, the gentiles and the people of Tyre and Sidon. I was inspired by his dedication and courage, and followed in his footsteps.

DC: Jonah?

JC: Jonah failed to listen to God's voice. He turned his back on God in an effort to save his life and avoid his destiny. In the story, Jonah is thrown overboard from his escape ship into the stormy waters and a whale swims up and swallows him. Jonah spends three days and nights inside its belly praying to God for deliverance. God hears his cries and the whale spits him out onto the shore. Jonah, now with ears to hear God's voice, bravely commits himself to the bitter end to minister to the ruthless and cruel people of Nineveh. Jonah was intimately guided by God along the way.

DC: What does the whale mean to you?

JC: The whale is a metaphor of man's corruptible nature. Being swallowed by the whale is a poetic way of saying the lower animalistic instincts and desires, whether carnal pleasure, greed, materialism or selfishness, control one's life. One so ensnared is blinded by these base desires, is driven mad and destroyed by them until the hand of God intervenes. The story reveals two points. The first shows Jonah's fear and unwillingness to listen to the voice of God and the consequences of walking away from that calling. The second shows redemption, second chances and a life guided by divine purpose.

DC: How do you relate to Jonah's story?

JC: Prior to my ministry I sought a name for myself; I wanted the riches of the world and preferred its status and pleasures over God. I embraced the world and evaded my destiny. God is not without a sense of irony. After I was swallowed, chewed up and belched out of life's mouth, I was guided back home to recuperate and heal. Later, I was boldly committed to a ministry of compassion, hope and renewal in the Father.

DC: Would you characterize Jonah and the Whale as your story?

JC: I see parallels.

DC: Would you agree that it foreshadows your descent into Hades after your death by crucifixion and then your resurrection after three days?

JC: I don't agree with the Christian analogy. Granted, at campfires at night or in my house in Capernaum, I quietly shared a few stories from my past.

Those stories got reinterpreted and applied differently than the way I told or experienced them. They drew on them and mixed half-truths, metaphor and myth to tell their Christian story. They had to rearrange and intensify my life; they had to rework and retell my wisdom and embellish my miracles in order to speak with foreigners and other halfhearted listeners. That is how the Jesus movement gained traction.

DC: I appreciate that because any story can be told in such a way as to downplay or sharpen it.

JC: History and telling a story are two different things and do not always match. I'll leave it at that.

DC: I'd like to get back to the Old Testament prophets; I'm almost finished with this part.

JC: Please.

DC: Each one was fearless in the face of terrible odds and circumstances but found the courage to minister.

JC: That is correct. There is something else I need to sharpen. This experience I'm about to mention happened to me as it happened to every man we spoke about. When God sets His eyes on you and He places His hand on your heart, speaks into your ear, or shows Himself to you, you have no other choice but to set aside your life and be of service to that calling. That is a condition. There is no other alternative, as Jonah discovered. Whatever you wanted to do in life, wherever you wanted to go, whatever *it* is, that part of your life is over and that becomes the living sacrifice. You no longer live for yourself or your family; you are an instrument in the service of the greater good whether it is for people, history or God. Every prophet you mentioned experienced the same thing. I have one other important point to mention: as much as the prophet gave to and gave up for God, in return God gave Himself to each prophet.

DC: I'm reminded of your saying, "Give, and it will be given to you. A good measure, pressed down, shaken together and running over, will be poured into your lap." (LK 6:38)

JC: You realize the principle underpinning this saying.

DC: You experienced it firsthand.

JC: I knew that truth was not a collection of words strung together that sounds profound. No! My words were truth.

DC: We touched upon this before, but I'd like to circle back to it again. Do you consider yourself a mystic? I would characterize you as such.

JC: I preferred the term *prophet* over mystic. After my NDE, my senses – sight, hearing, dreams, and intuition – awoke and were alive. The Father was alive in my life and furnished me with knowledge and wisdom that otherwise I would not have known.

DC: You didn't have this capability prior to your NDE?

JC: It was sleeping. Prior to my experience, I was intellectually sharp and argumentative. That's not to say that I couldn't remember a dream or two or that occasionally I was intuitive, but after my NDE event I was inclined. I was open and clear; my mind was on fire and I could make connections I had never been able to do before.

DC: Genius awoke.

JC: Or enhanced.

DC: Would you consider your life a spiritual odyssey?

JC: I consider life a gift of the Father.

DC: I want to ask you a few more questions before we wrap up this section.

JC: I'd like to change back into my robe. Hopefully, it is dry by now.

DC: All right. This shouldn't take long. When did you compose your Wisdom Sayings?

JC: Over time. There was no single moment when I composed them all. It is not as if I had access to a complete archive whenever I needed. That wasn't the case. I composed a few here and a few there; some at this time and others at that time. I created them one by one at different times over the course of years. I must admit that many were created while I ministered because I was faced with a current situation I wanted to address, and one way to address that was with a saying. But I worked out a few before my ministry.

DC: I see your Wisdom Sayings and teachings a bit like poems, and it interests me to know when the inspiration began.

JC: Upon my return home, after I healed and was working as a carpenter. An intuition or an idea would enter my mind and I would think about it for a while, and then I would shape it and rework it.

DC: You liked stories and you were a good storyteller.

JC: Yes.

DC: Did you look to the Torah, Psalms, of other wisdom traditions for inspiration?

JC: I reached a *fullness* and no longer needed scripture for guidance or inspiration. The Torah, law, wisdom literature and the "wisdom of Solomon" was a part of me and had merged with my heart and mind. I set aside books and learning to concentrate on self-discovery, the Father and my ministry. My imagination was on fire and I drew from my own wisdom and experiences, not from my ancestors'.

DC: As I gaze upon the books in my library, I reflect upon the long journey I travelled. Each book represents a single path of discovery and each collection represents a world of exploration. The man here with you today is not the same as the 19-year-old whose first step on his spiritual odyssey was an existential crisis. We are two different men, yet I see with the same eyes, hear with the same ears, feel with same heart and walk with the same feet today as I did yesterday. I'm no longer swayed by discovery as I once was; rather, I am more fascinated in applying and sharing my wisdom.

JC: The same happened to me.

DC: I'd like to briefly talk about your storytelling techniques.

JC: You want me to reveal my poetic magic? One isn't supposed to reveal his techniques and methods.

DC: Please?

JC: What do you want to know?

DC: You invented many characters, settings, and circumstances for your parables and teachings and inserted unexpected twists and surprise endings. Will you comment on that?

JC: I incorporated exaggeration, astonishment and the unpredictable into my stories and I did not draw many stories from Jewish history. My stories were new: notice the Sower, the Mustard Seed, the Rich Man, and the Woman searching for her lost coin. Also, the more I composed the better I got, and the better I got the greater my insight, and the greater my insight the more I improvised a saying on the spot.

DC: For anyone who has ever tried to do that it is a remarkably difficult feat. I grouped your sayings into six categories.

JC: Six?

DC: The Our Father prayer, Beatitudes, parables, Kingdom of Heaven sayings, and aphorisms.

JC: That's five.

DC: Six, your Wisdom Sayings in the Gospel of Thomas. Together, these form a diverse wisdom package.

JC: I used several rhetorical devices and I didn't discriminate in style or in content. If something was foreign I used it. If it were part of my literary heritage I used it. The point was to disrupt, confuse and upset my listeners. I wanted to awaken their curiosity. I wanted them to wonder, be amazed or be angry. I wanted them to see things they had not seen. I didn't want to be an ordinary prophet with expected ideas delivering a normal message. I acted differently, thought differently and spoke differently. I had to be new, novel and exciting; otherwise, no one would listen to or follow me.

DC: I created an exercise to help me determine the timeline of your sayings. I wanted to find out which were created before you met with John the Baptist, which were inspired because of John and which were inspired during your ministry. It's difficult to assess but at times I felt I could tell at least a few.

JC: Why is that important to you?

DC: I wanted to see your development and how you changed and why you changed. Your sayings represent an entire body of work, and it reveals your progression, inspiration and development. Did your thoughts or insights about a subject change? All this is evident in your sayings. You have early sayings, middle of your ministry sayings, and near or at the end of your life sayings. The challenge is to place them in chronological order.

JC: Did you put them in order?

DC: Partially.

JC: How did you do it?

DC: I asked, "Can Jesus have known this information prior to or after John?" Next I examined the context of the saying and asked, "What does the context tell me?" If the content and the context of the saying were known before you met John, I placed it in the Prior Category folder. If not, I put it into the Ministry Category folder. I discovered most of your sayings appear to be inspired by the context of your ministry.

JC: Give me an example.

DC: We don't have time to go through them all but here are a few. I suggest the Lilies of the Field, the Kingdom of Heaven is inside you, and the Our Father prayer and the *strong man* motif were conceived prior to your time with John the Baptist.

JC: I did not worry, I knew the Father was everywhere and inside of me; I started forgiving, I was thankful for my daily food, I accepted uncertainty in my life and recognized everything whether pleasant or painful, easy or difficult was a gift from the Father. Each of these I understood before I saw John.

DC: Let me repeat the *strong man* saying, "Or again, how can anyone enter a strong man's house and carry off his possessions unless he first ties up the strong man? Then he can plunder his house." (MT 12:29) I would suggest the strong man originates from this period we are discussing.

JC: This saying is comprised of three parts. The first part, "a strong person's house," represents Israel. Second, the "tying his hands" is a metaphor for Israel's persistent problems. The third part, "then he can loot his house," represents my ministry. The first two parts come from the time before John, while the third was motivated by the success of my ministry.

DC: I have one more saying I want to talk about. It, too, stems from this period and reveals your spiritual development and progressive insights.

JC: Which one?

DC: "The Kingdom of Heaven is like a mustard seed." (MT 13:31)

JC: The mustard seed is a two-part analogy wrapped within a progressive process. I realized that something very small could grow into something very big; that is the first part. The second part is that there is new life when the seed dies and grows into a bush. The mustard seed is tiny; it dies, it grows and becomes large for the birds of the air to make their nests. The mustard seed does not live for itself alone; it lives for others. It is one part of a greater whole. That is the larger truth, but in order for the mustard seed to be of use to the birds of the air it must die. It then gets transformed so that other life can live. Try to understand: everyone is a part of this larger unifying whole. We can't escape it and it is the Father's process.

DC: How do you see yourself in this analogy?

JC: How could I not? The steady effects and knowledge of the Father and of wisdom and compassion grew to a point where I had to share them with the world. Then I went to John the Baptist.

DC: You knew it was the right thing to do.

JC: Yes.

DC: Knowing something is right and doing something about it are not the same.

JC: One has to know and one has to act. I knew I had to start small.

DC: Did you imagine your ministry would turn into something larger?

JC: I thought it could happen, but I couldn't be sure.

DC: To summarize, you conceptualized a number of sayings or thoughts before John but you finished them because you discovered something new while you ministered.

JC: That tended to be the process. I learned by doing. Also, as I conducted my ministry I revised the content of a saying. I would think about it and work it out in my head while walking to a town or when I prayed or meditated in quiet and lonely places.

DC: Switching subjects, did it occur to you or could you imagine that you could make a name for yourself through your ministry?

JC: That was never my intent or interest. That's not to say I didn't want people talking about me, wondering what I was doing or what I had to say. That I wanted. My relationship with the Father deepened while I ministered. It was like a mesmerizing dance that captured my heart and imagination. As I danced my love increased. I didn't want it to end. The more I danced, the more I wanted to share the dance with others so they could know the Father as I knew the Father.

DC: I have to switch subjects again. I'm running out of time for this section but I find it important to discuss these thoughts with you now because the remainder of the interview involves other ideas and issues.

JC: Please.

DC: This too is a rather delicate subject because it involves an idea that meant one thing to you during your ministry and another thing to the Christians after your crucifixion. The original meaning is all but lost and what is left of this poetical term has been incorporated and appropriated by Christianity and the Church.

JC: What are you referring to?

DC: The Sacred Marriage.

JC: The Sacred Marriage! It is a weighty and alluring subject.

DC: How did it motivate you and how did you use it in your ministry?

JC: Marriage is a significant concept for Jews. One is married to another person, one is married to religious ideas and practices, and Jews are married to God. The idea has many applications. To your question, the answer is yes; it was important to my ministry.

DC: Because you wanted to marry the divine nature with the human nature?

JC: I sense another question in the back of our mind. Could it be, "Is there more to me than my physical body?"

DC: I'll go along with that.

JC: Notice our senses – I can see, hear, feel, touch and taste. Notice our imaginations – I can think this and visualize that. Notice our tongue – we can speak words of praise and encouragement or spew words of hate. Notice our feet – we can walk here or there. Notice my hands – I can build a house or a temple. Essence is not physical. The feeling of love in my heart is not physical. Ideas are not physical. Numbers are not physical. Words are not physical. The alphabet is not physical. The spirit that animates life is not physical. The presence in our body, heart and mind is not physical. The presence is in all things and all around. What gives the breath of life? The Father. The divine presence. We are filled and animated by the Father, and we can be in accord with the presence at all times. But something gets in the way and keeps us away from the Father.

DC: By that you mean the lower level of human nature: runaway desires, coveting, murder, deceit, lying, heartlessness and selfishness.

JC: We have a dual nature; the nature of man with all our base instincts, which is corruptible, and our heavenly or godlike nature which is love, creativity, and imagination. The point is to cultivate the heavenly knowledge – be less attached to our base impulses and their fiery desires and participate with the divine. The question to ask is, "Is that possible?" If you say no, then you have to ask, "Why?" If you say yes, then you have to ask, "How?" The issue at hand is the obstacle that keeps you from dancing with the divine.

DC: Our lower natures.

JC: Now we should ask a follow-up question: "How did we get in this predicament?"

DC: According to Genesis it was our first ancestors, Adam and Eve, biting into the apple of good and evil. (Gen 3:1-24)

JC: That was how the Jews understood this problem and it was a serious issue for the sages of Israel. They were thinking about this subject for a very long time and concluded that something started us down this road of ruin and death. They poetically termed it the Fall. The flip side to the argument was that something was needed to restore that which was fallen, otherwise the consequence was that we would continuously spiral down and never get back to our standing with God. I worked on the flip side of this argument.

DC: Restoration?

JC: Restoration was the theme and undercurrent of my ministry. I married the mind with the heart and encouraged people to set aside the lower nature and allow the heavenly nature to flourish. I wanted to offer another Garden of Eden where one could commune with the divine in peace.

DC: This is the Sacred Marriage.

JC: It is not the marriage of the church to God. That was taken out of context. It is the marriage between the lower nature and higher nature of man. These two natures cannot be separated; they need each other. The wisdom, knowledge and love of the Father have to be one's guiding light.

DC: I'm reminded of the saying, "When you make the two into one, when you make the inner like the outer and the outer like the inner, and the upper like the lower ..." (THOM 22)

JC: Our human nature – the heart and mind – is easily persuaded and corrupted by misguided desires and misplaced fear. The world is like a swift and strong current. When we get caught in it we are driven where it wants to take us and are helpless to stop it. The Father is of another nature, a nature that only appears inseparable, but since we don't know it or have experienced it, we don't cultivate it. I wanted people to know the Father as I knew the Father. I wanted people to know true wisdom and true love. To accomplish that goal, I became less interested in my needs and desires and more attentive to the Father's and the needs of the people.

DC: You became His instrument. It almost sounds as if the needs of the Father and the needs of the people are two sides of the same coin.

JC: That is the relationship. Growth in the Father begins with one's development and is completed by giving and sharing with others. I made the decision to be the Father's instrument and live according to it. I was the type of person who was decisive and lived by my decisions.

DC: Once you decided to travel down that road you wouldn't say, "I made a mistake" and turn around and walk back. You were "all-in" and allowed that path to lead into uncertain and unknowable terrain which, ironically, permitted another facet of divine revelation.

JC: I like the way you think. My family lived by the rule of commitment, as did I. If I said, "I'm going over there," then turning back wasn't an option. I know it happened to me before. I left home only to return. At that time, I felt I had no other choice, and I certainly didn't want the same thing happening to me again. I didn't want to leave home again, like I left home the first time and returned as one who fails. I tried to plan the ministry in a manner like planning a building, but that proved to be a mistake. Ideas, direction and words came to me without any pre-planning. My intuition was strong, my hearing exceptional and my eyes kept getting clearer. This was different than before and I was inspired. I felt the Father was fully present.

DC: Talk to me about the influences carpentry had on you and how it affected your ministry. Did the knowledge of carpentry provide you with something tangible for your ministry? Did it help you in any way?

JC: I appreciate that question. While I worked on a construction site I was exposed to different hardships. There was the heat and cold and the wet and dry climate. There was the physical demand of digging trenches, lifting and stacking material, cutting and chiseling wood, and assembling the parts. One had to focus, have vision, be able to plan and lay out a project and communicate with others. One has to know each step and plan accordingly. As you know, a building slowly develops. It moves one step at a time toward its directed end and I was committed to each tedious step. I cultivated endurance, determination and patience, and if something went wrong I had to know how to correct the problem.

DC: You do not have many construction references in your sayings, not nearly as many as robbery, money or food. But one comes to mind: "Why do you call me, 'Lord, Lord,' and do not do what I say. As for everyone who comes to me and hears my words and puts them into practice, I will show you what they are like. They are like a man building a house, who dug down deep and laid the foundation on rock. When a flood came, the torrent struck that house but could not shake it, because it was well built. But the one who hears my words and does not put them into practice is like a man who built a house on the ground without a foundation. The moment the torrent struck that house, it collapsed and its destruction was complete." (LK 6:46-49)

JC: You see I found wisdom in different disciplines. I had to learn the truth in each, I had to learn how to include that wisdom into my parables, and I had to learn how to apply that wisdom in my ministry.

DC: When I compare you to Paul I see difference. He copied the Pharisees in several respects. He was logical about the law, formed an argument, worked through it, was knowledgeable about the scriptures and conducted his campaign like a Pharisee teaching in the Diaspora, as if he were directed by Jerusalem. You on the other hand were an entrepreneur. You developed a product, made an investment and capitalized on the market. You saw an opportunity, seized the moment and delivered your product, which, in this case, is the Father.

JC: I compared my life to a plowed field sprinkled with seed. The plants grew and bore fruit.

DC: Did you see yourself as harvesting the fruit?

JC: Not only did I harvest the fruit, I ate it. Poetically, I was ready to minister to Israel as Israel was ready for my harvest.

DC: There's something else I see. You are known by your words, deeds and actions – by what you said and did. There is, however, another side to you and it is defined by what you didn't do. When I looked carefully I noticed you didn't moan or complain; you didn't lament your plight or Israel's; you didn't offer condolence or comfort. You were eternally optimistic yet candid; you had faith in your work and the people who followed you; and you believed in your ministry's effects. When I take notice, I see lamentation and complaint around me. I hear, "Why is this happening to me?" "The country is lost" "Why bother to do anything?" or "God is dead!" You saw and heard the same, yet you are not cynical. You are not pessimistic. You do not accept either cynicism or pessimism, and both are absent from your words, demeanor and action. Instead, you were positive, hopeful, and confident, with bold actions to match.

JC: That was the merchant and entrepreneur in me. To move in another direction where I fueled people's anger, frustration and discontent would have been counterproductive. Had I been different, other than what I offered through my ministry, I would have gathered followers who were socially discontent and politically suspicious and angry; they would have wanted to change the world rather than themselves. Had I appealed to that sentiment people would have acted accordingly. I wanted people to be healed, to love and to know the Father. That offering was different than what the other prophets of my time offered.

DC: Also, cynicism isn't effective when faced with conditions ripe for change. You elevated yourself above normal reactions. You wanted to be with the people but not act like them. You were a leader with a tangible mystique; the one to follow. You were different. People sensed your genuineness and strength.

JC: I led by example. I didn't ask for anything that I wasn't willing to do and I was willing to go to the end.

DC: So, the time arrived and you went to John the Baptist.

JC: I made my decision and left.

DC: Again, leaving your friends and family for the unknown.

JC: I didn't think about it in that manner. But now that you say it, I can see your point.

DC: When you went to John you were motivated, you knew the Father, you were filled with love and compassion and you embodied the New Wine metaphor.

JC: That characterizes it.

DC: You also had a deep connection to your Hebrew heritage and you wanted to bring the love of the Father to them.

JC: I had a heartfelt compassion for them.

DC: I've finished my coffee.

CHAPTER 6

JOHN THE BAPTIST

JC: I feel more comfortable now that I'm wearing my robe and tunic. Let me say a small opening prayer. "Father, renew our minds and fill our hearts with wisdom and love. Guide us gently by your hand and bless us with strength and courage as we continue along this road. Amen." I wanted to clear the air and start fresh once again.

DC: Notice the sun finally peeking through the clouds.

JC: So it is.

DC: Are you ready to continue?

JC: I am.

DC: Let's talk about John the Baptist.

JC: John is a good subject.

DC: You both ministered around the Galilee.

JC: Yes.

DC: I believe you were motivated differently but it's hard to see the truth of that through the lens of Christian theology and Old Testament prophecy. Apparently, John is the voice in the wilderness that makes the way for you because you are the fulfillment of prophecy. I must ask myself if I can understand your true motivation, or John's for that matter, in lieu of the Christian perspective.

JC: What are you asking?

DC: I want to know what inspired you to go to John. Do I have to rely on the Christian account or can I see your motive without it? What happens when I set aside the theological narrative? What can I see? Both of you are painted with a specific brush.

JC: I'm sure you tried.

DC: It is a challenge. Christianity is two thousand years old and when I examine you and your ministry I see what the Church, its theologians and historians want me to see. Before I started this interview, I sensed something was missing but I could not put my finger on it.

JC: You have the mind to see through the theology. Why do you think I went to John the Baptist? What is your gut feeling? I found the Father outside of scripture and I would encourage the same for you.

DC: My suspicion is that the gospel narrative does not reflect your true motives.

JC: You don't agree that I went to John to get baptized and receive the Holy Spirit?

DC: That is a story of convenience and more theology than history. There is more to this story than the Christian narrative.

JC: Where would you like to begin?

DC: I'd like to start by asking, "Why did you walked ninety miles from your house to the Jordan River to see John?" What motivated you?

JC: He baptized across the Jordan River in Bethany.

DC: Across the Jordan River in Bethany. The walk must have taken about a week.

JC: If I were walking leisurely. I shaved a day and a half. To your question, I was compelled to see John.

DC: Compelled? How so? What could he offer you that you lacked?

JC: Use your mind. I'm sure you can make an educated guess.

DC: To be baptized?

JC: That is a consideration.

DC: What else can I see in this story? Let's start with the basic nuts and bolts.

JC: Nuts and bolts?

DC: The nuts and bolts of practicality and method. You didn't live your life theologically. You lived your life in service, and that is a different motive.

JC: You'll have to explain yourself.

DC: You reached a culmination point and decided to go to John.

JC: What do you mean by culmination point?

DC: The point of no return – a now or never, a do or die moment when your wisdom and inspiration to conduct your ministry were at hand. Maybe the Father's voice was loud and pushed you forward. Either way, you were committed to your message of the Father and didn't have to learn it while you ministered.

JC: I won't disagree with that.

DC: I suggest you lacked the *how* to conduct a ministry not the *what*. You didn't know the steps involved because you were not exposed to it before. You are a quick study but not quick enough to learn something like a ministry from scratch. You needed some guidance. Simply, your message required feet to run.

JC: What else do you see?

DC: I suspect you wanted to witness John in action and see his practice up close. You wanted to know what he did and how he did it. When you saw, you recognized that he had developed an image, a method and a rite, and you needed something similar.

JC: He was dedicated with a meticulous sense of the peculiar. He ate wild honey, wore a sack cloth, and lived in the wilderness. He called people to repent and introduced the rite of baptism.

DC: How did you hear about John?

JC: Remember, John was my cousin and our family was aware of his ministry, but rumors and whispers spread throughout Judea about him. He became news. People returned to Capernaum renewed and reinvigorated. They were surprised by his cold-water baptism. That was unprecedented. Instead of a ritual purification bath his water represented renewal; a change of the heart from the inside, which leads to holiness and righteousness, and a clean body from the outside, which leads to purity. These changes worked in concert. It was said he was powerful, that his message of repentance was awe inspiring, and that he was Elijah resurrected. People felt he was different than the other prophets and thought he might be the Messiah. He did not advocate an armed resistance against the Romans; instead, he wanted people to return to God. His movement was extraordinary and captivating. I thought John could mentor and teach me, not about the Father but about a ministry.

DC: Before we explore this in more detail, I need to ask why you didn't think a school or an academy would have been a better solution than a ministry. You could have established a particular place for people to come. You could have taught your spiritual knowledge, revealed the Father and healed in one location instead of traveling around. The people could have come to you instead of you going to the people.

JC: I thought about the Greek academy, the synagogue and the Essene community, but none of these examples appealed to me. They did not seem appropriate. Traveling felt closer in nature to the Father than a school. I felt the Father in movement and action that seemed active and alive; it was not stationary. God goes to people where they are rather than waiting for people to come to Him. I emulated that facet. John's ministry was outside in the landscape not set behind walls, and his baptism practice and hands-on approach appealed to me. This was startling, provocative and new. His message and practice were shocking and gave people new hope and renewed expectations. He connected with those who felt God was on the verge of appearing.

DC: I'm reminded of his words, "Repent, for the Kingdom of Heaven has come near." (MT 3:2) There was immediacy and intimacy to his ministry. One difference between you and John, aside from his theology, is the location of his ministry. He ministered around the Jordan River whereas you took your ministry on the road and traveled throughout the countryside from village to village and town to town.

JC: I matched the challenges of a traveling ministry with my personality and, as I mentioned before, I modeled my ministry to my understanding of the

Father. I didn't want to be something I was not. I felt I needed to learn from John so I became his disciple. Unlike him, I wanted to incorporate healing into my ministry. I just didn't know how to put all the pieces together.

DC: What was your first step?

JC: I walked to Bethany to look him in the eye and to experience baptism.

DC: What did you find in him? Was there something in his eyes or something about him that resonated with you?

JC: Fire. Conviction. Certitude. Power. He knew he was doing the will of God. His ministry of baptism was his birthright; he was born to do it. His message was clear and his methods effective. His demeanor and conviction made a lasting impression on me.

DC: John paved the ground before you and led the way, in a manner of speaking.

JC: Many followed him and were inspired. I was one.

DC: When I compare and contrast your ministries, I notice both were fresh, novel and peaceful, and both required dogged commitment and determination not only for you but for your followers as well. They were not off the hook of commitment.

JC: John and I knew a gritty, single-minded commitment was needed during this time of turmoil and chaos. Being lukewarm was not an option for anybody. It would not have brought about the effective change we wanted to see in our society or in the individual person.

DC: You drew a line. Neither of you used your ministry, like Judas the Galilean, to force structural changes in society through murder, violence, mayhem and destruction.

JC: We didn't think it useful. In fact, we thought it dangerous. In this regard, John and I inspired each other. We were interested in a community of believers who had an internal change of heart.

DC: Is there anything else that John did for you?

JC: John was baptizing when I arrived and then the unexpected occurred. He stopped and we stared each other in the eye. He was delighted to see me and recognized my spiritual demeanor was strong. One recognizes that quality in another; it's a shared but rare experience. I went to him because I wanted to be baptized and to learn from him so I that would know how to minister. But what happened next surprised me. I didn't anticipate his revelation.

DC: What was that?

JC: There was something on his mind of which I was unaware.

DC: Which was?

JC: He was convinced I was the Messiah.

DC: Did you think that?

JC: No! He believed it. All along he said he was not the Messiah, that he was "not worthy to stoop down and untie" (MK 1:7) the Messiah's sandals, and that he was the voice in the wilderness making the way for the powerful one.

DC: How did you react?

JC: I was skeptical, yet I could not dismiss his conviction either. It was if his words were the voice of God. For a time, I wondered if I misconstrued the Father and wondered if I made a mistake. I knew I was inspired by the divine, but does that make me the Messiah?

DC: He thought it did. He also said of you that you were the "Lamb of God." Did that resonate with you? Why do you suppose he thought you were the Messiah?

JC: This is complicated. Our society anticipated the Messiah in times of trouble and people of my day expected him to appear at any moment. Excitement filled the air and the possibility of the appearance of the Messiah stirred people's hearts and minds. It was pervasive. Though this was in the air it was not on my mind. John's belief that I was the Messiah involves his Essene priest background.

DC: Explain what that means.

JC: The Essenes were a desert community of priests, scribes and laypeople living in Qumran near the Dead Sea. They were well versed in scripture. They believed a messiah would arise to lead the Israelite people back to God in the End Times and restore the Temple with proper priests.

DC: Who were proper priests?

JC: The bloodline from the Sons of Zadox. The Essenes believed they were legitimate heirs to the Temple. They alone felt responsible to regulate, manage and conduct the Temple practices, offerings and sacrifices, not the existing Temple priests who acquiesced to the Romans.

DC: I want to know more about the Essenes. Who were they? What did they want? What did they believe? What was their practice?

JC: They were a religious community who separated themselves from the rest of Israel. It was their belief that the time was near for Israel to be restored to its proper standing in the world and in God's eye. They also believed Israel was a wayward bride who strayed from God and was once again in immediate danger of being chastised by God. To countermand and counteract this growing problem they communed in the desert and initiated purity, devotion, and observance practices acceptable to God.

DC: They looked to the past for guidance and were committed to those old-school ideas and practices which we discussed before.

JC: You have an odd way of minimizing the issue.

DC: I'm trying to understand them. What were some ideas and practices of the Essenes?

JC: They thought pleasure seeking was a vice and regarded temperance and mastery of passions as a virtue. They shared belongings and wealth, observed the Sabbath religiously, and conducted ritual baths. They devoted themselves to the ancient Hebrew writers, did not steal, were charitable, desired the simplicity of life, and applied healing with stones and herbs. They ate and said grace together, thanked God as the giver of life, learned a craft, wore simple clothes, and did not take oaths. They thought the human body was a prison, conquered pain through willpower alone, and valued death more than life without end.

DC: You have several things in common.

JC: I do, but not everything is in common. We had our differences.

DC: Did you join them or spend time with them?

JC: Let me say that I was known by them as they were known by me, and I'll say I passed in and out of their community but I separated myself from them because we no longer saw eye to eye. I set aside several of their ideas and practices.

DC: Which ones did you set aside?

JC: I wanted to dance with God, to love and laugh; they did not. They believed in righteousness and purity; I believed in compassion and mercy. They traveled two by two and brought a weapon to defend themselves with; I did not. I knew the Father intimately through direct experience; they understood God and worshipped Him as the Creator who was all-knowing, strict, jealous and vengeful. I ate and drank with sinners, prostitutes and the unclean; they thought that distasteful. I have to emphasize that last statement.

DC: You also traveled throughout the countryside whereas the Essenes tended to stay isolated within the Qumran community. They wanted to restore the Temple priests; you wanted to end the practice, which is why you said, "The Kingdom of God is within you." (LK 17:21)

JC: I knew the body was a temple of the divine; they believed the body was a prison. They followed the Sabbath strictly; I saw it as a day of celebration and healing. The big difference was that I wanted people to love and embrace life; they wanted people to obey in order to resurrect an older religious order. They believed in the final Battle between Good and Evil; I believed the divine was in our midst. They believed in the Messiah and Savior; I believed in the restoration of the person and the community.

DC: In the Essene literature, there are two strong but opposing characters. One is the highly influential Teacher of Righteousness, and the other is his nemesis who left the community, the Wicked Priest. A tense rivalry ensued and persisted between them, which extended beyond the community. It shows a vibrant dichotomy within this community. There is a constant and fierce struggle throughout the Dead Sea literature between two opposing forces. There is a battle between purity and impurity, right practice and wrong practice, right thinking and wrong thinking, and between those who accept the community and those who oppose the community. In addition, to the battle between the Teacher of Righteous and the Wicked Priest, there is the coming battle between the Sons of Light and the Sons of Darkness. This is striking to me in several ways.

JC: Why is it striking to you?

DC: A similar pattern exists in the early Jesus and early Christian movement. One practice is to smear a person with a disparaging label, the other is to prop up, elevate or acknowledge a faithful adherent. Notice this practice in the New Testament canon; your detractors are disparaged with labels such as harlot, doubter, back slider, Antichrist, demon possessed, Pharisee and traitor. For those who follow and/or are important to the movement the moniker of the just, the rock, disciple, apostle, believer, repentant, and follower are used. The point I'm making is that the Essenes were guilty of stigmatizing another, as were the Christians; each pointed a finger and hurled insults at their opponents and their competitors.

JC: What does this pattern suggest to you?

DC: It illustrates the importance of group identity, of group adhesion, congruency and bond, of group unity and group think. It implies that the group accepts, acknowledges, and adheres to particular practices, rites, creed and dogma, and that the followers accept the hierarchical authority associated with that group.

JC: Is that all?

DC: There is a palpable tension between rival groups and individuals. The dynamic within this battlefield is implicit. It says this one is trustworthy and that one is not, this one is a true believer and that one is not, and this one is a member of the group and that one is not; and that one left but we stayed true.

JC: Let's examine in more detail the Christian rivalry before we jump back to John the Baptist. You point out the significance of the group. I must also point out that the leader of the group had to stand out in order to capture one's heart and imagination. The leader had to be intelligent, bold, dynamic, charismatic and inspirational, especially in times of chaos or crisis. I had to get that in as a commentary note. What do you understand in regards to the Christian rivalry?

DC: The early Jesus movement and the early Christians faced daunting and seemingly insurmountable challenges. The external forces against them were fierce. Here is a list: the ordinary Jews in general, the Jewish religious establishment of Pharisees, Sadducees, priests, and Temple High Priests and the Jewish political establishment, namely the Hasmoneans. In addition, I believe the Essenes were against them. Strangely, several Essene ideas get inserted and grafted into Christian literature and practice, but the other powerful force against the Christians was the Roman Empire. The Romans forced the Christians to develop yet another set of resistance tactics.

JC: Resistance tactics? What do you mean? What were they?

DC: The Christians didn't acknowledge or pay tribute to the Roman statue of Caesar, which was in every city in the Roman Empire. They didn't participate in the Roman-sanctioned religious festivals, and Roman women converts didn't want to have sex with their husbands, thinking it was impure. In a sense, the Christians turned the Roman social order upside down, which irritated and upset Rome greatly. There is one other thing the Christians did, which is rather covert and under-handed.

JC: Which is?

DC: The Synoptic Gospels were written in such a way as to show how a God is created, how a God operates in the world, how peace is established and how an alternative kingdom develops, and all of this is in competition and dissimilar from the Roman model.

JC: Rome had an emperor, who was a god, and an empire, which is the kingdom. The emperor did not always have longevity or a bloodline to draw from. It was not always clear who would rule the Roman Empire.

DC: For a Roman emperor, the average length of time to rule the empire was four years.

JC: And the matter now turns to succession. In Rome, there were several ways an emperor rose to or fell from the throne. One was disposed by force – a civil war broke out and the victor took the throne, or a powerful general marched up to Rome with his army and demanded the throne. One emperor succeeded another because of a bloodline or one rose through the ranks of the senate. Each of these practices was a typical Roman succession custom. In relation to peace and the building of the kingdom, the Romans employed their military to crush an adversary. When they succeeded they appointed a loyalist king or governor to rule that area, collect tax and maintain peace by brute force if necessary.

DC: That is one way to establish peace and a kingdom. I'd like to circle back and mention another obstacle the Christians confronted. Not only did they face the array we just mentioned, they fought against the existing political, philosophical and religious traditions and the theology and ideology behind them. As a new religion, they had to offer antidotes or alternatives to the prevailing customs, beliefs and practices. It was a tall order and something to admire from afar. In addition to the external struggles, the Christians also fought numerous internal battles among themselves.

JC: I'm enjoying your observations. They were busy fighting everything. Please continue. What was the internal strife?

DC: Christians were pitted against other Christians over theology, rites, practice and, specifically, your identity.

JC: You're speaking specifically of whether I was human, divine or both.

DC: I am. That was one point of contention, but there were others. We see over and over again in Paul's letters his fight with those who question his theology and his moral and ethical code. I'll mention three: "Should one eat meat if the animal was sacrificed to a pagan God?" "Should one be circumcised or not?" and "Who should be included in the Kingdom – only Jews or gentiles as well?" They don't appear to but this point to deeper factions and rivalries. Other rivalries involved theology.

JC: Such as?

DC: One group of Christians, the Pistis Christians, expressed their faith in you and that you are Lord, Savior and the Son of God who died for the sins of mankind. Another group of Christians, the Gnostic Christians, believed that you were a Savior because you revealed the way back to the Father and the way to know the Father was through some kind of mystical experience either of the self or of the Father.

JC: These two approaches put a wedge between those who wanted to find or have meaning and purpose in their life. It is an old problem: worship, practice and belief versus connection with the divine through direct personal experience.

DC: On a slightly different note, but consistent with the rivalry theme, I want to point out that a few scholars suggest you are the Essene Wicked Priest because you left that community, while others suggest Paul was the Wicked Priest because he twisted the meaning and intent of your ministry into something you did not advocate. There is a lot going on during this early phase of Christian development and it is similar to the infighting between the various Jewish sects. I see them yelling over, fighting over and killing each other over theology and practice as each promoted their respective position while discounting or supplanting the other.

JC: I experienced a similar pattern and thought it counterproductive. I was too much of an individual and free thinker to be concerned with the needs of the group. Instead, I advocated the need of the individual. Group infighting and rivalry is another matter altogether.

DC: I'd like to return to John the Baptist, discuss his relationship with Herod Antipas and tie it together with his conviction that you are the Messiah.

JC: All right.

DC: John accused Herod of adultery and Herod responded aggressively by arresting John and punishing him by chopping off his head. An alternative reason for John's execution exists which I'd like to address. The rulers worried John was raising an army of believers on the other side of the Jordan River, ready to overthrow Herod and oust the Romans. If enough people were saved a new, large, restored and free people of God would exist creating the possibility of another Exodus. The reigning and enslaving pharaoh, in this case the Romans, would be swept up in God's wrath. People hoped John's army would initiate the End Times and force the hand and appearance of the Messiah. With that the Promised Land could be resettled and populated with new holy and righteous believers and the unrighteous and unholy unbelievers, Gentiles and illegitimate rulers would be gone. This may be the reason for John's execution and his expectation that you are the Messiah.

JC: What do you know of the Jewish End Times and the Messiah?

DC: The End Time was the period of wickedness, debauchery, idolatry and waywardness just prior to the appearance of God's revenge and wrath. Many Jews of the first century understood that a cycle of time had reached its fullness, like a baby about to be born, and that a new cycle was to start. Jewish people looked for the Messiah to overthrow the Romans. John the Baptist could have been the anointed one or you could have. Another facet of this story involves the one who initiates the revolt and gets it started. Afterward the Messiah, like Moses before him who confronted the pharaoh, would miraculously appear, take charge and lead the way. He and his army of true believers would fight and destroy the Romans, thus saving Israel from annihilation. The Messiah would place himself on the throne of David and Israel would once again live peacefully in accord with God.

JC: John's theological message and his baptismal practice ignited his followers to imagine such an End Time scenario.

DC: Was your ministry guided by such intention and sentiments?

JC: My ministry was geared toward the restoration of one's heart and mind through compassion and wisdom. I wanted people to come together through love and compassion and to experience the divine within. Love is an active process and requires effort. I was aware of but I did not agree with the idea of a Messiah who would restore Israel by military force. That was never my intention.

DC: It doesn't appear that John's message was geared toward love as much as it was geared toward repentance and getting back in alignment with God. There is other side to him, however, that expects a miraculous appearance of the Messiah since he is making the way for him. What did John expect to do when the Messiah arrived? Take up arms?

JC: He thought he could offer his devout followers to the Messiah. Then he would step aside and allow the Messiah to work his miracles of restoration.

DC: The names of your brothers suggest your family's attitude in this regard, and your ministry certainly had the means to change people's hearts, minds and outlook.

JC: Is that what you think? That I wanted to participate in an insurrection? Or that I wanted to lead it?

DC: I'm playing the devil's advocate.

JC: Don't! I wanted to share compassion and my wisdom of the Father. I had to get involved because I couldn't watch the rising anger, frustrations and hatred any longer. I had to do something and I knew I could offer something.

DC: Did John's power and conviction captivate you?

JC: Generally or specifically?

DC: Start with the general and end with the specific.

JC: Generally, I couldn't take his words lightly. His message was convincing and his baptism rite was powerful. Together they struck a deep chord in a person and it changed them.

DC: What are the specifics?

JC: I was surprised, even stunned, when he used the terms *Messiah* and *Lamb of God*. I didn't anticipate these titles and didn't want to accept them. Occasionally, *Messiah* flashed across my mind but it was brief. What else could I think with the power of the divine inside of me? Remember, John was an Essene priest. In the beginning I tried to live up to his mantle, religious ideals, inspirations and hopes. Over time they didn't feel right and I couldn't reconcile them with my understanding of the Father. As my voice strengthened, the Essene influence withered. I was not willing to dedicate my life to the ideals of another person or sect. I just could not do it; besides, the Father was guiding me in another direction.

DC: One has to have courage to allow a new path to unfold and to change direction, because the ambiguity and uncertainty that comes with it can be unsettling or distressing.

JC: At times choices are made for us. Is that Fate, destiny or the Father? At other times we choose and our choices prove astute and beneficial. The challenge comes when a decision is made but the result is different than what was anticipated. Then what do you do? Is that what you mean when life changes direction?

DC: Partially. But I'm thinking specifically of your departure from John the Baptist. At first you felt compelled to know his teachings, rite and methods, but something changed. Did he serve a purpose? Did something feel askew? Or, as the gospels state, did you simply move on after you received the unpredictable infilling of the Holy Spirit? You weren't bound by John or owe him anything, did you?

JC: I no longer needed John's counsel or assistance. I received his gifts and was on my own.

DC: Like a ship leaving the harbor and heading out to open water.

JC: Yes.

DC: After you left, I believe you received two gifts. Maybe you realize what they were, but maybe you did not.

JC: What were they?

DC: Clarity to know what to do and, just as important, clarity to know what not to do.

JC: Excellent point. Let me talk generally about choices. Choices always appear in life and decisions have to be made. One can make them or Fate and circumstances can make them for you. If you sit and do nothing you end up over there. If you choose, you end up over here. I preferred to make decisions; rarely did I enjoy the consequences from a forced decision. Later, I found the usefulness of thinking through a choice and understanding its implications beforehand.

DC: You imagined the outcome.

JC: The more informed I was the better the choice I made, and the better the choice I made the more effective the result.

DC: Another question is, "Are you comfortable making a decision and accepting the outcome?"

JC: Or, "Can you accept the unknown and all that transpires from a decision?" Acceptance has to be cultivated, as do the emotions. One can't always control events, but one can control the emotional response to them and not get swept into a torrent.

DC: The Our Father prayer ties in nicely with our current discussion.

JC: Let's talk about its importance.

DC: Tell me if I am wrong but I believe the Our Father prayer was inspired by several factors. One was the aftermath of your NDE and the direct effects and changes that resulted from it; we already discussed those. But here is a list of the other influencing factors that you unconsciously incorporated into the prayer: the events leading up to John, your separation from John, and the events that unfolded after John. You are the type of person who needs to understand and appreciate how the world works and how you fit into it. From the moment you left home and then returned, to your decision to see John and then leave him, and straight through your ministry and into the final stage of your life you encountered turmoil, ambiguity, uncertainty and unpredictability. The pattern repeated throughout your life. The Our Father prayer originates here and composing it was your way of confronting and accepting that persistent condition. You minimized the effects by narrowing your vision specifically into guidelines.

JC: I offered this prayer because one disciple asked for it. (LK 11:1) John was in the habit of praying and giving his disciples prayers to pray. This particular disciple wanted one from me and by the time I had given it to him I had eyes to see and ears to hear.

DC: I also believe you accepted your many and varied experiences, whether ambiguous or uncertain and pleasant or painful, as the Father's gift. You also simplified your life, and the more simplified it became the easier it was for you to make uncomplicated but clear decisions. You simply went to one village to teach, heal, confront and encourage. You gathered disciples and followers and when you finished you went to another village, repeated your process and got similar results. The Our Father prayer acknowledges God in all things and asks for daily bread, not to be tested and to forgive those who harm, injure or insult you. This was your guiding principal and it worked.

JC: My truth was simple and by practicing it daily I experienced the hand of the Father.

DC: I'd like return to the titles John the Baptist gave to you because they are pregnant with consequence. I see a beginning. This is the moment when titles and symbolic metaphor start in your life. I can't see it any other way. You went to John and he immediately conferred highly significant and charged titles upon you. Maybe you didn't agree with him, but it nevertheless started a trend. From then on symbolism and titles were incorporated into your ministry. What can you tell me about that?

JC: Initially, I didn't fully appreciate this feature and didn't think much about the symbols and titles or their importance. Not at first; that came later. As I mentioned earlier, I didn't think I was the Messiah and I didn't expect people to put their hope in me as such, nor did I embrace the sacrificial Lamb of

God. You become a living sacrifice when you dedicate your life to God. The sacrificial Lamb is a Christian invention, not mine.

DC: Though, after John, you realized the power of titles?

JC: I did. I was drawn to the titles Son of Man and Son of Adam. I noticed these titles had unexpected psychological effects because people stopped, wondered and listened. They were mesmerized. They identified with and remembered me. I'd hear whispers, "There's the Son of Man." It meant something to them.

DC: As opposed to, "There's that guy who said, 'Turn the other cheek.'" You also referred to yourself as prophet.

JC: Yes. I'd like to address another effect of titles. This had two faces. I wanted to embody a particular ideal, but others wanted to see me in their light and used their monikers.

DC: You were called Messiah and addressed as lord, teacher and rabbi.

JC: Those are the ones who liked me and felt I could offer and deliver something of value to them. Those who didn't like me called me a blasphemer, a drunk and a glutton. I wanted people to listen to my words, get healed and apply my knowledge, so I did not dissuade them from seeing what they wanted to see. Titles also made the distinction between me and the other men claiming to be messiahs and prophets who ministered throughout Judea and Israel more pronounced. I sought after any and all extra advantages; there were many competing voices and one had to stand out from the crowd.

DC: John was a colorful character and many things went into his prophet persona, from the clothes he wore, to food he ate, to the fiery words he said, to the rite he performed and to his title.

JC: He was called the Baptist and his appearance matched the rawness and power of his words.

DC: I'm beginning to see that titles, clothes, words and rites were necessary components of getting your message across.

JC: They worked together in tandem and none of the elements could conflict with any other.

DC: What did you wear?

JC: An ordinary tunic and robe. I didn't wear fine cotton or colorful clothing. That was not as important as what I did or what I said. People remembered me for my miracles and perplexing teachings. Like John, my clothes were raw and ordinary and they contrasted to the powerful miracles I performed and the bewildering words I spoke.

DC: What did baptism do for you? Did it accomplish anything?

JC: I didn't imagine a single act like that would do anything but since I was ready for a miracle the remarkable transpired. I felt peace. Washed. Renewed. Emboldened. I felt new and awake.

DC: Was your baptism an act of acceptance?

JC: Acceptance? I like the meaning of that word. Before my baptism, I sensed my path; afterward I knew my path.

DC: The gospels mention that a dove descended and landed on you.

JC: I felt touched by the divine and something astonishing occurred, as I rose from the water a pair of doves landed on me. Many saw and interpreted it as a sign from God.

DC: In other spiritual literature and in other religious practices the symbolism of water and fish are intimately interwoven. In the Babylonian account Oannes, the Fish Man, emerges out of the water to teach the arts, sciences and letters. There is the Hebrew story of Jonah and the Whale, which we spoke of earlier, and Christian converts were likened to fish that at baptism are returned to the sea of Christ. Various forces in the invisible world work in the visible world, as seen when you emerge from of the Jordan River. As you ascend out of the water, a dove comes to you, and you take your rightful place in the world. In this story, we see the symbolic interplay between the invisible divine forces manifesting in the visible world, and once this transpires you begin your ministry. Would you characterize your baptism as a symbolic gesture as I mentioned or would you characterize it differently?

JC: By your logic all of John's followers and disciples must be considered the same as me. Did they not go into the water as I did, and did they not come back out of the water as I did? Does that make them God? Does that make me a god? One can say it is symbolic. Fine, but that does not mean that I am by nature or constitution any different than any of the others who were baptized. Immersion into the water was the same for me as it was for everybody else. For some, baptism was extraordinary and truly profound and meaningful.

DC: Thank you for clarifying that point. Every time I come across symbolism or metaphor in reference to you I see less of you and I see more of the authors' intent to make you into something else. In this case the Christian writers want to make a theological point. In the Gospel of Mark, it is written when you emerged out of the water, "You are my Son, whom I love; with you I am well pleased." (MK 1:11) I see something different. I see a man accepting his calling and being filled with power to follow it. I like symbolism and can appreciate it, but not here. Instead, I want to get at the heart of the man, not at the heart of theological metaphor.

JC: I don't want my life to be diminished through symbolism, yet I did become a symbol of change and a new voice.

DC: When I contemplate the initial phase of your ministry and the journey or process to get it up and running, I notice John's pivotal role. His influence is hard to see at first but the deeper I looked the more I saw.

JC: What did you see?

DC: I see three facets. First, I see a bridge. Before John you were one thing, after him you were another. All the New Testament gospels agree that your ministry started after you saw John. I can't argue or question this point; it makes sense and follows the nature of transition.

JC: What do you mean by the nature of transition?

DC: "What goes in is not what comes out." For example, a seed, once planted in the ground, emerges as a flower, tree or plant. It transitioned into the thing it was meant to become or has the potential to become. For humans, the seed enters the womb and emerges as the infant. What goes in is not what comes out; the first thing turns into the second thing. I see a similar process with you and John. Before John you were a man living his life as a carpenter near his family; after John, you were a prophet and a living sacrifice for God away from his family.

JC: You mentioned three facets of John's influence. What are the other two?

DC: Second, I see the use of titles and a new rite; I see the significance of demeanor, conviction, food, clothing, home, ministry location, teachings, disciples, transformative experiences, leadership, and a few other intangibles. Third, when I review some of your sayings and practices I see John's influence.

JC: John showed me the techniques to be a powerful prophet.

DC: What technique?

JC: He evoked confidence. He was a leader who spoke clearly and directly. He was filled with fiery passion and conviction; he spoke his mind and did not mince words. My words, however, were more lofty and intelligent, and not as sharp. I was gentler and softer but that is not to say that I was less forceful or charismatic.

DC: When I examine this period in your life, read your sayings and review your practices, I am hard pressed to distinguish the direction of influence. Did he influence you or did you influence him?

JC: I don't know what you mean by the direction of influence.

DC: This is delicate. *Direction of influence* is another term I coined because I cannot determine from which direction the pattern originates.

JC: Do you have any examples?

DC: John's ministry and baptismal rite prepares the way for the Messiah. While you ministered, you sent your disciples ahead of you to towns and villages. (LK 10:1) The same occurs during Passover prior to your crucifixion. You ask two of your disciples to go ahead of you into Jerusalem and prepare the upper room. (MK 14:13-15) These accounts portray the act of preparing the way for you; one is John's method while the other is yours. Now I must ask whether John inspired you to send your disciples ahead of you or did your technique inspire the words to be put into John's mouth by the gospel writers after your death. The gospel writers were in the habit of inventing and exaggerating when telling your story and the first written account, which is the Gospel of Mark, was written roughly forty years after your death.

JC: Enough time to forget or overlook that kind of detail. What other direction of influence examples do you have?"

DC: John the Baptist says, referring to you, "He must become greater; I must become less." (JN 3:30) In this one statement two actionable parts move in opposite directions. You employ a similar or parallel structure in your sayings, "So the last will be first, and the first will be last" (MT 20:16) and "Whoever finds their life will lose it, and whoever loses their life for my sake will find it." (MT 10:39) The same logic applies to the Father's influence – His influence becomes greater while yours becomes less. So, my question is, did John influence the structural format of these sayings or did your words inspire the gospel writers to put this type of structure into John's mouth? It's difficult to determine the direction of influence. That is what I mean.

JC: Does it matter?

DC: Yes it does. You are a source of great inspiration on many levels, especially to those who followed in your footsteps after your crucifixion. Your teachings, practice, method and examples inspire people to this day.

JC: John's influence in my development as a prophet cannot be underestimated. He was consequential and important in my life despite our theological and practical differences.

DC: I see his influence in your sayings. In one "you began to speak to the crowd about John: 'What did you go out into the wilderness to see? A reed swayed by the wind? If not, what did you go out to see? A man dressed in fine clothes? No, those who wear fine clothes are in kings' palaces.'" (MT 11:7-8) Or you said, "Foxes have dens and birds have nests, but the Son of Man has no place to lay his head." (LK 9:58) And again you said, "Therefore I tell you, do not worry about your life, what you will eat; or about your body, what you will wear. For life is more than food, and the body more than clothes." (LK 12:22-23) Would you agree with this?

JC: John's ministry, style and words influenced me. He wore a robe wrapped with a leather belt, ate locust and wild honey, didn't have a permanent place to stay, and spoke with fiery words. People came to hear him and they listened. He baptized people. He was captivating. Later, when I was on my own I incorporated parts of his ministry into my mine, but I still had to develop my own style, practice and teachings.

DC: Elaborate on your differences.

JC: I used titles, performed miracles, fed people, healed people and shared my Beatitudes, parables and teachings. Unlike John, I was not concerned with holiness or righteousness. John's message of repentance and baptism was straightforward and clear, while many of my sayings, teachings and practices were puzzling. John ministered around the Jordan River to be near water for his baptismal rite. I, on the other hand, traveled from synagogue to synagogue, house to house, village to village, town to town, countryside to countryside and beyond into Tyre and Sidon. He preached repentance, baptism and the End Times. I spoke about the Father, of love and compassion, and wisdom. I knew my teachings and practices were incompatible with his. I taught the measure used is the measure used on you. I taught the practice of turning the other cheek, of mercy and forgiveness. I taught the nature of inheritance and the manner of investing. I taught the Kingdom of Heaven is like a mustard seed. My teachings and John's teachings were not the same even though our goals were similar.

DC: What were they?

JC: To get people to think and act differently.

DC: Is there anything else that was different between you two?

JC: I ate and drank wine with the dispossessed, infirmed, tax collectors and harlots, much to the chagrin of the Pharisees and Essenes; John did not. I had women disciples, John wouldn't allow it.

DC: What were the similarities?

JC: Like John I didn't have a place to stay when I ministered, I wore mundane clothes, I didn't eat much and I gathered disciples. He challenged Herod Antipas' adulterous relationship with his brother's wife. I challenged the Pharisees on ritual practice and I turned over the money-changers' tables at the Temple during Passover. He performed baptism; I performed miracles. He spoke about God in relation to repentance, holiness and righteousness; I spoke about the Father, love, compassion and forgiveness. He was killed by Herod Antipas. I was judged by Herod and then handed over to Pilate to face my death. (LK 23:2-12) His dead body was removed by his disciples. (MK 6:29) My body was removed from the cross and placed in a tomb by the people I knew.

DC: Maybe you can clarify this since the accounts conflict with one another. After your baptism and temptations, the Synoptic Gospels tell of your return to the Galilee and Nazareth. (MK 1:14, MT 4:12, LK 4:14) The Gospel of John tells a different story. After your baptism, you quickly gather disciples and perform your first miracle at Cana during the wedding by turning water into wine. (JN 1:35-2:11) Instead of detailing the historical timeline and subsequent events, can you give us insight into your thoughts and intentions? Also, can you discuss the point at which you started your ministry? There is a fine line, but I like fine lines.

JC: There are four periods to keep in mind – the time when I decided to see John, my time with John, my time in the desert after John, and my time as I ministered aside from John. Confusion arises in relation to my time with John and the purpose of my desert experience.

DC: The desert experience is another name for your temptations.

JC: If that is what you wish to call it. My temptation/desert experience was not only pivotal in defining and separating me from John but also in purging me of my attachments.

DC: Is it correct to assume that it was necessary for you to overcome your human temptations rather than separate yourself from John? Or, at some point, did you follow in John's footsteps and act like him?

JC: I thought my time had come while I was with John. I was wrong. At first I put aside the Father and love and compassion to preach repentance and baptism as John did. He was a mentor and teacher. I did what he did. I said what he said. The time arrived when I didn't feel right about that any longer. I wanted people to know the Father. There was a dimension to his method that I agreed with but not for his reason. My religious position was different than his; that is not to discount his heart for God. Truly he was a man after God's heart.

DC: He was an Essene priest who was versed in scripture, wanted people to become holy and righteous, and expected the Messiah to solve the problems of your time. As an Essene, was he interested in restoring the proper priestly and royal bloodlines?

JC: I wouldn't say that was in the front of his mind or that he was guided by it, but that is not to say it wasn't there.

DC: Why ask people to repent and live righteous and holy lives? After all, there is an underlying urgency to his message that judgment was around the corner. "Repent, for the Kingdom of Heaven has come near." (MT 3:2)

JC: I concluded that John's message of repentance and baptism, along with the hope and expectation embedded in it, was misguided. People weren't healed or feed; they continued to walk in the dark, they lacked wisdom and failed to know the love of the Father. The purpose of my ministry was to address each of these issues.

DC: Not only were you compelled to separate yourself from him and change course, you could not accept his opinion that you were the Messiah or Lamb of God.

JC: We wanted two different things, but unfortunately some of our language was similar and that became a source of confusion. I had to determine the right thing to do for my message. I was committed to the end just as he was. I didn't want to start a ministry and then leave it. I had to feel what was right in my heart. Once I came to that conclusion and my confidence grew I knew I had to leave and find my way. I could no longer be his disciple. He had one message, I had another. To find the solution I went into the desert. I needed to hear the quiet voice of the Father.

DC: So, another dimension of your temptation/desert experience was to clarify your position from John.

JC: Yes, aside from my physical and spiritual purging.

DC: What happened?

JC: Imagine the forces bearing down on me. I wanted to be of service to the Father. I felt John could help. When we met, he called me the Lamb of God and Messiah. I was baptized and a pair of doves flew directly overhead. These affected me in ways I was not fully prepared for. I followed in his footsteps and did what he did. After a while, this started to feel wrong; the feeling crept in and continued getting stronger. All that I had come to know about love, compassion, mercy, justice and the Father I set aside while I was with John. John did not completely embrace these issues in his ministry. He preached repentance, a changed heart and getting right with God through right living; he was not addressing the need to join the heart of God to the heart of man. For me to know the Father was not necessarily through the mind, it was through the heart – an open heart. It may appear as if there is no difference but there was. Because of it I felt I needed to seek the silence of lonely places to hear the voice of the Father for guidance.

DC: I found that solitude and silence still the heart and clear the mind; they allow other unforeseen forces time to marinate and cook.

JC: It allowed me to feel what is right and to see what I needed to see. Things became visible and focused.

DC: Would you agree that your ministry started during your time with John?

JC: That was my first attempt and it taught me a great deal. I also learned what not to do, which is also very important. My ministry, for which I am known and remembered, didn't begin until after I had made my last renouncement of myself and the world in the desert and after I had recovered from that ordeal.

DC: I'd like to explore your desert experience in more detail. It is said you spent forty days in the desert without food. Let's talk about this first. Forty days is another way of saying a long time.

JC: Yes. It was an extended period of time and the number is symbolic.

DC: I want to understand the subtle issues about this experience.

JC: What subtle issues?

DC: The smallest of details. I appreciate your first attempts to follow in John's footsteps and that later you realized you needed to separate from him. At that decisive moment, did you have his same fiery conviction and dogged determination?

JC: That is a perceptive point. I carried with me a slight hesitation. My conviction wavered. I thought to myself, "Can I really do this?"

DC: What was going through your mind?

JC: I had to face my fears and concerns and address my commitment and attachments. When I looked to John I saw that he was willing to wear a basic tunic and eat wild honey and locust. He needed very little. He didn't have a home; home was where he slept or a cave he found. He needed very little in terms of material wealth, clothes and food. He was a man possessed by the spirit of God and that passion nourished him. It gave him life and made him distinct. He was a man of absolute conviction.

DC: He pushed his chips into the center of the poker table and said, in essence, "I'm all in." Maybe you felt you were not.

JC: I don't know "poker table" or understand what you mean by "I'm all in."

DC: Poker is a gambling card game of chance. When a player pushes his chips into the center of the playing table, he is betting that his one hand is either going to win the entire pot of money or he is going to lose everything and walk away from the game. That is what I mean by "all in." It's all or nothing.

JC: I see the point you are making. That is commitment. Events can turn either way.

DC: I surmise when you went to John you were motivated and committed but after spending time with him you realized the difference between his commitment and yours.

JC: I realized the discrepancy and knew there was still work to be done. I was not completely ready.

DC: Would it be right to say that at this point your heart was in the right place, your knowledge and wisdom were in the right place, but your willingness or commitment vacillated and that you questioned yourself? Maybe you felt you couldn't abandon everything altogether and take that leap of faith, the one that would take you to the very edge of your being and hurl you toward your death.

JC: I wouldn't disagree with that assessment. However, I was willing to face myself and ask, "What do I need to do?" I took stock and re-evaluated my situation and commitment. I didn't completely like what I saw.

DC: Did you think maybe service to the Father wasn't for you?

JC: That crossed my mind, but I couldn't give it much thought. The Father's voice roared in my ear and I couldn't ignore it. I had to do something.

DC: You went out into the desert to isolate and purge yourself from the last vestiges of ego and fear.

JC: I didn't go out into the desert specifically for those reasons, but that is not to say that did not occur. I purged my fear, quieted my ego and lost my attachments. There was another reason for the desert. When I went out into the desert I did not have a gauge to test my commitment. I had a desire to conduct a ministry but I was also filled with confusion. I had no reference point to gauge or measure my desire, determination, resiliency or courage.

DC: In other words, you needed something to compare them to. You needed a bar to base the intangibles.

JC: That is correct. I felt something was needed and I also felt it was important not to be overwhelmed by such emotional turmoil and uncertainty. I had to cleanse myself of these debilitating dynamics.

DC: To do this you put yourself to the test by exploring the edge of human potential and endurance. It is one thing to say you are dedicated to a cause; it is quite another to be dedicated and willing to face unknown challenges, dangers, obstacles and even death. One is either all in or all out. I imagine being in the middle wasn't going to do you or anybody else any good.

JC: The spirit and the body have different needs and desires. To prove the level of my commitment I did the unthinkable. I smothered the needs of my body. I quieted my concerns, silenced my ego, and centered myself on the Father. I had to find out if I had what it takes to go the distance. Parts of my personality had to increase while the other parts had to decrease. After my beating and robbery, I wasn't afraid of physical pain or death. That I put to rest. I knew life carried on beyond death so I was not gripped with fear on that front. The issue was getting everything in alignment – commitment, knowledge, desire, ego and heart.

DC: You had to die to yourself so the Father could live.

JC: Yes.

DC: When I study your ministry I notice it is punctuated at the beginning and the end with extreme feats of human endurance, deprivation and agony. Here is another term I coined. I call these extreme exploits feats of endurance. I can't say I've gone to the extent that you have but I experienced periods of physical deprivation and I've been alone for long periods. During times like these the mind attempts to make connections with incongruent ideas and emotions. I recalled dreams, re-experienced intense emotions, and saw my shortcomings; I felt the pain I've caused another and I felt the pain someone or a situation caused me. My mind cleared and I saw the positive and negative consequences of my decisions.

JC: I know exactly what you mean. Self-reflection is a necessary facet along the path. I observed my past and relived prior situations and events. I discovered my innate inclination for food and how I was governed by it; I discovered minute resistance to the Father and my lack of faith, and when I was a young man I was convinced I should be ruler of the world.

DC: You? I think that odd. You acted exactly the opposite. Then again one of your temptations, as recorded in the gospels, is to rule of the world. In the gospel Satan took you to the top of the Temple, showed you the world and offered it to you but you refused. As a boy and young man, I was convinced I would change the course of history; not be a part of history, mind you, but change it. Painful and sobering experiences broke that spell.

JC: I too thought I was special. I possessed a special personality, with special gifts and special insights into the mind of the divine. I assumed that should account for special dispensation.

DC: Why not? The plaque on your cross reads, "Jesus, king of the Jews."

JC: Don't be glib. I didn't write that; nor did I think that.

DC: Sorry. I didn't mean anything by it.

JC: You should learn to say what you mean. It clarifies the mind. I want to mention that the ambition and intention of my followers and disciples was for me to rule Judea as the king or High Priest. I thought that a mistake and I didn't entertain that notion. I thought it problematic, unsound and foolish.

DC: Why?

JC: Leaders focus on social, cultural, political, military and religious issues rather narrowly. For instance, I constantly fought against the Pharisees because I didn't agree with their thinking or practices. They were prideful and arrogant men who pursued power and privilege. Is that the kind of leader we needed?

DC: People who are leaders are prone to be like that. That said, I can imagine if a dogmatic and religious individual were king or High Priest they would rule with an iron theocratic fist according to their strict beliefs and practices. There wouldn't be much tolerance or diversity.

JC: I didn't think it a good idea to elevate a spiritual sage into a leadership role.

DC: Fair enough. We got a little off track. As I mentioned before, I refer to your desert temptation as a feat of endurance – one of three.

JC: I'm thinking about what you mean. If I would guess I'd say that one feat of endurance was my desert experience, the other was my death at the hands of the Romans, but I'm hard pressed to understand the third.

DC: I see it as your ministry.

JC: You do?

DC: These three required extraordinary commitment, dedication and hardship.

JC: As I think about it further, before I went into the desert, I had a chance to examine my options; I believed I had two. I could quit and do something else with my life, which reminded me of Jonah. I didn't want to follow in his footsteps. Or I could minister and be as committed as John. I chose the latter. The voice of the Father was just too loud.

DC: You've said that a couple of times. Can you explain its meaning? Are you hearing voices?

JC: Not voices, a roar. It wasn't distinct like, "Go over there, now over here, do this, now do that, say this, and now say that." It wasn't like that. It wasn't like the voice of an angel giving a set of instruction for me to obediently follow. It was an indistinguishable roar that wouldn't quiet. When I ministered it subsided. When I sought solace from lonely places it increased. I listened to it like Moses listening to the burning bush. I accepted it as the voice of the Father and I followed it from my heart.

DC: Did the roar provide you wisdom?

JC: I don't doubt that. I learned to listen through silence. I learned to listen through feeling. I learned to listen through intuition and I learned to listen through action. I cleared my heart and mind to receive the Father; I wanted to be an empty vessel so He could fill me up. One might think I was completely out of my mind; I was accused of such. For obvious reasons, it was a practice that ran counter to common sense and our religious practices. When people saw me sitting motionless and being quiet they stopped and wondered what I was doing. From an outsider's point of view my act of listening was irrational.

DC: Back to the roar. How did silence prepare you for the Father? I'm reminded of a bride on her wedding night waiting for her groom.

JC: I wouldn't say that, but silence gave me the ability to receive insights, and the quieter I became the more insights I received. I can also say that as I got quieter directions became clearer. Silence gave me a greater sense of what to do and when to do it, what to say and when to say it. It also increased my joy. I felt happiness. I felt laughter. I felt love. I felt wonder. I felt peace and I felt like sharing all of this.

DC: Would you say by being quiet and seeking solitude you became emboldened?

JC: That practice was integral and I wouldn't disagree with your statement. What started off as a gentle intuition became stronger, and as I followed the insight my confidence increased. As my confidence increased I became bolder and more determined.

DC: I'd like to swing back to your desert experience and temptations and talk about a few specifics. According to the Synoptic Gospels your first temptation involved food. I suspect food was particularly important and satisfying to you.

JC: Without food, we die.

DC: I'm not dismissing its necessity. What intrigues me is that food meant something more to you. Food was a pleasure for you, possibly a sensual delight.

JC: I liked everything about it. I liked growing and harvesting food. I liked its texture, flavor, aroma and taste. I liked how I felt after a meal. Sometimes I ate too much and felt bloated. Other times I felt I didn't eat enough. Taste was a sensory experience I liked and looked forward to each day. There is another thing I liked about food aside from its flavor, texture and aroma; I enjoyed the conversations I had over a meal.

DC: During your ministry, you didn't want it motivating you. Eliminating the pleasure and desire for food was a necessary sacrifice.

JC: I realized my ministry involved depravation. I didn't want to be tied to my cravings, nor did I want distractions to be a point of focus.

DC: You felt it was necessary to eliminate any temptation.

JC: For my ministry to succeed I wanted to be filled exclusively with the Father. I had to set aside my pride and ego. I had to set aside my sense of importance and my inclination to challenge the divine.

DC: What? Did you wrestle with God like the patriarch Jacob? Ok! From the look on your face you didn't find that comment amusing.

JC: I didn't.

DC: The Synoptic Gospels describe your desert experience as tests.

JC: It was a test. The desert experience involved my temptations and attachments. Food was one of the attachments I had to address and face. To overcome this I fasted during my entire stay in the desert. I wanted to be in control of my body. The other seemingly insurmountable issues were my inclinations to test God and my sense of importance. These too were challenged and defeated through extreme depravation.

DC: After your desert experience the gospels never mention you fasting again. The Pharisees question you about this and you dismiss fasting as unnecessary or inconsequential.

JC: After the desert experience, I discarded the practice of fasting because it was of no value. I was alive in the Father and felt that particular practice was tied to an older religious tradition. My concerns changed. My emphasis changed. My body changed. I was moved by new wine and new wineskins.

DC: Did you have any idea what was in store for you when you went into the desert?

JC: How could I? No one can know the exact particulars. No one knows what is in store on a journey. There is a relationship between the hidden and the revealed. The time arrives when the hidden is made known. It is odd, isn't it?

DC: What?

JC: When I went out into the desert I saw myself in a particular light. I envisioned myself as privileged, intelligent, proud and extraordinary. During this ordeal, I realized just how ordinary I am, yet, oddly, no two people are alike. Something gives us a unique and individualized quality. A journey into the desert draws us out and shapes us to become the one we are supposed to become. By choosing to do it I became alive. I drained myself of my attachments, and had I not done it I would have lived a false and moralistic life without being able to connect to myself or to the people to whom I ministered. I would have been flat. The necessary changes for me to grow and become robust in the Father would have been limited and I doubt whether I would have been able to experience the miraculous.

DC: This is one phase of the Hero's Journey. That is the terminology we use today. Sometimes the journey is chosen, other times it is thrust onto us, but once it begins other forces act on us. Part of it can be controlled, other parts cannot.

JC: I'll let you in on a secret: when the quest gets underway you see the world differently and the world sees you differently. You may be judged falsely for what you are attempting to accomplish or you may be accepted under false pretense. Notice the response I received while I hung on the cross. On one hand I was mocked and ridiculed, while on the other I was cried over. Regardless, people's response and reaction of adoration or hatred is a fate that is out of your hands and there is little you can do or say about it. When that occurs to you my advice is to attend to the task at hand. Just keep moving forward.

DC: I haven't gotten that far on my journey.

JC: Yes, you have. You've gotten pretty far; otherwise you would not be able to conduct this interview with me. There is one more turn in your transformation. You just haven't reached it yet.

DC: I'm swept up in the current of history, I'm not making it. And I still haven't found my place in the world.

JC: That saddens me. Knowing one's place in the world is a sacred experience. Not knowing is nightmarish; life and the world don't feel right. Everything is out of joint. I felt this way before I went to John. One of my hopes and what I imagined is that my ministry would solve that issue.

DC: Did it?

JC: My time with John and learning from him was one thing. I taught what he taught. I baptized as he baptized. I did what he did, but something was missing.

DC: I can picture you were going through the motions but it was not your calling. His ministry was his ministry, not yours. You followed in his footsteps; you imitated him but it was not in your heart. As a side note, for my readers to understand, the Gospel of John states that you and your disciples baptized upon returning to the Judean countryside after meeting Nicodemus and your trip to Jerusalem. (JN 3:22-24) I'd like to know what you thought was missing.

JC: It's difficult to put into words. The best I could say was that I was not ready to conduct a ministry. I had to undergo another transformation but I didn't know what that entailed or what to do to accomplish it.

DC: I think I understand. I had several apprenticeships under my belt when I graduated with my master's degree. Even with these I felt I wasn't ready to teach; technically I was. My rationale was different than that of my fellow classmates who applied for and landed teaching positions. I really didn't have a lot of real-world experience. It's odd but I didn't think it fair to teach the words and knowledge I learned from my professors without fully absorbing and knowing the subject. I wanted to make it my own before I could teach it, and to do that I needed the wisdom from experience. I didn't think it fair to my students if I didn't fully appreciate the subject or know the ins and outs and ups and downs. I wonder if my reaction and thoughts were similar to yours.

JC: Your truth is not mine.

DC: How did you go about the transformation you thought necessary?

JC: I don't recommend a self-prescribed technique or method to transform oneself. Ultimately that leads to another facet of you. You simply discover another facet of the ego, with its wants and desires. Little changes; you only move one part from here to there or you suppress it, which in the end makes matters worse. That said I felt I needed to be alone for a very long time and I went out into the desert. While out in desert I became clear with a singularity of purpose.

DC: Tell me about that.

JC: The desert was a cauldron of hardship, purging and revolution. I went in as one thing and came out another. If I had not had my desert experience I would not have been able to conduct my ministry.

DC: Why?

JC: I discovered I was attached to old habits, old visions, old ideas, and old preconceptions about the world, my religion and myself. I thought of myself and perceived myself one way. I knew how to do this but not that. I wanted to conduct my ministry as I saw fit. I couldn't see straight because I was in the way. I held onto non-essential ideas, issues and habits. The desert clarified that and transformed me. It wasn't enough to see into my soul; I had to be cleansed of the inhibitors. If I had not gone through that ordeal I would not have been able to see as clearly or act as powerfully as the Father wanted.

DC: This is important. You were spiritually purged. I know we've touched upon this but from your last comment I'd like to know what the desert sharpened. Will you elaborate?

JC: I was isolated and without comforts. I didn't hear another human voice. I didn't hear laughing, singing, crying or yelling. I didn't see another human face. I did not see a smile or frown. I didn't have contact with another person. That affected me. After a while, the deprivation caused me to realize the depth of the mystery.

DC: What did you realize?

JC: That I am the divine and the means to animate it. I was its legs, arms and voice. I was its instrument; I was the place where the infinite makes itself known, the place where eternity meets the present. I was the revelation of the Father and that the Father and I were inseparable. That made my decision to minister more palatable. I was a sacrifice and the animating principle of the Father. In essence, I was becoming nobody. I wanted to tame all my desires – my body and its needs, and the needs of my ego. The desert excised those things.

DC: You became like the lilies of the field, which do not toil; they grow of their own accord and, in your case, you grew in the accord of the Father. You also said, "Whoever finds their life will lose it, and whoever loses their life for my sake will find it." (MT 10:39) This speaks to the falsity of the ego. Did this understanding come from your temptation/desert experience?

JC: The desert was a catalyst.

DC: What happened afterward? Were you ready to minister on your terms?

JC: I knew what I had to do, but I had to recuperate from my ordeal. I was exhausted and malnourished. My health deteriorated and again I found myself needing to be healed. At the same time events unfolded quickly for me and John.

DC: This is the point at which events turn in another direction and speed up. Let's talk about this further. What happened?

JC: I got what I needed from John and used his wisdom wisely.

DC: I meant what happened to John?

JC: He made a turn in his ministry. As mentioned, he preached and taught righteousness and holiness, repentance, baptism and turning back to God. He pivoted from this ministry to attack and challenge Herod Antipas, the tetrarch of Galilee, and the second son of Herod the Great.

DC: What was the reason?

JC: Not only did John refuse to accept Herod as the legitimate ruler, but to complicate matters he was disturbed and upset that Herod Antipas was lawfully married to the "daughter of King Aretas of Petrea" before he discarded her for Herodias – Phillip's wife. (*History of the Church*, p. 62) This was an act of adultery and a very serious violation of Jewish custom.

DC: Who was Phillip?

JC: Another son of Herod the Great and tetrarch of Iturea and Trachonitis.

DC: You didn't want to get embroiled in John's affairs.

JC: The consequences were dire and serious for several reasons. John dedicated his life as a sacrifice to God. He wanted what was right and good, but he found Herod's marriage sacrilegious and impure and leveled charges against him for adultery. That was a grave accusation and didn't sit well with Herod, his court, military advisers, or his new wife Herodias. They sought revenge. They also felt Herod's power and prestige were violated, that John did not accept or endorse Herod's authority. And since John had many followers and had authority over them, they worried John would instigate a revolt. Herod got ahead of John and stopped the potential revolt from occurring by arresting him. With a twist of irony, the arrest was done reluctantly because they thought John was Elijah resurrected from the dead. They knew the history of prophets, how the prophets were treated, and the consequences for that treatment. The entire episode was puzzling and disconcerting for everyone. I did not want to get bound up in it.

DC: You were discerning and realized the Father's message needed wings. Had you fought on John's behalf and accepted his outrage toward Herod Antipas as yours, it's possible you might not have conducted your ministry and then we would not be having this conversation.

JC: Upon my return from the desert and upon hearing John's news I went home to the Galilee. I needed to restore my strength and health. Spiritually and mentally I was ready to conduct my ministry. The desert experience was spiritually transformative, but it took a severe toll on my body. When I recovered, I took advantage of a particular development within the religious community. There was a realization that the divine voice was active and alive, and that it was not constrained to our ancestors. A new practice developed allowing one to speak in the synagogue. One could voice one's opinion and teach. That was new and something I had never taken advantage of until then. I started my ministry not at the Jordan, not with water, but in the synagogue.

DC: How did that work out?

JC: I was not well received. But that did not discourage me. I then took my miracles and teachings of the Father out into the countryside.

DC: During this period, you were alone. I mean were you without followers or disciples.

JC: I was alone. This period was crucial because it distinguished me from John.

DC: I surmise that, like John, you became the news; word spread across the land attracting many for various reasons. You were original, you could feed and heal people and you worked miracles. Some thought you were another Messiah and therefore wanted to be a part of your movement. I can hear the whispers in the back of people's minds: "Is this really the one?" "Can we hope that God will save us with this one?"

JC: This is true. People were interested in me for several reasons. Some thought I was the Messiah because of my words and miracles. Other came to listen because John said I was the Messiah. What is important is that my ministry got underway and gathered momentum. My message expanded; I developed more teachings and performed more miracles. Finally, I knew what I wanted to accomplish.

DC: What did you want to accomplish?

JC: Peace with one another and with oneself, restoration and healing of the individual and a relationship with the Father. I was not interested in restoring the Davidic or priestly throne. I wanted a change of heart. I wanted to heal the sick and the brokenhearted; I wanted to re-establish the dignity in each person because that had fallen asleep; I wanted each person to discover the pearl lying hidden and buried in their heart. Heart speaks to heart, and the Father is full of heart. I knew the healing touch of the divine. I knew what it was to be lost, without direction, without hope, and then to be restored through love, compassion and forgiveness. I needed it and when I received it I was restored and renewed. I felt the need to share that with others. That was the revolution; it was a revolution not by militant action designed to gain power and freedom from the Romans but a revolution of the heart and mind, to free each person enslaved by a closed mind, hard heart or a ravished body. I ministered to the confused, marginalized, dispossessed, conflicted and sick. I welcomed my leadership role but I did not welcome the leader who advocated or endorsed violence to usher in the Last Days. I was not that kind of leader. I made that distinction clear. Others might have seen that in me, but I did not see it in myself.

DC: You obviously felt you could not continue your ministry alone, and you looked for disciples.

JC: The task grew beyond my physical abilities. I saw an enormous field without enough hands to minister to all the sick, needy and dying. Like John I needed disciples, but there was a difference. I was not going to baptize or preach about repentance; rather, I was going to teach the Father and perform miracles.

DC: And you gathered a series of disciples from the surrounding Galilean countryside.

JC: Yes.

DC: During this initial phase, John the Baptist sent you a delegation of disciples to determine if you were the Messiah, or if they should expect someone else. (LK 7:20)

JC: I responded that, "The blind received sight, the lame walk, those who have leprosy are cleansed, the deaf hear, the dead are raised, and the good news is proclaimed to the poor." (LK 7:22) My ministry was not designed as an insurrection or military coup, but, I must say, it was unpredictable.

DC: Your calling card and trade secret.

JC: People were perplexed.

DC: Not long afterward John met a grisly fate. What did his death mean to you? How did you feel when you learned that Herodias' daughter asked for John's head as payment and gift for an erotic dance she performed for Herod Antipas?

JC: Give me a moment to gather my thoughts. (*Jesus sips his water.*) Yes that is what was said. I wept. People were outraged and shocked. It tore one's heart apart. It was difficult to imagine John's beheading was the fulfillment of a flippant drunken pledge and oath – a gift – due to an erotic dance.

DC: I can see why the New Testament says not to take an oath. It binds one to act in a way that can be shortsighted, troubling and detrimental.

JC: Herod Antipas was not discerning. He was impulsive and brash and couldn't see the consequences of his words and actions. John's beheading at the fortress Machaerus was demeaning and degrading, vacuous and cruel, and a cynical dismissive taunt. It ridiculed everything John believed and accomplished. When Herod came to his senses he understood the seriousness of his actions.

DC: How did John's disciples respond?

JC: They "took his body and buried it" and came and told me. (MT 14:12) Herod was afraid John's death would instigate a revolt. I went to the other side of the Galilee. I thought that expedient. I didn't want to be the source of violence. I didn't want people to look at me for direction or rise up in an armed revolt. I already knew what I was doing was dangerous. But this calloused and ridiculing act made me realize that my ministry held a similar fate. If John could be killed for following God and by baptizing and having followers, so could I.

DC: What did you do?

JC: Again, I had to make a choice – continue or stop? I faced a dilemma and needed to find direction and a ray of clarity. I sought the solitude of lonely places. My heart and wisdom were in conflict with Hebrew traditions and past revelations. I knew the Father is alive and that revelations occur naturally as figs grow on fig trees. I found the clarity to continue and the compulsion to share my vision and knowledge. I also knew my ministry would lead to my demise.

DC: History was rather cruel to Herod for his "outrageous treatment of John." Instead of John's followers rising up against Herod Antipas, a war broke out between Herod's former father-in-law King Aretas of Petrea over his slighted daughter. "The war ended with a pitched battle in which Herod's army was totally destroyed.... Herod was deprived of his throne on the account of the same woman, with whom he was driven into exile and condemned to live in Vienne, a city in Gaul." (*The History of the Church*, p. 63)

JC: John's followers saw it as Herod's "richly deserved punishment." (*The History of the Church*, p. 63)

DC: Moving on. You continued your ministry, attracted more followers and Herod "heard about all that was going on. And he was perplexed, because some were saying John had been raised from the dead, others that Elijah had appeared, and still others that one of the prophets of long ago had come back to life. But Herod said, 'I beheaded John. Who, then, is this I hear such things about?' And he tried to see him." (LK 9:7-9)

JC: We finally met at my trial. Pilate sent me to him. Like many of the people of the day, they were only interested in witnessing a miracle or asking questions. They had heard about me and wanted to see me perform a miracle, as if I were an act or novelty. Answers or miracles in times like this did not produce fruit as they did when one was in legitimate need. When I refused Herod's wishes I was "ridiculed and mocked," dressed "in an elegant robe" and sent "back to Pilate." (LK 23:6-11)

DC: That was the distinction – you discerned the difference between the gift of a charlatan and the gift of a doctor. You did not satisfy the curious with acts of the Father merely to prove a point. It was not a show to unveil the hidden nature of the Father. It was not to say the mystery exists. The mystery is known through the heart; the mind tends to get in the way, yet a renewed mind can see clearly into the heart of the matter. That's rather an ironic twist.

JC: I performed miracles for and answered questions to those who sought with the heart, not with the mind. I discovered that one's mind tends to fill with a big ego and becomes blind.

DC: And you knew the difference.

JC: My heart was open to experience another heart. This is wisdom. When one experiences the heart one experiences the Father, and the Father moved through the heart of the infirmed and the heart of the seeker. The Father's work was the work of restoration and renewal – of the heart, mind and body – and I could feel the movement. I knew it. My mind quickened to answer the question or my hands became hot so as to touch the sick and heal them.

DC: Is this available to everyone?

JC: The same Father is in you as He is in me. He is all around. Every person has a heart and a mind.

DC: Then it is up to each individual to –

JC: One must be open and willing to cultivate, nurture, bear fruit and reap the harvest. It is a narrow road and few are willing to walk it.

DC: And the road to destruction is vast. Yes. It is a challenge. Before we continue to the next topic I have a few remaining questions concerning John. While John was alive you conducted your ministry. The two of you were working in different fields, so to speak, but after his death you were the sole prophet in Galilee. And to the authorities you became as much of an enigma as John.

JC: I was. John's disciples were naturally confused and upset. John thought I was the Messiah. As I mentioned earlier I did not accept that mantle. Others were willing to grant me that title, but I did not accept or declare it. I knew the Father and his wishes. That I will accept. I allowed the Father to live in me as I lived in Him. I was not the message. I was the messenger of the Father. Many of John's disciples came to me on account of John, others retreated deeper into the desert and into the Eastern Parthian Empire because I did not live up to John's ideal, while others who remained angry with Herod came to hear my words, be healed and follow me. Herod Antipas' actions, unfortunately, had unintended and dire consequences. He was central to John's death and an instigator of mine. The two Galilean prophets who loved God conflicted with his sense of greatness and authority.

DC: He is hardly known whereas you are world renowned.

JC: Well, all right.

DC: I can appreciate your wisdom, "So the last will be first, and the first will be last." (MT 20:16)

JC: It is difficult for one as Herod to know the Father. He had to invest heavily to maintain his empire, leaving no room to know or invest in the Father. There is earthly treasure and there is heavenly treasure. Earthly treasure is not transferable in the Father, while heavenly treasure is transferable to the heart and mind.

DC: I'm a bit struck by Herod's response regarding Elijah and imagining you as John who was raised from the dead. Can you explain? What transpired at that time regarding the afterlife? I thought the Jews did not believe in immortality; that God had given them the Promised Land as his gift and that was enough.

JC: During my time immortality, resurrection and the afterlife were topics of discussion and belief. Much of this came about during the Seleucid tyranny, the massacre of Jews, and the Abomination of Desolation. My ancestors came to understand the exile into Babylon around 565 BCE as chastisement for going astray, for losing the heart of God. After we returned, with the permission of the Persian King Cyrus the Great, we built the second Temple; the Temple of David and Solomon was destroyed by the Babylonians. After Alexander the Great died, remember he conquered the known world, the Seleucid Greeks wanted to eradicate the Jewish religion. They thought it backward compared to Greek philosophy and rationality. They tortured and killed many devout Jews for following their ancient religion. Our scribes and elders could not reconcile the injustice with the quantity of spilt blood and the desecration. After all God is a source of justice and mercy and these acts were unjust and barbaric. If people died because of their faith in God, then how does one receive justice from God? It was concluded that there must have been a life beyond death. It was from those days that the afterlife crept into our language and dialogue. This was the beginning of our awareness of the soul. Many accepted it, others did not.

DC: The soul is Greek and Egyptian.

JC: Ironic, isn't it. These were our ancestral enemies.

DC: You became aware that life continues after the death of the body.

JC: The Father is living. I am living. The source of life is living; I did not differentiate living here or living there as dissimilar. Rather, I experienced them as the same. "I am that I am." I exist. The Father is both existence and nonexistence simultaneously.

DC: I have a story to tell in this regard.

JC: I'd like to hear it.

DC: I was standing at the edge of a cliff overlooking the Pacific Ocean, Santa Catalina Island off on the horizon, when I had an epiphany concerning the relationship between the wave and the ocean.

JC: What was the implication?

DC: The wave moving across the ocean experiences itself as a wave. It knows itself as a wave; whether big or small. It believes it is separate from the ocean, but when it crashes and returns to the ocean it realizes it isn't separate; it realizes it isn't just an expression of the ocean. It realizes something new altogether and this is the most profound reality.

JC: Tell me.

DC: The wave finally realizes that it and the ocean are water.

JC: Now you see. You have eyes. Both the wave and the ocean are one regardless of motion. For me the Father was the ocean. That is how I understood it. One doesn't need a physical death to realize that truth; one needs an open mind and heart.

DC: We've covered a lot of territory. I'd like to take a break.

JC: I'd like to go outside and watch the thundershowers and lightning.

DC: When we resume, I'd like to discuss some of your teachings.

CHAPTER 7

TEACHINGS

JC: We're in the middle of a torrential deluge and the mountain range is obscured by the rain and dark clouds.

DC: The storm is more severe than I thought. The wash at the bottom of the hill will flood. We can drive down to see it.

JC: I'm comfortable sitting here with you.

DC: Have you ever experienced a hard-driving monsoon rain before?

JC: Not in the Galilee. This rain is different. I'm listening to a loud, hard patter beating on the roof.

DC: Sounds like a hundred hands pounding a tight drum.

JC: Yes.

DC: I've grown accustomed to it. I never experienced this kind of weather at the beach. When I first experienced it I was astonished. Now I welcome it.

JC: Had we experienced this kind of weather one would have assumed the End of Days was upon us.

DC: Maybe for some it is an omen of things to come.

JC: I didn't think like that.

DC: Is that because you wanted to make a difference in people's lives rather than conceding to the whims of Fate or the wrath of God's judgment? You don't seem to me to be the type of person who would wait for something to happen and say, "I told you so."

JC: Our world was out of balance. Some thought God was going to intervene, rebalance the world, punish the wicked, and save the righteous.

DC: That is the Old Testament image of the avenging tribal God.

JC: The Father was neither jealous nor avenging. I did not teach about impending doom or disaster; rather, I taught and showed the Father's love, mercy and compassion.

DC: I see God's wrath and punishment in the story of Noah and the flood, Lot and Sodom and Gomorrah, and Moses and the Exodus.

JC: That is my heritage and I faced that sentiment daily. It is what I wanted to countermand.

DC: You offered people a new relationship with themselves, with their neighbors and with the Father. It was relational rather than transactional. Rites, practices and beliefs are transactional, while the relationship with a person to another person or to the Father is relational.

JC: I was thinking that a new relationship would create a new person and enough restored people would generate a new group.

DC: The new group would usher in a new community.

JC: Correct.

DC: That was your equation.

JC: What do you mean by *equation*?

DC: A simple equation is A plus B equals C, or A minus B equals C. When variables are plugged into the left side of the equation the answer is seen on the right. It is straightforward logic.

JC: All right.

DC: Your logic system was more complicated because it involved real people in real circumstances. In your case, you taught people about the love of God and the love for each other. If one was changed by love the dynamics of your society would change. One, two, or three like-minded people couldn't make a difference, but a large group could generate the transformation you thought possible.

JC: I knew that one person could captivate another and together they could captivate others. Those in turn could captivate even more and so on; the process grows.

DC: Again, I'm reminded of your mustard seed parable.

JC: Things start small and grow until the birds of the air can make their nest. It was a simple principle I applied in my ministry.

DC: I'd like to ask what you wanted people to do with your knowledge.

JC: I wanted people to recognize its truth and I wanted them to apply it.

DC: Let's discuss your sayings and teachings in more detail. Again, I'd like to understand their origin, but I'd also like to explore their meaning.

JC: The Jews have a long story and wisdom tradition. I drew from that history as I drew from my social conditions.

DC: We spoke previously about the "house divided" and "giving to Caesar what belongs to Caesar." What other sayings are inspired by social conditions?

JC: "Beware, you who call yourself perfect in the obedience to the law. You pay the tax on mint, dill and cumin, but you ignore justice, mercy, and honesty." (Q43) And "A prophet is not without honor except in his own town, among his relatives and in his own home." (MK 6:4) I experienced this directly around the Galilee. Another is, "Why do you wash the outside of the cup? Don't you understand that the one who made the inside is also the one who made the outside?" (THOM 87)

DC: The latter refers to the religious practices you thought were ineffectual, misinformed or governed by entrenched historical traditions. You wanted to break that apart and you introduced a new vision of God and established a new set of actions and practices.

JC: That was my goal, and some sayings were created to address that blindness. For instance, I addressed confrontational Pharisees with, "To what, then, can I compare the people of this generation? What are they like? They are like children sitting in the marketplace and calling out to each other: 'We played the pipe for you, and you did not dance; we sang a dirge, and you did not cry.' For John the Baptist came neither eating bread nor drinking wine, and you say, 'He has a demon.' The Son of Man came eating and drinking wine, and you say, 'He is a glutton and a drunkard, a friend of tax collectors and sinners.' But wisdom is proved right by all her children." (LK 7:31-35)

DC: You confronted the religious authorities one way and your followers another. To your detractors, you didn't have time to craft a saying. You responded to the immediate situation with your quick rhetorical wit and impromptu style in order to point out institutional deficiency. To your supporters, you spent time crafting your parables and other short sayings in order to surprise and teach, educate and instruct.

JC: I had two styles and two audiences. To the religious authorities, I confronted their theology, hypocrisy and inadequate practices and pointed out their corruption. Rarely did I offer advice. To my listeners and followers, I challenged their ingrained and imprudent beliefs and offered wise alternatives. I had a rhetorical style for each party.

DC: Aside from your teaching style I see your technique in gathering people to listen to you. You didn't always go to them; they came to you. I wonder if this technique was revolutionary or if you were inspired by someone.

JC: What are you referring to?

DC: I see something subtle. You would go near a town or village and wait outside in a field or hilltop. I suggest you directed your disciples to go into a town or village and bring people back to you.

JC: Why would you assume that?

DC: The parable of the Great Banquet suggests such a technique. (LK 14:16-24) In the parable the master of the house prepares a banquet but none of the invited quests attends, so he orders his servants –

JC: – Let me finish. I said, "Go out to the roads and country lanes and compel them to come in, so that my house will be full." (LK 14:23)

DC: I don't believe you imagined that technique and inserted it into your parable. I appreciate your intelligence and observational skills, but this technique appears very specific and real. The relationship between your stories and real-life events is not coincidental. What is difficult to determine is whether the events and techniques are yours or someone else's.

JC: I was creative, inventive and open to experimentation. I wanted to continuously invent new parables and conceive new techniques. My mind was complicated in that manner; if something became routine I would change it because I didn't enjoy the expected.

DC: Wisdom is universal yet personal, and is cultivated by life experiences. It is not learned or known from books or traditions, yet both can inform wisdom.

JC: Is there a question?

DC: Not a question but a point of observation regarding the details in your parables. I see trace elements of your life in them. For example, I see you in the rich young man who wanted to follow you but couldn't when you told him to sell everything; you knew what he was going to face and you forewarned him. I see you as a bridegroom, as a father with a child, and as one who bought a house and was obligated to attend to the business and maintenance of domestic bliss.

JC: Is that puzzling?

DC: No. When you spoke you spoke with authority and certainty. You didn't say, "Well, let me think about that" or "I think it is this way." You spoke directly. You spoke powerfully and convincingly and that didn't come from reading.

JC: I did not waver. I spoke as a leader and from a position of authority and conviction. I learned much from our stories, from the Torah, from my father Joseph and from life. These are the ingredients of wisdom.

DC: Is there a mystical literary tradition you drew upon?

JC: Such as?

DC: The Book of Enoch, the visions from the prophets, Ezekiel, Egyptian or Greek mystical traditions? I'm also wondering if there is anything from the orient.

JC: I was aware of the hidden wisdom traditions. One needed to apprentice with a master to know the wisdom contained within that tradition and only a few could apprentice with a master. I also knew that such wisdom takes years of training and a grueling initiation rite.

DC: I don't see that in your ministry.

JC: I was open and inclusive to everyone. I did, however, pull certain people aside who I thought capable, like Thomas, and shared deeper wisdom, but there was nothing formal or strictly structural in the training.

DC: Underlying the mystical Hebrew tradition is the realm of the alphabet and words. Each letter is a magical world or universe of its own accord. Stitching letters together creates a word, stitching words together creates a sentence, stitching sentences together creates a paragraph, and stitching paragraphs together tells a story that expresses wisdom and may even reveal a hidden mystery. Words are powerful agents of the divine.

JC: The Hebrew creation story places God beyond the void of darkness; he hovered over it. God created the heavens, the world, and everything in it through the sheer pronouncement of words, "Let there be light." (Gen 1:3)

DC: From the Hindu perspective, the divine is nothingness and creation is existence, being, sustainability, all processes, numbers, life and death. Time and the forces and cycles within time continuously repeat. Life emerges, is sustained for some period of time and is inevitably destroyed. Then the process repeats over and over again, and it is not linear; rather, it is circular.

JC: I saw the mind like the void. Speaking divine words quickens and illuminates the potential of darkness and transforms it into light.

DC: Ah, hence your Wisdom Sayings.

JC: I drew on another mystery. It wasn't hermetic or Kabalistic. Rather, it was the experience of the Father and the self.

DC: I don't see this as part of your daily ministry.

JC: I shared deeper layers of wisdom to a few I thought were capable, as I previously mentioned.

DC: There is a tendency in the gospels to share knowledge with your disciples when you were alone. Inevitably they'd ask for clarity on a particular teaching. The most obvious that comes to mind is the parable of the sower. (MK 4:3-20, MT 13:3-8, LK 8:5-8) The tendency also exists in the Gospel of Thomas.

JC: Some ideas are best shared during quiet moments with a select few who have ears to hear.

DC: I've noticed that an audience has to be ready to receive deeper knowledge and it has to be the right audience. Otherwise, words fall on deaf ears and time and effort are wasted. Nobody gets anything out of it. Something is given but nothing is received.

JC: You bring up an important point in the mystery of knowledge. If one were a seed, then that seed has to be planted in fertile ground and it must be watered. Growth occurs for the teacher when knowledge is given to the student and the student grows as he or she receives that knowledge. An exchange must transpire for growth, fruit and the harvest to occur. Wisdom and knowledge are relational; they cannot be one-sided. If there is a teacher without a student there is no growth. Likewise, if there is a student but no teacher there is little growth. The two work in conjunction with each other.

DC: Even though two people are at different ends of the knowledge spectrum they complete a circuit and provide the other with what they need.

JC: The teacher teaches to a student and the student, if wise, listens and applies the lessons.

DC: I see you as a poet using words like a painter using a brush. Wisdom was your canvas and the Father and life were your inspiration. You were head and shoulders above your contemporaries.

JC: I was merely doing what I could and sharing what I knew.

DC: Many of your parables did not draw upon the stories from your ancestors; they were new. How did your parables come to you and what information was new?

JC: Most parables took time to craft while others came promptly. At times, my intuition was clear and I could get them out of my head and into my mouth swiftly. These tended to be the shorter sayings – "Seek and you shall find; knock and the door will be opened to you." (LK 11:9) Or "Salt is good, but if it loses its saltiness, how can you make it salty again?" (MK 9:50)

DC: You knew how to relate to your audience, and you knew which words to use to address them.

JC: My mind was sharp as a knife and sliced into the darkness of the divine. You called me a poet. I considered myself a blacksmith and my words were my blade. I fashioned my sword differently from the blades of old; I created a new shape for a new world. The wisdom traditions that I was born into speak of holiness and righteousness.

DC: And this tradition is filled with lament, suffering, hope and the desire for external change.

JC: Job, Psalms, Proverbs and Ecclesiastes address many problems: some involved the problem of being surrounding by enemies, of being alone, of being disturbed by life's unfortunate situations, or seared by the sense that life is meaningless, while some wisdom offered hope and comfort to the weary and distraught. I knew something else and wanted to bring that to my followers and disciples.

DC: You brought a new color weave into the world by considering strangers your brothers and sisters.

JC: I knew the Father intimately and knew each person was a child of God. My relationship with my father, mother and brothers and sisters was similar to my relationship to the Father, and this family relationship extended beyond the border of my immediate family. I knew everyone was my brother and sister. We were one large family.

DC: Elaborate on this point and how it relates to the Father.

JC: I experienced the Father as a vast living tapestry and life woven in it. The tapestry is a dynamic, living, breathing and energetic interaction between heaven and earth, the heart and mind, and the heart of Father and the heart of man. The Creator and the creation are inseparable and the two are joined seamlessly together regardless of appearance. Everyone and everything is a different color and thread within the tapestry. From this new insight, I fashioned a sword that I wielded and plunged into the heart of my society. I wanted my listeners to experience a new creation, a new temple, and a new wisdom tradition without lament, agony and suffering.

DC: Wisdom was an essential pillar of your ministry. What are the others?

JC: I had three pillars – teaching, miracles and sayings. With these I constructed a new temple for anyone to enter. Once inside, the divine could be known and one could be healed, restored, renewed and fed.

DC: Several ideas circulated around the fundamental concept of the temple during your lifetime. I know of three and they could not be more dissimilar – the Jerusalem Temple, the temple to which you speak, and the Essene temple. Your temple is not the same as the Jerusalem Temple, particularly in the practice of knowing God. Your practice was relational – one to God and one to another – while the Jerusalem Temple was transactional; animals were sacrificed for the sins of the nation. At the same time, your ministry wasn't fixed to any one physical location. It was mobile because it was inside each person; wherever they went the temple went with them. The other version of the temple was expressed by the Essenes. They envisioned each person a living stone, metaphorically speaking, and when laid side by side and one on top of another a new temple was constructed.

JC: I was not averse to that concept. Many ideas circulated at that time in reference to the divine; the temple was only one. I incorporated a portion of that into my ministry. I wanted restoration. I believed a new person was created through wisdom, love, compassion and knowledge of the Father. Just as the Temple was rebuilt and restored during King Herod's reign so too I rebuilt and restored the individual so they could experience the divine.

DC: The new person in essence was fashioned into a living stone for a new temple.

JC: I didn't draw the same conclusion as the Essenes in regards to the divine, nor was I interested in their practices and I did not accept their beliefs. In addition, I did not want to continue the belief in our traditional Jewish temple practices. I wanted to wrench the veil in the temple that separated the Holy of Holies chamber from the Holy chamber.

DC: The temple system separated people into camps; clean from unclean, sin from sinless, righteous from unrighteous, holy from unholy, chosen from Gentile, purified from unpurified.

JC: Yes, an unseen veil separated people throughout my society and divided them.

DC: You wanted to eliminate that barrier.

JC: I want to mention another point.

DC: What is that?

JC: Privilege and benefits resided with the authoritative side of society while neglect and the curse of burden resided on the remainder and not so fortunate. I knew the Father was available to all and in all.

DC: Yet, at the same time, your words and actions were deliberately challenging and confusing. It perplexed people and made them unsure.

JC: I defied expectations and disrupted preconceived notions. Following the divine is not easy, and the Father is not about religious rules and practices. It involves an individual person in relation to him or herself, and it involves a relationship between that person to another and that person to the Father. My vision and conviction was that these relationships worked in mutual support in a manner similar to carved stones stacked on top of one another erecting a temple.

DC: Was that the nature of salvation?

JC: I didn't incorporate that term into my sayings. I didn't see it in that manner. Rather, I knew God resided in each person, not unlike the darkness that "was over the surface of the deep." (Gen 1:2) Divinity waits in silence. When God's word is spoken, the person awakes and stirs alive like creation.

DC: You saw man as the ground needing to be prepared and God's word as the seed waiting to be planted. Once all is ready and the word is spoken, the seed inside the person is activated and begins its creative transformation.

JC: Each person is asked to cultivate that seed into a living plant for the birds of the air to make a nest.

DC: This is the deeper meaning of the mustard seed, and it relates to the sower parable.

JC: Recall the parable. "Listen! A farmer went out to sow his seed. As he was scattering the seed, some fell along the path, and the birds came and ate it up. Some fell on rocky places, where it did not have much soil. It sprang up quickly, because the soil was shallow. But when the sun came up, the plants were scorched, and they withered because they had no root. Other seed fell among thorns, which grew up and choked the plants, so that they did not bear grain. Still other seed fell on good soil. It came up, grew and produced a crop, some multiplying thirty, some sixty, some a hundred times." (MK 4:3-8)

DC: I see it.

JC: The ground must be prepared to receive the seed.

DC: Two forces are at work in your teachings – restoration and renewal.

JC: As a people, we were overly burdened by the effect of sin, and the subsequent duty, rites and practices that regulate or manage it. Everyone was overly concerned that they would say the wrong thing, do the wrong thing, think the wrong thing, and commit the wrong act. Everything was wrong. Everything was placed on the negative. No one could stretch and breathe. We were burdened by law and shackled in chains to debt, fear and practice. Whatever one thought of sin, however one missed the mark, a pure heart and a clear mind counteracted the effects. A heart filled with hate and violence continues acting in hate and violence. A mind entrenched with preconceived ideas and notions and attached to them continues seeing and experiencing the world in exactly the same manner. How does one break free from these bonds?

DC: It was said you would tell people who were sick or had done something wrong that their sins were forgiven.

JC: Yes, that was simpler. The point was to restore them – get them back on their feet, preferably with an open heart, walking toward the Father. But my people were punitive, afflicted by the sickness to punish and seek revenge.

DC: An "eye for an eye."

JC: Yes.

DC: I appreciate your motive when you speak of children, "Let the little children come to me, and do not hinder them, for the Kingdom of God belongs to such as these." (MK 10:14)

JC: Watch children at the age of four, five and six and pay close attention. They love, play, laugh and run. They are pure of heart. They are honest. They trust. They are not burdened by the demands of life. They do not worry what to do or what to say. They do not fret. They forgive and forget. They cry and fight, and move on because they are not attached to hate, ideology, or "this is right and that is wrong." They are not politically or religiously motivated. They may not always share and at times they are selfish and stubborn, and they push and shove, but they live closer to the divine than adults.

DC: Their playful demeanor is what adults lost, and you felt one could revert to that child-like state.

JC: As we mature we carry pain and the heavy burden of life. We embrace bitterness, anger, and disappointments and the supple heart turns into a hard, calloused rock. We hold onto our self, accept traditions of our fathers as real, and embody the ideals of the nation. We say, "This is mine," "You are wrong, I am right," "You will die but I will live," "I am rewarded but you are punished." We live life through fear – fear of death, fear of the unknown, fear that something bad will happen to us, fear of punishment, fear of shame and guilt, fear of ridicule, fear of failure, fear that life might be pointless, fear of losing our possessions, fear we are not the person we imagined, fear of what others think, fear of loneliness.

DC: It is sobering to recognize the truth of that statement. It is nightmarish. We are locked in a cage of our own making. You saw a way out. You saw a way to experience the Father, to enjoy life and to live without fear and hate.

JC: It was important to know love, be washed and renewed in the light of the divine, cleansed of the things that burden the heart and freed from the preconceptions of the mind. "Enter through the narrow gate. For wide is the gate and broad is the road that leads to destruction, and many enter through it. But small is the gate and narrow the road that leads to life, and only a few find it." (MT 7:13-14)

DC: What is the narrow road for you?

JC: Practicing love over hate, discernment over judgment, forgiveness over condemnation, unity over exclusion and peace over violence.

DC: There is a driving force that ensnares everyone – power, lust, greed, ego, food, vanity, clothing and fear. Those can be minimized and replaced with love, brotherhood and unity. I'm reminded of the Beatitudes from the Sermon on the Mount; the ideas and practices you taught where inspirational and mitigated the negative influences of one's primal nature.

JC: The Beatitudes were on my lips at every turn and I spoke of them everywhere I traveled.

DC: Did you have an affinity for mountains?

JC: I did. I also liked the mountain as metaphor. They made my teachings more authoritative and credible. People have an innate sense that a mountain is closer to heaven and a source of revelation. My ancestors had divine encounters on the mountain – Noah, Abraham, Moses and the prophets.

DC: Here is a collection of your sayings from the Sermon on the Mount: "Blessed are you who are poor, for yours is the Kingdom of God." (LK 6:20) "Blessed are the pure in heart, for they will see God." (MT 5:8) "Blessed are you who hunger now, for you will be satisfied. Blessed are you who weep now, for you will laugh." (LK 6:21) "Blessed are the meek, for they will inherit the earth." (MT 5:5) "Blessed are the peacemakers, for they will be called the children of God." (MT 5:9) These sayings move in another direction from your Hebrew wisdom tradition.

JC: Notice the nature of action. One must do; one cannot sit. Also, notice it is not about ritual practice; it is about relational practice - one to another and one to the Father.

DC: I also want to point out that these saying are not simple words but teachings. What you taught is what you did. You were poor but the Kingdom of God was yours, you were gentle and inherited large followings and disciples, you were pure in heart and saw the face of God, and you were a peacemaker and called the Son of God.

JC: I understood the reciprocal relationship between giving and receiving. Words, actions and deeds have consequences.

DC: One saying points to this: "For if you forgive other people when they sin against you, your heavenly Father will also forgive you." (MT 6:14)

JC: "Give, and it will be given to you. A good measure, pressed down, shaken together and running over, will be poured into your lap." (LK 6:38)

DC: "For with the measure you use, it will be measured to you." (LK 6:38)

You received a greater measure of the Father the more you encouraged, healed, forgave and taught.

JC: The difficulty lies not in the hearing words - although for some that was difficult - but in applying the words.

DC: I imagine this knowledge and technique was not a common practice and must have come as a surprise and revelation.

JC: Yes.

DC: Contrast your practice to the practice offered by the religious authorities. You viewed their practices inherently as incorrect and you confronted them on that.

JC: Their path to the divine was imprudent, their results unsatisfactory and they perpetuated the same misunderstanding. It was a case of the "blind leading the blind." (MT 15:14)

DC: Here is one saying from the Lost Gospel Q: "Beware, you who call yourselves perfect in your obedience to the law. You pay the tax on mint, dill and cumin, but you ignore justice, mercy, and honesty. You should practice these things first. You wash the outside of your cups and plates, but inside you are filled with thoughts of greed and theft. Didn't the one who made the outside make the inside too? Wash the inside of the cup and it will all be clean." (Q43)

JC: Here is another, "You who claim to be the most devout are hopeless! You love sitting in the front row of the synagogue and having people bow down to you in public. You are like whitewashed tombs – beautiful on the surface, but filled with death and decay. Beware of those who load people down with the crushing burdens of laws and regulations but do nothing to help them. You have taken away the key of knowledge, but instead of unlocking the door, you have blocked the way for those trying to enter." (Q44)

DC: In spite of the clarity and simplicity of your teachings, you didn't want to make it easy for people. You didn't want them to be lulled asleep, yet you didn't want them to be overly upset and walk away either. Knowing the Father is hard work and requires commitment.

JC: By walking the narrow path with me one would come to know the Father as I knew the Father. This path was not about morality, ethics or ritual practice. Like the Temple in Jerusalem my temple radiated outward and like the Holy of Holies the closer one got to the center, the closer one got to the Father, and getting closer to the Father one discovered the self. Renewal and restoration followed and set in motion the Kingdom of God.

DC: And that is a living presence. Does the Father have a center?

JC: *Center* is a figure of speech. The center is everywhere and nowhere simultaneously. I was aware my language and metaphors conveyed several meanings and were confusing, yet I had to stay within prevailing boundaries and ideas. If I went too far no one would grasp the concepts, nor make it real by applying it.

DC: What happens when I follow you and practice your teachings? Where is the 'I' or the self at this point?

JC: It disappears into the Father. The deeper one goes into the Father the more real He becomes and the less you become. You are filled with the living presence of the Father and distinctions dissolve.

DC: What did you mean by this saying? "Seek and you shall find; knock and the door will be opened to you." (LK 11:9)

JC: That should be evident by now. It is the Father of whom I was speaking and the culmination of one's search. The Father is hidden but, paradoxically, can be found.

DC: I want to switch over and talk about faith. You are quoted as saying, "Truly I tell you, if you have faith as small as a mustard seed, you can say to this mountain, 'Move from here to there,' and it will move. Nothing will be impossible for you." (MT 17:20) Take me back. What do you mean? I also recognized that faith ties into the parable of the talents. (MT 25:14-28)

JC: My ministry was an act of faith. I was bold, courageous and fearless. I taught and performed miracles and the more I did the more treasure from heaven I received.

DC: The treasure wasn't of the earth?

JC: Not necessarily.

DC: It wasn't the riches of money, kingdoms, jewels, silver, gold or the status that comes from them?

JC: It was the treasure of the Father and his kingdom. Again, I want to point out that I did, I performed, I taught, I said and I was involved. My ministry was a sacrifice of compassion, of mercy, of devotion and of love. The more I did the more I received of the Father, and the more I received the more I felt alive – more than I had ever been. I said, "Whoever has will be given more." (MK 4:25) This was due to my faith.

DC: What do you mean, "People do not pick figs from thornbushes, or grapes from briers"? (LK 6:44)

JC: The fruit one wants to harvest is gathered from the plant from which it grows. If you want to know the Father it is not through violence, killing, hating and condemning. If one wants to know oneself, it is not through the pursuit of wealth or in correct and prescribed conduct of ritual practice. If one wants an open mind it is not through attachments to preconceptions, through the rationality of an argument, or through the defense of a position. Neither is it through "I am right and you are wrong." It grows from a mind present in the moment. If one wants an open heart it is not through fear and callousness; it is through love, compassion, peace and mercy.

DC: I'd like you to address, "Again, the Kingdom of Heaven is like a merchant looking for fine pearls. When he found one of great value, he went away and sold everything he had and bought it." (MT 13:45-46)

JC: The saying is simple, but there is much to unravel in relation to the merchant, the pearl, prudence and the purchase. One has to ask, "What is the pearl?"

DC: It is created in an oyster that lives in the sea.

JC: It has a hard, unattractive outer shell.

DC: Yet inside lies hidden a sphere of opulence.

JC: A desirable commodity for the one who knows where to look.

DC: Like the oyster, one has a hard outer shell and the pearl cannot be found by gazing at or being allured by it. If I understand correctly, attending to the outer shell is equivalent to the wide road that leads to destruction.

JC: The pearl is not out there, or there, or over there. It is right here. The pearl is inside of you. Now ask, what is the pearl?

DC: Oneself and the Father. It is both, isn't it?

JC: What do you do when you find the self and the Father?

DC: Be prudent and buy it, as you did.

JC: That is the treasure. One must sort through a lot of merchandise and look in the right place. One can't look outside. One can't go here and there or over there to find the hidden treasure. The point is to discover the pearl that is hidden inside of you. I did. Notice the Father working through me. Look at what I did. You see it is not so hard to understand. I didn't make it complicated.

DC: Once you understand and have the key to unlock the mystery. I want to switch subjects and talk about money. You speak of it often and it raises some concern. You seem to be for it and against it simultaneously.

JC: This too has two sides and faith is tied to each. The pursuit of money, which is a type of faith, directs one to money's outcome while it imperceptibly shapes the heart and mind to see and know the world from its perspective. People are seen and judged through money. Life is seen through money. "This is expensive and that is cheap." We compare ourselves through money: "That person has expensive things. That one over there does not have expensive things." Then we judge, which leads to condemnation. In addition, we see our successes or failures through the lens of money and from here we form an opinion. We secretly say, "I am successful and worthy of admiration and praise because I have money." This inflates the ego. Conversely one might say, "I am nobody because I do not have money and no one cares about me." Both are unfortunate fruits of money. The Father is neither known nor unknown because of money, but the pursuit of money challenges one's prospects of knowing the Father intimately.

DC: Will you explain the other side of money? You speak of it in terms of investing. I'm thinking about the parable of the talents. (MT 25:14-28) How is this parable relevant and meaningful? What is its intention?

JC: Anyone who invests money expects the day to come when it makes a return. Expectations can be high or low; the investment can be a hit or a miss. There might be a big return; there might be a small return. One can't say for certain what the outcome will be, but one must be willing to invest in an endeavor and be willing to cultivate and tend to its needs. Regardless of outcome one has to have faith in the process. I applied the same investing principle to my ministry. I invested everything I had in the Father. I invested in teaching, healing and the restoration of others. I walked from village to village and town to town. I had faith in my ministry. I had faith in myself, in what I was doing, what I could accomplish and what I set out to do. If I did not have faith, if I wavered and was blown here and there, or if I chased after this or that, I would not have accomplished anything. I was committed. This is the faith to which I kept referring. I invested all of my talent. Does that answer your question?

DC: Yes, it does.

JC: I see it has stopped raining and the clouds are breaking up.

DC: The sun is peeking through.

CHAPTER 8

DISCIPLESHIP

DC: We've covered a lot of territory; now I'd like to turn and discuss the nature of discipleship. Disciples and discipleship are considerable ingredients to your ministry. They embody and reflect your wisdom, the Father, compassion and community. And, to sharpen the point, your legacy continued beyond your death because of your disciples.

JC: Without my devoted disciples traveling throughout Judea and the Roman Empire, my teachings and ministry would not have spread, my wisdom would have died and the Father would not have been remembered. People's hearts were opened and their imaginations stirred because of their dedication. I am known because of my disciples and without them my name and legacy would have been a mere side note to history.

DC: What do you imagine that side note would say?

JC: "A Jewish prophet named Jesus spoke of the Father in a soft but powerful voice and people throughout Judea who heard him speak were encouraged. He was a man of God. Many followed him; hundreds loved him, still hundreds more listened to his sayings. He was crucified by Pontius Pilate for disrupting the peace during Passover at the Jewish Temple in Jerusalem and his body was buried in a shallow grave never to be seen again."

DC: After your crucifixion, your disciples fled back to the Galilee to fish on the Sea of Tiberias, (JN 21:1) probably in fear and confusion. Later, something happened and they overcame their fear and charged fearlessly into the world as you had done.

JC: That's right. They learned the secret of dying to themselves and finding the life of the Father.

DC: I'm interested in knowing if there was something particular you were looking for in a disciple. Did you have criteria? Was there such a thing as an appropriate or ideal disciple?

JC: Such as?

DC: Did one have to be a certain age or have a particular background; did they need to be working people, uneducated, poor, religious or female? Were you looking for leaders or religious elders?

JC: I was interested in people who were committed and as passionate as I was. I was not interested in anyone's background, temperament, age or persuasion. Men and women followed me from many walks of life; some were young, some were old; some were intelligent, some were naïve; and some were rich and most were poor.

DC: This spectrum seems to have represented a cross section of your society, at least of the bottom or middle tier. I see fishermen, tax collectors, harlots, zealots and demon possessed. You were a carpenter and one of them.

JC: Think about what I said in this regard, "It is not the healthy who need a doctor, but the sick." (MK 2:17) My disciples represented those of our society who were vilified, poor without a voice and already judged because of prevailing attitudes.

DC: I see that they were judged for being alive.

JC: If that is how you want to put it. But yes, in our society one's place in the world had overtones; one was either judged or accepted depending on what they did or where they found themselves.

DC: Like the sick and infirmed, or sinners, tax collectors and harlots. Prejudice was built into your society.

JC: Prejudice was ingrained. The people and issues you mentioned were viciously stigmatized. Sickness was a sign that the person was sinful and judged by God. That prevailing attitude upset me.

DC: You provided hope and solace; a sense of belonging and a sense that not all is lost. People simply had to follow you or listen to you.

JC: And I was a healer.

DC: You flipped metaphorical tables and you flipped literal tables in the Temple. Your Beatitudes speak powerfully to conditions we previously mentioned: "Blessed are you who are poor, for yours is the Kingdom of God," (LK 6:20) "Blessed are you who hunger now, for you will be satisfied. Blessed are you who weep now, for you will laugh," (LK 6:21) "Blessed are you when people hate you, when they exclude you and insult you and reject your name as evil, because of the Son of Man." (LK 6:22)

JC: I knew the relationship between cost and benefit.

DC: You appreciated and understood the nature of risks and rewards and of loss and gain; that nuance was incorporated into your ministry.

JC: The business of agriculture and the business of the merchant motivated me. Each knew how to work their field and make it financially viable. I emulated that in my ministry.

DC: Your mindset was entrepreneurial and you cultivated it.

JC: I had to. How else was I going to bring my message to the people? Also, look at my success in gathering a range of followers and disciples.

DC: Did you have any success gathering followers or supporters from the upper classes? Were religious people interested in your teachings and ministry?

JC: That depends on what you mean by interested. I was a curiosity. My ideas were new and many threatened the existing establishment. For my brazenness, the establishment came out to listen to my sermons. Some wanted to catch me make a mistake so they could point and shake their finger or hurl insults at me. They wanted to say, "See, he is a fraud!" Others invited me into their homes to discuss the finer details of the law. If they didn't come to me I went to them in their synagogues. Most would not listen and nearly all challenged, threatened or argued with me. Unfortunately, anyone from within the establishment willing to follow and learn from me constantly looked over their shoulder.

DC: Why?

JC: Because they were afraid of the wrath and consequences leveled against them from the elders and ruling council. There was a brave man named Nicodemus who was a Pharisee and "member of the Jewish ruling council," who genuinely wanted to know more from me. (JN 3:1-2)

DC: A few recorded lines from history say that when he was discovered to be a secret follower he was swiftly ousted and sent into exile. He paid a high price to be associated with you.

JC: He ran for his life. Such was the fate of any who had much to lose in this life and little to gain from my wisdom.

DC: The Gospel of John sums up the sentiment, "Yet at the same time many even among the leaders believed in him. But because of the Pharisees they would not openly acknowledge their faith for fear they would be put out of the synagogue; for they loved human praise more than praise from God." (JN 12:42-44) I can appreciate the depth of your saying when looked at from this perspective: "Do not be afraid of those who kill the body but cannot kill the soul. Rather, be afraid of the One who can destroy both soul and body in hell." (MT 10:28) And another: "Do not store up for yourselves treasures on earth, where moth and vermin destroy, and where thieves break in and steal. But store up for yourselves treasures in heaven, where moths and vermin do not destroy, and where thieves do not break in and steal. For where your treasure is, there your heart will be also." (MT 6:19-21) These last two sayings seem specific to a target audience that includes the leaders, wealthy and religious authorities.

JC: Following me was costly particularly for the educated, successful, privileged and religious. "Enter through the narrow gate. For wide is the gate and broad is the road that leads to destruction, and many enter through it. But small is the gate and narrow the road that leads to life, and only a few find it." (MT 7:13-14)

DC: The truth behind this statement doesn't just apply to the rich, privileged or religious.

JC: That is correct. Anyone is susceptible in following the road to destruction.

DC: Your message neither drew nor appealed to the rich, privileged or religious.

JC: That is not altogether true. A few were swayed or interested, but for the most part, my wisdom was contentious, controversial or inadequate for them.

DC: Quite the opposite for the demoralized, downtrodden and outcast who felt your message was liberating, dynamic and hopeful.

JC: My message was open to anyone and everyone regardless of age, gender, status or wealth. I didn't discriminate. I knew, however, that my message was more acceptable to the dispossessed and downtrodden than it was to the upper class. Anyone who was comfortable and was not willing to accept the conflict that my ideas, messages and practices provoked and engendered would not follow me, at least not publically.

DC: To know the depths of your knowledge they had to follow you.

JC: They had to allow me to teach them about the ways and knowledge of the Father. They had to be willing to receive, to give and to do. To get the most from my wisdom they had to be involved with all three.

DC: You didn't want lukewarm or wavering people; or someone looking over their shoulders thinking they should be doing something else. You were committed and wanted the same from your audience and followers; it was either all or nothing.

JC: Go back to my sayings. "No one can serve two masters. Either you will hate the one and love the other, or you will be devoted to the one and despise the other. You cannot serve both God and money." (MT 6:24) And "As they were walking along the road, a man said to him, 'I will follow you wherever you go.' Jesus said, 'Foxes have dens and birds have nests, but the Son of Man has no place to lay his head.' He said to another man, 'Follow me.' But he replied, 'Lord, first let me go and bury my father.' Jesus said to him, 'Let the dead bury their own dead, but you go and proclaim the Kingdom of God.' Still another said, 'I will follow you, Lord; but first let me go back and say goodbye to my family.' Jesus replied, "No one who puts a hand to the plow and looks back is fit for service in the Kingdom of God.'" (LK 9:57-62) These sayings speak for themselves.

DC: It is said by some that you created a cult of dedicated but narrow-minded followers, but I would argue against that accusation. To learn any trade or know the depths of anything requires dedication and commitment. If someone came to me and asked, "Teach me to be a good woodworker," and I replied, "It's easy. Just push the plank of wood through the table saw and everything will take care of itself." That would be misleading. To be good at and knowledgeable about anything requires ten thousand hours and that does not include the financial investment. I see something similar with your teachings and understanding of the Father. People might have been inspired but you wanted committed and dedicated people who, through thick and thin, would stay and learn from you.

JC: You see my point. I felt it was important to know the Father and the only way to do that was to follow me, listen to my teachings and apply my wisdom. If one wanted to see a miracle and they happened to be at the right place at the right time, then they witnessed a miracle. If they wanted to know how to perform the same miracle, however, then they would have to follow me because it takes a lot of hard work and guidance. And the only way to get that was to be a follower or disciple.

DC: You had women followers.

JC: My mother Mary, along with Mary Magdalene, "Joanna the wife of Chuza, the manager of Herod's household; Susanna; and many others." (LK 8:2-3)

DC: These were women of means.

JC: Whose service and support was crucial.

DC: This was unheard of for your time. Was it sacrilegious?

JC: This goes to the question of what I wanted to accomplish. I wanted to be inclusive, not exclusive. I wanted to challenge barriers and the status quo, to include people who were voiceless and provide them with a voice, a direction, a purpose, and a vision of the divine that was different than the one they were born into and lived with every day. What better way to accomplish this than within our religious patriarchal society? I wanted to shatter barriers, push new, more inclusive ideas, and show people new possibilities. After all, my society was closed, narrow-minded and blind.

DC: Did your disciples feel the general sentiment of the society? Were they prone to grumbling or resentment? Were they angry or frustrated with the current state of affairs? In the United States, it is our pastime and birthright to express and vocalize our opinions pretty much about everything but specifically about the government and current events. Everybody has an opinion and it doesn't take much to get someone to express their thoughts or feelings on a particular subject.

JC: Most had misgivings and preconceptions, and many were prone to grumbling. Remember, we faced serious issues that led to several discussions involving Roman rule, taxation, the direction of the Israel and the End Times. Some people expressed resentment and the need for direct action against the establishment while others questioned how my ministry would change anything.

DC: Aside from these issues, I would like to know how people responded to your message of the Father. It is not a concept they would have known. It was new and it must have been hard to accept and appreciate and, I imagine, when you spoke of the Father it mystified your listeners.

JC: Even though I was guided by the Father I did not discuss Him openly with everybody. My experience and understanding of the Father was very different from the Hebrew concept of the divine, or from the Hellenistic religions, and from the Mystery Religions and paganism. As such there was no common ground to grasp the Father or make sense of Him. The concept was too abstract, yet ironically the Father was very personal to me. My followers and disciples greeted me with confused eyes and blank stares when I spoke about Him. Early in my ministry I learned only a select few were capable of comprehending my vision and knowledge of the divine.

DC: Would the Father have been a discussion at night around the campfire?

JC: The best one can do when it comes to the knowledge of the Father is point to it rather than explain it. Words simply fall short. I want to mention that the topic of the Father was not the only subject hard to grasp. Many of my parables were difficult to comprehend and forced me to explain myself over and over again. Few appreciated or comprehended my insights.

DC: There was no reference point. Your topics and themes were as foreign as the Roman occupiers. The themes you taught couldn't be understood from the perspective of one's upbringing, traditions and customs. Somehow one had to step outside the known, which at best is tough and demanding. I wonder how many of your followers or disciples were inclined.

JC: Yet the truth was that I was the door and foothold into that world. I was the bridge between the world of the familiar and the world of the unfamiliar. People knew me and knew my Jewish heritage, but the words I spoke were not ordinary or customarily Jewish. My words and ideas were confusing and they couldn't reconcile them with my Jewish nature.

DC: I think this explains the meaning of the saying in the Gospel of John, "No one comes to the Father except through me." (JN 14:6) I believe this idea was taken out of context and flavored theologically. The writer expresses a theological certitude, but I think he is speaking more truthfully of a social condition. It appears to me that the more accurate meaning of this saying involves context; at that time, you simply possessed knowledge of the divine that few others, if any, possessed.

JC: There was no other person, whether sage, elder, Pharisee, Sadducee, priest or Essene living in Judea who could tell you what I meant by the Father or the Kingdom of Heaven. These were types of experiences and truths were not morality tales. They did not stem or originate from our history or traditions. I was the only one who understood them and I tried to share them with my tribe.

DC: I'd like to briefly discuss the Kingdom of Heaven. Paul believed the kingdom was holiness and righteousness, while John the Baptist believed in repentance and that the kingdom was near. Both felt the End of Days and God's judgment were near. You don't speak like that.

JC: My sayings regarding the Father and the Kingdom of Heaven speak of the mustard seed; of a woman carrying a jar of meal on a distant road; of yeast, leaven, and meal; of "someone who wanted to put a powerful person to death" (THOM 96); of treasure buried in a field; of a pearl; of planting and sowing; and that the Kingdom of God is everywhere. My experience of the Father and my understanding of that mystery are very different from those two men's. One is hard-pressed to find holiness and righteousness in any of my Kingdom of Heaven sayings.

DC: If the Kingdom of Heaven is not holiness and righteousness or repentance as suggested by them then what did it mean to you? Please explain.

JC: It is not one thing; it is several things simultaneously.

DC: The Kingdom of Heaven gets associated with and confused by location. It is the place one goes after death.

JC: That is not what I meant! The Kingdom of Heaven is here and here and here. It is inside us. It is around us. It is everywhere. It is the means of divine expression. It is divine. The divine is not a being; it doesn't have form or substance. The Kingdom of Heaven is being and becoming, action and non-action, and energy and consciousness. One has to stop and think about that deeply. One must clear one's mind of everything it thinks and knows and become empty. Eventually, the Kingdom of Heaven makes itself known.

DC: The movie *Star Wars* uses the term "the force."

JC: All right. You can call it whatever you want. Changing the name or calling it differently doesn't change its inherent nature.

DC: Your disciples were hard-pressed to grasp the Father and the Kingdom of Heaven.

JC: That is correct.

DC: Even though they were confused, I sense they liked being around you because you were so unusual. I don't believe that is the only reason they followed you, but it certainly was one.

JC: My followers and disciples enjoyed knowing they were a part of a group who had special access to divine knowledge that the rest of our society did not.

DC: Your ministry contains two parts: theology and application. One part was words and ideas and the other was action. This is unique because the alternative would have been a school building or an academy. You could not have taught application and action as you knew it in such an institution. An academy could not have taught one how to treat another, how to react to harassment or slurs, or how to work a miracle. Your ministry was a real-time interaction with people and your teaching method included a hands-on and show-and-tell approach. This makes me wonder if people followed you to hear about your spiritual philosophy or whether they followed you to learn about the intangibles.

JC: I don't know if I agree with your last statement. Crowds gathered around me to listen to my stories and to hear my parables and Beatitudes.

DC: And they came to witness the miraculous or to be fed. Your followers and disciples got close to you and you taught them theology and practice in real time on the run.

JC: On the run?

DC: It's a figure of speech. You didn't have a fixed location because you went around the countryside and taught and practiced wherever you found yourself. That said, some of your more in-depth discussions occurred at night around a campfire in between towns or villages.

JC: At times I taught at night. I might be asked about something I said during the day or I might be asked about a deeper subject. I found it hard to teach while walking from village to village or town to town because of the many distractions. Instead I taught when we camped for the night because that was the time I had everyone's most undivided attention.

DC: How many would listen?

JC: Sometimes all of them, sometimes a handful, and many times one or two. It varied. A few had ears to hear the more profound wisdom of the Father and Kingdom of Heaven.

DC: You must have made a strong impression on a person like Thomas since he is the one attributed with compiling your Wisdom Sayings into a gospel. The Gnostic Christians continued your practice of teaching deep "spiritual philosophy" to those seeking hidden wisdom.

JC: Unfortunately, the Gnostic Christians didn't fully recognize or appreciate the power and intelligence of the heart as I had taught. The mind and heart have different intelligences and both were important to me, but my preference and my leaning toward the heart overshadowed the mind. I found the heart more effective than words in getting people's attention and keeping them together. I knew the heart is a place where things are born. One needs to experience the power of the heart. I wanted people to circle around a pure heart; to be drawn and moved by it.

DC: "For where your treasure is, there your heart will be also," (MT 6:21) and "For the mouth speaks what the heart is full of." (LK 6:45)

JC: My words were clear on this point.

DC: I'd like to switch gears and mention that your ministry must have galvanized your audience to think big. What you said and what you did was novel and extraordinary. You also had a particular mystique and identity to rally around. You were charismatic and bold and you spoke eloquently. You performed miracles, confronted religious authorities and were fearless. That made a lasting impression.

JC: It did. I was respected and considered a leader who had knowledge and authority. I knew, said, did, performed and confronted. That instilled confidence, and it inspired and brought my people together.

DC: Maybe one was also motivated by, "What on earth is he going to do next?" and "Whatever it is I want to be there to watch it happen."

JC: I smile at that because it was true. But, let me remind you, I sent my disciples out two by two to teach and perform in the same manner as me. Then it was they who were talked about, not just me. If they wanted to be included in my ministry they had to do what I did and in this way, I turned the tables on them. It was one way for me to separate the wheat from the chaff.

DC: When they went out two by two, villagers or townspeople must have known they were your disciples and must have anticipated your arrival because you followed behind "to every town and place" they went. (LK 10:1) Like John the Baptist they prepared the way for you.

JC: That was one of my practices.

DC: Some of your disciples came from John the Baptist.

JC: They did. "Andrew, Simon Peter's brother, was one of the two who heard what John had said." (JN 1:37-41)

DC: Did you only have twelve disciples or were there more?

JC: I had as many as seventy-two. (LK 10:1)

DC: Yet only the twelve are mentioned. Can you name them?

JC: "Simon (who is called Peter) and his brother Andrew; James son of Zebedee, and his brother John; Philip and Bartholomew; Thomas and Matthew the tax collector; James son of Alphaeus, and Thaddaeus; Simon the Zealot and Judas Iscariot, who betrayed" me. (MT 10:2-4)

DC: Is this the order in which these twelve were sent out two by two?

JC: It is.

DC: The Gospel of Luke mentions them in similar order but without the two by two connotation, and there is another slight variation. "Simon (whom he named Peter), his brother Andrew, James, John, Philip, Bartholomew, Matthew, Thomas [these two are reversed from Matthew's Gospel], James son of Alphaeus, Simon who was called the Zealot, Judas son of James, and Judas Iscariot, who became a traitor." (LK 6:14-16) Thaddaeus is replaced by Judas son of James. The fundamental account of the original twelve varies, and the person who is missing and one who becomes very important and the leader or father of the Jerusalem Church is your brother James.

JC: You are correct in saying he was my brother. I didn't ask him to be a disciple but that didn't mean he wasn't a member of my ministry.

DC: I'd like to move on to another topic. You advocated something I'd like to quote. "For all those who exalt themselves will be humbled, and those who humble themselves will be exalted." (LK 14:11) I see this statement directed to various people.

JC: You don't see it as a general human condition?

DC: Not completely. Just because someone is arrogant or prideful doesn't mean they will be humbled. Maybe some people will have a change of heart but I have not seen that switch firsthand.

JC: Then who do you think it addresses?

DC: First, I believe this saying is autobiographical, so it is about you. Second, I believe it is directed to your disciples and third, I believe it is about the rich and powerful people in your society. The hope in your saying is that some unfortunate event would befall them and they would be humbled and quieted as they "fell from grace."

JC: Did you wish to address any of these?

DC: Yes. I'd like to address the first two and start with you. As we discussed earlier, you underwent a severe transformation. I believe you were once prideful and arrogant, had a number of unfortunate but necessary and painful experiences after which you found yourself on the road to humility. You weren't born humble.

JC: No I wasn't; quite the opposite.

DC: You humbled yourself to conduct your ministry.

JC: That is correct, and to hear the voice of the Father.

DC: The humbling process is dreadful. Many of my life's lessons included an element of anguish and sorrow. After I had gone through many painful experiences I imagined I was beyond the process. Much to my chagrin I was wrong. It continues to this day. What I'm discovering in my transformation is that I'm becoming more limber, more sensitive and more aware. I'm also willing to listen and, oddly, I'm becoming more resolute. You aptly said, "Be as shrewd as snakes and as innocent as doves." (MT 10:16)

JC: Easing the grip of the ego is agonizing and terrifying. It kicks and screams and says constantly, "I am me. I am terrific. I am important. I am smart. Look at me. I know everything. I know what God wants." Eliminating that voice and subduing it required extraordinary means and my ministry was one method to help facilitate that process.

DC: Expand on that issue. How did your ministry help temper or quiet the ego?

JC: The purpose of the ministry was bigger and more important than any individual, including me. One had to conform to the ministry's goals and be shaped by its interests and needs.

DC: Tell me how that worked.

JC: The question to ask is, "What was the purpose of my ministry?" I had to be clear on that point and I was.

DC: I know we've spoken a lot about your society, how you wanted change, how you introduced the practice of love, mercy and forgiveness, and how you initiated the new concept of the Father. But talk about the goal of your ministry.

JC: I wanted to offer hope and wisdom. I wanted people to be free from ignorance and inadequate religious practices. I wanted to bring love, peace, mercy and forgiveness. I wanted to offer healing; to reunite people together in love, and to let people know the dynamics of love, forgiveness and mercy. I wanted people to know the mystical nature of the Father and that there is a personal connection to that mystery. I wanted to feed those who were hungry both literally and figuratively and I wanted to restore and uplift the downtrodden. I wanted to be inclusive rather than exclusive, and I didn't look to the past for direction as we stepped into the future.

DC: For the first time, I see that your ministry had more than one purpose. It had an exterior focus by ministering to others and an inner focus by ministering to your needs and the needs of your disciples. This begs the question of how your disciples and followers were affected by your ministry. Were they humbled by it?

JC: No. Their attitude and demeanor upset me many times and my patience was tried.

DC: I see their lack of faith, persistent questioning and desire for power; I see fear, judgment, condemnation and ignorance. I see zealotry, infighting, hate toward women, combativeness, competitiveness, stealing, grumbling and denial.

JC: They missed the point completely. What I taught and embraced was difficult to accept and practice for everybody – disciples, followers and listeners. They had to overcome those tendencies, which they did not. After my death, however, many achieved it by conducting their own ministry. Then they realized what I taught and remembered what I said and allowed themselves to be changed.

DC: Let's go deeper into your ministry in relation to discipleship. Your ministry instigated and addressed society's ills and practices; at the same time, it addressed ingrained personal habits and prejudices. Your disciples were affected by similar egotistical issues. In effect, your disciples reflected the makeup of your society, and I would say the two reflect each other.

JC: When it came to my society I was faced with four primary challenges. First, there was the growing tension and ambiguity people felt about themselves and the future. Second, there was a lack of compassion coupled with an inflated amount of judgment, condemnation and argumentation. Third, I felt our religious understandings, rites and practices were limited and in cases ineffectual. Fourth, I experienced the living reality of the Father. This knowledge was very different from the traditional Hebrew God, and I wanted to introduce my understanding of the Father into my culture. My ministry addressed each of these issues through compassion, teachings, healings, miracles and discipleship.

DC: That was an exterior focus. Did you have a similar strategy with each of your disciples? Did you address each uniquely in a manner similar to the way you addressed your society?

JC: I wanted them to know what I knew so I taught them. I wanted them to stop judging and condemning. I stopped judging and condemning. I wanted them to see; I could see and showed them how to see. I wanted them to love; I loved and showed compassion. I wanted them to follow me and do as I did.

DC: We have a saying, "Be the change you want."

JC: That is what I did. I started with myself. I allowed my ego to be crushed, I was mentored and I went out into the desert to purge myself. I never asked my disciples to do anything that I was not willing to do. I did and asked them to do the same.

DC: Your faith was unshakeable and steady like the flow of a mighty river.

JC: It had to be. The task at hand was immense as the Father's heart. I knew what I wanted to accomplish and I set my heart to do it. I made small but significant steps. I was persistent, consistent and determined. The result is that change happened. It happened to me. It happened to my society. It happened to my disciples. And change slowly but progressively gained momentum.

DC: I'm trying to grasp how seventy-two disciples changed and what they did after your crucifixion. They are not mentioned in the gospel canon, the Gospel of Thomas or any of the other gospel accounts. I surmise they faded into oblivion, lost the fire and left, or started another faction, possibly the Gospel of Thomas community. In any event, they were forgotten to history. How did you treat them? Did you treat them differently than the twelve?

JC: I tried not to single anybody out. I didn't want anyone to be special or have special privileges, otherwise rivalry and jealousy would spread and cause discontent. I didn't want that, but that wasn't always the case. I tried to focus on the ministry and what we could accomplish.

DC: I see an element of favoritism when I read the gospels.

JC: I was the leader. People looked to me for guidance, direction, advice and wisdom. They wanted to be near me and get to know me. It was natural for my followers to want to be near me. I was their teacher and friend. When I smiled on someone they became alive and happy. When I looked on someone sternly they became sad or upset. It happened that some of my attention became more focused if someone stayed with me everywhere I went. I began to trust them and befriended them.

DC: I can accept that. I'd like to mention, as a matter of record, that I see succession. Someone had to succeed you and take your place.

JC: After my death, some of my disciples banded together, agreed on their authority and moved out into the world with my message.

DC: All right. Of your many followers, you chose some, others chose you. Some were dedicated to the end while others were not, and I would surmise some left but maybe, at a later time, came back.

JC: That is a fair assessment. The range of discipleship varied. I couldn't be concerned with every wrinkle. Instead I was concerned with my approach and the achievable results.

DC: I see two parts – discipleship and audience – and you dealt with both from two angles.

JC: I'm getting to understand you. Your mind works by understanding how parts work and you isolate and separate this thing from that thing.

DC: Isolating things helps me see them. When I see the parts I can dismantle and examine them more closely. I can reassemble them like a puzzle. Then I can see how the entire thing works as one thing. That is my inner engineer.

JC: We were speaking about the relationship between discipleship and audience. At times, these two were entwined.

DC: Will you elaborate?

JC: Many times when I was alone with my disciples I taught, shared parables and stories, and revealed the nature of the Father. They asked questions and I answered. This was another practice that bonded us together and we became friends. We shared our struggles and concerns, and we shared our frustration and hopes. They got to know me and I got to know them. Because of this they understood my intentions and expectations more clearly. We started to know each other and to act in concert.

DC: I can see how your disciples gained hope, confidence and faith. I can see how their spirits renewed as if given new life.

JC: People felt hope, love and compassion. My ministry was different than people expected or anticipated. People felt the groundswell of a movement.

DC: I can see that.

JC: My ministry was a place in which one felt a sense of belonging. My ministry did not endorse ritualized practices, customs and calendar-day observances. People could speak their minds. They felt free and gained confidence. They felt they were doing God's work. The feeling of unity and purpose was awe inspiring, and people's composure went from drudgery to excitement and from disheartenment to encouragement. I saw it and felt it, and so could they.

DC: After your crucifixion, your movement was called "the Way." (Acts 9:2)

JC: My ministry was a way and that term expresses yet another title that, as you know, I found useful in distinguishing this from that and this one from that one. It had identifying effects.

DC: I want to go back to the relationship between ministry, disciples, followers and audience. Your words challenged, your parables confused and your miracles stunned. Your ministry was not easy or comfortable. Again, I think of the Israelites in the desert with Moses. It was hard and uncomfortable.

JC: That is the path to God. I advocated transformation, and transformation was always possible in my ministry. It can be quick and instant, or it can be slow and incremental. It's not the same for everyone.

DC: I'd like to swing around because I'm interested in the logistics of your ministry. How did this work? Did your disciples and followers stay with you? Did they go home at night? Did they meet you in the next town or village? Did they stay with someone in the village or town and meet up with you the next day, the following week, or month? Was it a hard-and-fast rule that they must stay with you at all times, or was there an allowance for time off? What was your policy regarding that eventuality, and how did you deal with that?

JC: Typically, we traveled together in a group and were away from home and family. Some brought their family along. Each of us agreed beforehand to think and act like a group, to focus on the purpose and goal of the ministry, to stay together and minister for a period of time, and not allow personal egos and preconceptions to dictate our behavior. In this regard, our dedication to the purpose and goal was not that different than a Roman military campaign. Not everyone was capable or accustomed to withstanding hardship. It was tedious and grueling. It was stressful and uncomfortable, and we, mainly I, were threatened. It was a daily struggle and it was something that had to be endured.

DC: You knew how to manage your misery and hardship. You had done it before with your desert/temptation experience.

JC: My ministry was difficult on many levels and it separated the wheat from the chaff. People put in what they could and got out what they could. Not everyone could follow me to the end.

DC: You said, "You are those who have stood by me in my trails. And I confer on you a kingdom, just as my Father conferred one on me, so that you may eat and drink at my table in my kingdom and sit on thrones, judging the twelve tribes of Israel." (LK 22:28-30) Aside from the daily hardship, you experienced the miraculous. I imagine it was similar to Moses and the Israelites while they were in the desert. Each day they received manna from heaven, each day they were led by the light of the divine, yet each day they grumbled and hoped for something other than what they received. They looked for the way out rather than the way into the heart of the matter.

JC: Miracles had a rejuvenating effect, as did my words, stories and actions, though not everyone felt that way.

DC: It appears in this recorded account, "From this time many of his disciples turned back and no longer followed him." (JN 6:66) Getting back to the original question regarding one leaving and returning.

JC: I didn't have an overarching policy. I dealt with people individually. At the same time I had to determine if the group had changed and whether the one returning was in the right frame of mind with the rest of us. When someone breaks a simple agreement by saying yes to discipleship, it's hard to accept them back and it's just as hard not to judge them. I was confronted with the integrity of the group and I was confronted with the change of a person's heart. I had to carefully consider and weigh each accordingly.

DC: This, too, interests me and is delicate, so I want to be diplomatic. The parable of the Prodigal Son is about forgiveness, but your message was also about commitment. You told one to leave everything behind to follow you and you told others to forgive one another. Your message of commitment and forgiveness boxed you into a contradictory position. Did you have a middle ground?

JC: What do you mean? Can you explain that point further?

DC: You spoke of forgiveness, mercy and love. It was embedded in your message. At the same time you asked people to leave everything behind, to be committed and follow you. So how did you reconcile these two opposing views when and if a disciple or follower left and decided to come back?

JC: I allowed for a follower to be a follower and a disciple to be a disciple. To be a disciple they had to be committed and a greater demand was placed on them especially with regards to love. Being a follower had another, less stringent, set of requirements.

DC: You had two grades of people?

JC: Not everyone could follow me as I wanted and I wasn't going to disallow it. The meat of the ministry required a very dedicated person and there was an internal reward for that commitment. I didn't give the reward. It came as riches from heaven.

DC: There's always a level of ambiguity, and there is tension between ideology and reality. One wants one thing but reality dictates something else.

JC: At the same time, to achieve fundamental or transformative change, principled rigidity and inflexibility had to be built in and maintained.

DC: If someone left and decided to come back, did you prefer to make one judgment over the other?

JC: Every situation was unique, but usually I was forgiving and welcomed the individual back into the fold. After all, forgiveness was mixed within my message.

DC: You navigated those turbulent waters rather well. If you were absolutely rigid, hardly anyone would be capable of following you. There had to be a porous give and take.

JC: It was not as porous as you suggest. Don't underestimate the power of one's imagination and heart to be sparked by something special. One wants to be a part of something bigger and to live up to that standard. Being a disciple gave the men great pride and a sense of purpose. The ministry was bigger than any one individual and after awhile they felt slighted if I was unduly forgiving. It wasn't hard for the dedicated to feel they were doing all the hard work while another who left and came back got off for free.

DC: Another thorny issue rose during your ministry. It is written, "An argument started among the disciples as to which of them would be the greatest." (LK 9:46)

JC: To which I responded by taking "a little child and had him stand beside" me and I said, "Whoever welcomes this little child in my name welcomes me; and whoever welcomes me welcomes the one who sent me. For it is the one who is least among you all who is the greatest." (LK 9:47-48)

DC: As you travelled with your entourage new people came into the fold. Did you have a benchmark to determine who was trustworthy, responsible or committed?

JC: There is no set answer. Some followed without waver. Some followed without heart. Others followed for a time and then left, while some returned after fulfilling a personal obligation. Commitment as a whole varied. I preferred unwavering loyalty and commitment day in and day out but that did not always occur. I had to accept what people could contribute and acknowledge that people were changed because of the ministry. The rest was in God's hands.

DC: In other words, a follower received what they needed and contributed what they could and you accepted that.

JC: Yes. I could ask only so much.

DC: In the end, though, it seems to have come down to the twelve male disciples. Were the women pushed aside or dismissed?

JC: The twelve have a special function, but other disciples and followers went out into the countryside, villages and towns as I taught.

DC: They are not historically recorded but maybe this passage from the Gospel of Mark alludes to this condition. The gospel states there was "someone driving out demons in your name" and your disciples "told him to stop, because he was not one of us." (MK 9:38)

JC: To which I replied, "Do not stop him. For no one who does a miracle in my name can in the next moment say anything bad about me, for whoever is not against us is for us." (MK 9:39-40)

DC: I wonder if they took this to heart. I also see the role of women in your ministry as rather suspect.

JC: For the generations who came after me, who didn't experience the movement from the beginning, that statement is more accurate than inaccurate. Many of my disciples, unfortunately, didn't think women should have a leadership role in the ministry because they thought it was the domain of men. They couldn't appreciate the full scope of my mission. Peter and Mary Magdalene fought about many things. She was principled and vocal, and she felt strongly that men and women were equal in the sight of divine. Women needed a voice in our patriarchal society and my ministry attempted to cure this ill. Silencing and relegating them to a specific domestic role, not granting them education, and preventing them a greater role in the ministry were not my intentions.

DC: Ingrained patterns are hard to break. It takes something phenomenal to break them.

JC: Not necessarily. It can be systematic and gradual, but a revolutionary transformation is effective and quick.

DC: The "quick turn-around event."

JC: You like that term.

DC: It's descriptive. While you ministered, you ate together, camped together, and laughed together; you shared your lives; you were bound together by a common mission. Did you teach or reveal new wisdom on the side when you weren't ministering or healing during the day?

JC: During quiet moments when I felt inspired I revealed more profound mysteries.

DC: The Gospel of Thomas contains teachings about the Father, eternity, and self that are not found in the canonical gospels. Did you teach these ideas to your disciples?

JC: I taught the more difficult ones privately, but they were not the only ones.

DC: Contemporary Christians state the Gospel of Thomas is Gnostic, which suggests a heretical nature. It is difficult for me to accept that position. One-third of the one hundred and fourteen sayings in the Gospel of Thomas are directly quoted in the Synoptic Gospels, and you are the central figure in both traditions. I can't square the circle. It doesn't make sense that your sayings in the Gospel of Thomas were inspired by a person outside the original group or the early Jesus movement. Someone had to get the ball rolling and that someone is either you or someone close to you who listened and understood your words.

JC: My teachings were thought-provoking and inspirational at a time when people were thirsting for something momentous to happen.

DC: I believe stories about you and your teachings evolved within communities according to their roots and temperament. The Thomas community embraced one set of teachings while the Jesus movement community embraced another. In the long run, these two groups had legs and feet that moved in opposite directions.

JC: Using my agricultural metaphor, each tradition had unique soil and each contained wisdom I seeded. The seeds fell on prepared soil, they were watered, the seeds became plants, and the fruit ripened and was harvested each according to their understanding received from me.

DC: Something nags my mind. It is assumed, that you taught people in the mountains, in the desert, in the countryside, in synagogues and in towns and villages. I had a flash of intuition just now and I'm rethinking your audience.

Your parables and Beatitudes were chiefly directed to a random audience and your followers and disciples were part of that audience, and they were just as much your targeted audience as your random audience. This point cannot be underestimated.

JC: I repeated the same sayings and parables in every village and town we entered. I spoke to my disciples, followers and audience. Everyone heard the same thing. I was indiscriminate. When I created a new saying and spoke it to a new audience my disciples heard it for the first time. Then they wanted to know more about it. My wisdom was etched in their memory because I repeated my stories over and over. That is how I learned and memorized the Torah – through constant repetition, and that is how I taught. Later, they wrote my sayings down. They could recite them because they heard them so often. I shared deeper knowledge, especially at night, around the fire. I answered many questions. This was the time when their attention was the greatest and they could listen intently.

DC: This is a little off topic but I'm now thinking about it. Did you have friends?

JC: This is off topic! I need to gather my thoughts. (*Jesus sips water from his glass.*) People with whom I worked before my ministry were friends as were the people I knew in my youth. When I started my ministry, I had to separate my past from my future. I had to separate those who I knew from those I would come to meet, know and lead. It was important to be alone in this matter; I refused familiarity.

DC: Can you explain that in more detail?

JC: I didn't want my life and past interfering with the ministry. I embarked on a mission that was focused. I was determined to initiate a new understanding of the divine and a new practice suited for that understanding.

DC: New wine and new wineskins.

JC: That took precedent. The life I knew and the people from that life had the potential of undermining the ministry – whether through gossip, idle talk, insubordination, lack of participation, or resistance to my message – and those attitudes and sentiments would erode people's confidence.

DC: Your previous life along with your friends and family had the potential, at the very least, to distract and, at worst, to undermine you and your ministry. Words and attitudes have consequences whether deliberate or unintentional.

JC: I didn't want to afford that opportunity. I didn't want a close friend who had known me before my ministry or a family member tell a follower "Jesus once did this," or "Jesus once did that." Nor did I want a friend question me with "No respectable prophet would do that or say that." Had those words spread among my disciples or followers my credibility would have evaporated and so too my message and ministry.

DC: There was enough to overcome without having to deal with that.

JC: People are innately obstinate, set in traditional beliefs and practices, engrossed with preconceptions, and filled with lust, anger, and greed. They are defensive, aggressive or argumentative. I didn't want to glance over my shoulder wondering if someone from my past was with me or against me, or say something that would sow confusion or distrust. I had to exude confidence, authority and faith at all times.

DC: You could not show any vulnerability. This leads to another facet about your ministry. In the Synoptic Gospels, you rarely mention the personal pronoun I. You prefer titles – Son of Man, Son of Adam and the like – and your parables and sayings always use the third-person singular – a rich man, a slave, a servant or a manager.

JC: Yes.

DC: Your followers addressed you as Lord or Rabbi, and you asked a rhetorical question, "Who do you say I am?" (MK 8:29) And "When Jesus came to the region of Caesarea Philippi, he asked his disciples, 'Who do you say the Son of Man is?'" (MT 16:13) You don't give a straight answer. You ask others to answer for you. To the question above "Peter answered, 'You are the Messiah.'" (MK 8:29)

JC: It was necessary to eliminate the *me* from my personality. I employed theatrics to get my message across. Images, words, deeds, actions and titles were designed to shock, confuse and startle. I wanted people to get out of their daily routine and experience the sensational.

DC: Let's take another break; I need another cup of coffee. When we return I'd like to talk about a few disciples.

CHAPTER 9

FOUR DISCIPLES

DC: Before we discuss your disciples I'd to talk about nicknames and name changes. What can you tell me about each?

JC: A nickname is important in that it embodies a new persona for a person and gives that person an opportunity to view themselves from a new perspective. And a nickname has an endearing and personal quality.

DC: You called Simon, son of John – Cephas – which is Peter and means *rock*. He was known as the rock upon whom the Church will be built (MT 16:18, MK 3:16, LK 6:14, JN 1:42), and the sons of Zebedee, brothers James and John, you called the "sons of thunder." (MK 3:16-17) John is also referred to as the "disciple most loved by Jesus." (JN 13:23, JN 19:26) I see these monikers as appealing and representing positive character traits. Aside from nicknames and from the scriptural point of view, there is actually a name change. For example, Saul becomes the Apostle Paul, Abram becomes Abraham, Simon becomes Peter the Rock and Jesus son of Joseph becomes Jesus the Christ. I notice when this occurs it signifies a change in the status of that person and it means that the person plays a more active role in service to God. I'd say the former self and inclinations no longer suit the new self with the new role.

JC: That is the tendency.

DC: Not all nicknames are positive. I see several instances in which a nickname was given to cast suspicion, dispersion, and disparagement, or to cause doubt about a person and their character. When I see this I'm hard-pressed to believe you gave such nicknames or monikers.

JC: Which nicknames do you see that are uncharacteristic of me?

DC: Son of Simon Iscariot – Judas Iscariot – the traitor who betrayed (MT 10:4, MT 26:14, MT 27:3, MK 3:19, LK 6:16, LK 22:3; JN 6:71, JN 18:2); Mary Magdalene – the demon possessed (LK 8:2); Simon the Zealot (MT 10:4, MK 3:18, LK 6:15); Doubting Thomas, also known as Didymos/Didymus Judas Thomas, which means twin (JN 20:24, JN 21:2, THOM 1:1); and your brother James the Just. (THOM 12:1-2) Each has a particular untold connotation and a few suggest character flaws. Even the moniker James the Just possesses an overly legalistic tone.

JC: I see your point.

DC: For a man advocating compassion and the cessation of judgment and condemnation I'm surprised to see these labels and nicknames. Not only do they raise questions – they raise my eyebrow. Should I take these disparaged people seriously? Can I trust them? Are these disparaged ones inferior to Peter, Paul or some other unmentioned disciple? The intent of these nicknames engenders suspicion and mistrust. Instead of seeing Christian unity, I see strife, power struggle and slander with such names. These words ring in my ear, "Watch out for these. Even though they were original Jesus disciples you can't trust them." The very things you embraced – wisdom, compassion, love, forgiveness, brotherhood – are destroyed and replaced with judgment, anger, scorn and separation. This practice appears to have metastasized throughout the Christian community after your death and become routine.

JC: That is unfortunate. A series of problems persisted and proved distracting throughout my ministry and continued beyond my crucifixion. That was one such practice.

DC: What other practice did you believe was unfortunate?

JC: The nature of the Father didn't make sense to the majority of my people.

DC: Your understanding of the Father was inconsistent and incongruent with the traditional Hebrew concept of Yahweh, Elohim and Adonai.

JC: My concept of the divine differed from normal expectations. The Father and the Kingdom of Heaven didn't quite fit into their understanding, and the deeper subtleties were missed and overlooked.

DC: As was the concept of the Messiah?

JC: Not particularly. But it was misapplied to me. The Messiah is a concept rooted in Jewish history and tradition. It means deliverer, the expected king, the anointed one filled with God's spirit, the leader of the cause who ushers in peace.

DC: You had a cause. You were filled with God's spirit. You were a deliverer – a deliverer of love, compassion and mercy. Your message was a message of renewal and you had compassion on the people you saw "because they were harassed and helpless, like sheep without a shepherd." (MT 9:36)

JC: The term *Messiah* had a variety of connotations; one was religious, one was political, one was expected change and another had a subversive tone. I was not the solution to the political problems. I addressed the spiritual needs of the sick and dispossessed and I brought a new concept of the divine to help and heal my people.

DC: Your disciples seem impressed by their importance in your kingdom after you and Yahweh overthrew the Romans. (LK 22:24) The mother of the sons of Zebedee – James and John – asked a favor from you: "Grant that one of these two sons of mine may sit at your right and the other at your left in your kingdom." (MT 20:21) The account in the Gospel of Mark records James and John, the sons of Zebedee asking, "Let one of us sit at your right and the other at your left in your glory." (MK 10:37)

JC: They were misinformed and I swiftly corrected them.

DC: It's easy to appreciate their hope. You were remarkable and they felt they could ride on your coattails straight into power positions. Think of that, a bunch of fishermen imagined they would rule Israel with a carpenter. I believe their sentiment was counterproductive. Not only are you addressing the society at large, you are working against the conviction and prejudice of each disciple.

JC: Yes. I was looking at the entire Field to see how I could manage my ministry effectively.

DC: I'd like to switch topics. Our time is limited and we can't discuss every disciple in detail, so I'd like to talk about a few.

JC: Which do you have in mind?

DC: Simon Peter, Thomas, Judas Iscariot and Mary Magdalene.

JC: Why these?

DC: Each brought a particular point of view and understanding to your ministry, each provided a significant yet unique contribution, and each came from a different spectrum of Jewish society.

JC: Very astute. I want to emphasize that each person was Jewish and was raised with Jewish customs and traditions. As such our Jewish heritage was common ground for every one of us. At the same time, each reflected a social problem and concern I experienced and addressed.

DC: Let's start with Peter. What was he like?

JC: Simon – the fisherman. Peter liked being on the water and liked fishing. I did too. A fisherman is different from a carpenter but each requires a similar approach and attitude. Each has to be determined, patient and skilled. A fisherman has to know the habits of fish, how to repair the boats, mend and wash the nets, and read the weather and wind. A fisherman has to be strong to row the boat and to pull in the catch. He has to be tough enough to withstand the rigors of the weather – the harsh sun glaring off the water and blinding the eyes or the biting cold of winter's early mornings before the sun rose. A fisherman faces this daily.

DC: What was it about fishermen that appealed to you? Did they have a particular temperament?

JC: The ones I knew tended to be unruly, prideful, tough, quick-tempered, strong-headed and opinionated.

DC: When you called the fishermen to your ministry I wonder if you couldn't resist the analogy – "fisher of men."

JC: I knew I needed to have men of this ilk for my ministry.

DC: You knew you couldn't accomplish or succeed in your mission alone and that you needed help.

JC: After my desert/temptation experience and after I recovered from that ordeal I was flush with enthusiasm. I went to the Galilee to teach in the synagogues and the countryside. Later I walked to Nazareth to teach but, to my dismay, my teachings were not well received, so I left and traveled to Capernaum.

DC: Were you upset with the cold response?

JC: When I think about it I'd have to say no, but my heart did ache and was perplexed. I thought to myself, "The Father is telling me to share my knowledge with them but they won't listen and receive it." I was versed in the Levite tradition and had read the prophets. I knew they weren't well received either. I saw myself as a prophet. I couldn't let rejection or hostility bother me. I had to keep moving, so I went to from one town and village to another. I was the metaphorical sower sowing many diverse grounds.

DC: With your disciples, you had many roles to fill – you had to lead, gather, administer, teach and perform simultaneously. You had to captivate them, speak to them directly, make them believe in you and make them believe in the cause.

JC: I learned from previous mistakes, when I was younger and pursued another life, that I needed to be more resolute, decisive, present and commanding. I needed to step into the shoes of the teacher and leader. I had to be fully engaged like John the Baptist. I couldn't be absent and leave it to someone else like I had done before.

DC: John must have had a large role to play in that regard. Was leadership a challenge for you?

JC: Yes, but I learned quickly. As I taught and ministered I was attentive to what worked and what didn't. I figured out the technique of going out two by two and providing a set of specific instructions. As the disciples trained to minister, I learned to lead, to use a tone of voice and to foresee the effects of my decisions beforehand.

DC: You called Simon Peter while on his fishing boat on the Lake of Gennesaret with his brother Andrew. (MT 4:18-22, MK 1:16-20, LK 5:1-11) Yet each of these accounts differs significantly from John's account. Let me quote: "Andrew, Simon Peter's brother, was one of the two who heard what John had said and who had followed Jesus. The first thing Andrew did was to find his brother Simon and tell him, 'We have found the Messiah.' And he brought him to Jesus, who looked at him and said, 'You are Simon son of John. You will be called Cephas.' (which, when translated, is Peter.)" (JN 1:40-42) In the Synoptic Gospels Simon was fishing with his brother Andrew casting nets, but in the Gospel of John Andrew fetches his brother while you were with John the Baptist, presumably baptizing. Later you went to the Galilee. I can't reconcile the differences.

JC: Different stories developed depending on the storyteller. At first this particular detail didn't seem important. Later it did. Remember the first gospel, the Gospel of Mark, was written nearly forty years after my death. By that time memories faded, stories changed and other stories had to be written with convincing detail.

DC: I suggest there were various traditions or that there were two different historical sources with different understandings. I'd like to continue and expand on this point; there is confusion in the Synoptic Gospels about the order of Peter's calling. In the Gospel of Matthew, you call Peter (MT 4:18-20) and his mother-in-law's fever is not mentioned. In the Gospel of Mark, you call Peter (MK 1:16-18) and later heal his mother-in-law's fever, (MK 2:29-31) while in the Gospel of Luke the order is reversed – Peter's mother-in-law is healed (LK 4:38-39) and then you call Peter. (LK 5:1-11) In any event Peter was called. At least that remains consistent. How did he respond to your call?

JC: It was mixed with shame and astonishment. Peter fell at my "knees and said, 'Go away from me, Lord; I am a sinful man!' For he and all his companions were astonished at the catch of fish they had taken." (LK 5:8-9) News about me had not spread like it had with John the Baptist. Rumors and whispers persisted but I wasn't as accepted or known as him. To be sure something was in the air that made my request common rather than peculiar. So when I called him to be a disciple he was caught off guard. That didn't last long; he was enthusiastic after I grabbed his attention when I healed his mother-in-law from her high fever. (MK 1:30-31, LK 4:38-39)

DC: What lessons did he learn from you?

JC: That question is appropriate for all involved. Each disciple was distinct. If they stayed with me to the end, eventually they had a profound experience of the Father. At first, most followed because my ministry was exciting and unusual. People were naturally curious and interested because my ministry lent itself to talk. My followers and disciples also felt that I was on a course with destiny; that God was behind me and that I was on a mission. They saw that I had command over situations and events that seemed impossible. They instinctively knew I was unique and that my ministry was exceptional. As a result, they felt compelled and encouraged by my ministry and wanted to be associated with me.

DC: They were also enthralled by your miracles – you walked on water, calmed a storm, healed the sick, lame, and blind, and raised the dead.

JC: One couldn't follow without a sense of awe. Others followed simply to be healed, to be given food, to hear an answer to a pressing concern or to listen to my baffling wisdom.

DC: I'm sure it took them away from the routine of their lives, which tended to be tedious, boring and all too familiar.

JC: Some followed me halfheartedly even though I warned them of the dangers. Excitement and concern mixed like leaven in flour.

DC: Did Peter experience anything specific because of you?

JC: The answer has a general side and a specific side. Generally, one doesn't know what a day will bring. Each of us has a life to live. But I found that life changes quickly and that change doesn't come with a set of wisdom sayings that tells you how to proceed or what to do. Maturing and bearing fruit in the Father requires a willingness to step into the unknown and allow life to proceed along a path that is different from the familiar path; at that moment one does not always know what to do, where to turn or what is required. One has to learn how to feel; in other words, you have to feel your way through the uncertainty.

DC: I can testify to that. I had to walk a path to understand the direction and potential outcome. At times, I didn't know the purpose or the direction in which I was headed. I just felt compelled to stay on the path.

JC: You see? One does not always know what is around the corner.

DC: Some of your Wisdom Sayings were born from ambiguity. The wisdom you knew from your youth, which was taught to you from Jewish history and religion, and the wisdom you knew subsequently from your NDE was diametrically opposed, and one perspective did not connect to the other. Once you stepped out of your near-death grave and after your mind cleared, you were forced to recalibrate your thinking. You created a new set of Wisdom Sayings from your new perspective.

JC: That was my course. Understand, at that time, wisdom was personified as Sophia.

DC: Excuse me. Let me stop and ask you about Sophia. Who is Sophia?

JC: Sophia was considered the feminine personification of wisdom. The Greeks represented her as a goddess and created statues of her. Some cultures represented her as a dove, some depicted her with a cluster of stars surrounding her head, while others considered her the mother of God, the mother of creation or the divine feminine. Wisdom was very important in ancient cultures, the Jewish culture included.

DC: The Hebrew wisdom tradition consists of Job, Psalms, Proverbs, and the writings of King Solomon – Ecclesiastes and Song of Songs. I'd like to quote from the book of Proverbs: "Does not wisdom call out? Does not understanding raise her voice?" (Proverbs 8:1) and "Listen, for I have worthy things to say; I open my lips to speak what is right. My mouth speaks what is true, for my lips detest wickedness." (Proverbs 8:6-7)

JC: I'd like to add another quote: "I love those who love me, and those who seek me find me. With me are riches and honor, enduring wealth and prosperity. My fruit is better than fine gold; what I yield surpasses choice silver." (Proverbs 8:17-19)

DC: The opposite of wisdom is folly. Proverbs speaks on such issue as well. "Folly is an unruly woman; she is simple and knows nothing. She sits at the door of her house, on a seat at the highest point of the city, calling out to those who pass by, who go straight on their way." (Proverbs 9:13-15)

JC: Inside Proverbs are short and quick life instructions and insights. "Lazy hands make for poverty, but diligent hands bring wealth" (Proverbs 10:4) and "The wise in heart accept commands, but a chattering fool comes to ruin." (Proverbs 10:8)

DC: Wisdom can distinguish relationships and inner qualities, and it can penetrate the veil of illusion. You had that ability.

JC: It was an important element of my ministry.

DC: I see your wisdom involved with how to live, how to pursue the divine, how to love one another and how to see. It could be said that you embodied Sophia. In fact, the Christians said you personified Sophia.

JC: My wisdom also involved do not judge, do not condemn, turn the other cheek, walk the extra mile, the Kingdom of Heaven is within you, find the pearl, invest in life, recognize blindness, consider the lilies of the field, and where your heart is there is your treasure.

DC: Your wisdom was not pessimistic or cynical. It was positive and hopeful.

JC: Neither pessimism nor cynicism was helpful or productive, nor was lament, moaning or wallowing. Before continuing with Peter I want to add that it is one thing to have experiences and to gain wisdom from those experiences; it is quite another to put wisdom in motion and allow yourself and the world to be transformed by it. I was willing to flip "tables" in the heart of my society. The world changed because I brought something to it that it lacked. That is wisdom.

DC: I appreciate your words. Shall we get back to Peter? We were talking about the general and specific things he learned from you.

JC: He respected and listened to me because I took an interest in him. I took an interest in each disciple and follower; I would listen to them and make them feel included. I had an open heart for them and they sensed it. I didn't judge or condemn them, and that affected the dynamic of our interaction.

DC: What more can you tell me about Peter?

JC: He had a small inclination for the mystical but he was plagued with doubt, fears, and preconceptions. He was not an educated man and he was blunt without a sense of irony or sophistication. He was stubborn, judgmental, impulsive, and patriarchal to the point of being misguided. At times he was the most resistant and on numerous occasions questioned and challenged my direction and authority. I had to chastise him. At my critical hour in the Garden of Gethsemane he was not vigilant. He acted violently and impulsively toward the detachment of soldiers, pulling his sword and striking Malchus the servant of the High Priest, cutting off his ear. Later he denied me. In spite of his shortcomings he was willing to try new things, his heart was large, and he was passionate. When he made up his mind he did not waver and he could "move a mountain." Upon my death he was shocked, disturbed, fearful, angry, shamed and mortified.

DC: He wasn't the only one. All your disciples must have felt the same.

JC: All were shocked, stunned and perplexed. All mourned. It was a terribly sad time. Afterward every disciple re-evaluated their life and their time spent with me. They had to come to grips with the seriousness of my ministry and had to re-evaluate the worth and risk of being my disciple.

DC: They faced the similar questions you faced when John the Baptist was killed.

JC: Everything comes into focus when your life is at risk.

DC: It is not fun and games.

JC: It is serious and deadly business.

DC: I see your resurrection appearance to Peter as described in the Gospel of John (JN 21:15-25) differently today than when I was young man. Then I took it at face value, but today, now that I am older and a little wiser, I sense Peter was profoundly riddled by shame and guilt and crippled by fear.

JC: He was.

DC: He probably thought he would suffer a similar fate as you and didn't want it. I can imagine that he examined your commitment to your ministry and compared it with his lack of faith; as he compared himself to you he saw inadequacy and weakness.

JC: He felt a tangible and dreadful fear. He recognized his deplorable actions leading up to my death and he found the entire lot irreconcilable and overwhelmingly troubling. He fell into a pool of self-loathing.

DC: In time, Peter set aside his burning emotions and overcame his shame. When he did he was transformed.

JC: The full extent of his transformation happened when his heart opened, when he finally felt and knew the depth and truth of my ministry. He had forgiven himself, swallowed his guilt and shame and stepped forward to meet the uncertainty and ambiguity of the Father.

DC: I imagine he was flooded by memories of you and the time you spent together. When he remembered your teachings and ministry he was encouraged and his confidence grew.

JC: He re-examined everything in his life and he re-evaluated the Father and my sacrifice.

DC: He too faced a similar choice as you: continue in the Father and Jesus and step into the unknown or go back to the Galilee and fish.

JC: When he processed all of my life and ministry, and absorbed them in his heart and reconciled them in his mind, his transformation was complete. He died to himself and started his ministry.

DC: It didn't occur while he ministered?

JC: The process of transformation continues while on ministry. Confidence, knowledge and wisdom build, but the initial event that removes or minimizes doubt and fear and provides clarity happens beforehand. Peter was transformed as I was transformed, and he did what I did: attempt to change the world by changing one life at a time. He started with himself.

DC: Did your wisdom and ministry affect each disciple the same way? Or did it affect them differently? Was Thomas' transformation more cerebral and intellectual? Or was his heart stirred?

JC: To answer, no two people are alike; each changes according to the grain of their character and personality. Also, no one can go out into the world and do something amazing without heart. A heart for the divine is like a burning fire. Without it, little can be accomplished. One needs passion. Some people are passionate, others mental. That is a strand in the divine fabric. Thomas doubted but his doubt is born from a different mother; it originated differently than Peter's.

DC: Tell me how Thomas' doubt was unique. What were his challenges? How did you try to neutralize his ingrained patterns?

JC: One can't break another's patterns or behavior; that kind of change happens inwardly either with an insight, an epiphany or some kind of divine experience.

DC: Do angels have to appear?

JC: You are being sarcastic again.

DC: Yes I am. My personal experience is that my patterns and behaviors changed for a variety of reasons. One is self-appraisal and reflection. Another is when the world pushes back unexpectedly. If it pushes back hard, the moment arrives for you to take things into account. For me, recognition and self-awareness was the first step of transformation.

JC: Quick transformation occurred for me with forgiveness, with the cessation of judgment and condemnation, with love and compassion, by eliminating preconceptions, and by applying wisdom.

DC: Your wisdom?

JC: Yes – forged in the crucible of the Father.

DC: All right. What did you offer Thomas?

JC: I offered him an assortment of gifts. First, I nourished his mind with the philosophy of the Father. I wouldn't acknowledge his doubt, and I wouldn't accept, as he did, that nothing could be done to help people. He couldn't see the miraculous. Second, he had a propensity to over-think a problem. He was in the habit of responding by doing nothing.

DC: He sat on his hands?

JC: I pushed him to act and do. Third, I encouraged him to find the path to his heart. He had to feel and to love.

DC: You provided him a "first cause" shove.

JC: You can say that.

DC: I've learned an open heart expands in two directions simultaneously – inward and outward.

JC: Thomas did not fully connect to traditional Jewish thinking even though he was Jewish. His mind leaned toward the Greeks and Hellenism. He felt forced to accept societal issues – rites, practices, arguments and religion – for what they were, but his mind was sharp. He saw through that paradigm as did I. He enjoyed being with me because we had moments alone to discuss the philosophic nature of the Father. I opened him to the realm of the self. He sat at the table I set for him and ate everything I offered him. He had deep insights into the Father, the self, and the Kingdom of Heaven. Thomas is of the head – knowing, thinking and rationality – of philosophic doubt and of argument. I had to flip the tables on him and present the heart. He needed a dose of compassion and a dose of being alive in the body.

DC: Explain that last part to me. What do you mean to be "alive in the body?"

JC: Our body is the point of contact with the world, with others, and with oneself; it is the temple of the divine; it houses the heart and seats the mind. If all I have are questions I can't connect to the heart. If all I have is heart I can't fully connect to the mind. If all I have is a connection to the divine I will disconnect from humanity and myself. After all, I am human. The point is to feel and know all parts of life – the divine, the heart, the mind and the body. This point really sharpened for me during my desert experience. This is when my perception of the body came alive. I abused it to gain something else but I came back with a greater appreciation of its needs. I didn't mind pushing the body to its limits. I didn't mind feeling sore or feeling pain. In this sense, I was like a Greek athlete. I knew I was alive and each component was awake and kicking. I wanted to channel each wisely and use it to its maximum potential.

DC: Thomas was disconnected from his body. He wasn't a fisherman like Peter who was accustomed to being physical. Thomas was cerebral. His body got in the way. It must have been difficult for him because your ministry was physical. You walked from village to village or town to town in the heat and the cold. After a while that wears you down. He probably didn't appreciate the physicality let alone your message of love and compassion. Both must have challenged him.

JC: They did. I tried to address each disciple in a manner suited to their need. I have to emphasize, however, that the ministry was challenging in every manner for every person. We went without. We did not always eat. Our mouths were parched. Our feet ached. We did not always have a roof over our heads. We were exposed to the elements. Danger lurked on the roads due to bandits, highwaymen, wild animals and Roman soldiers. We were not always welcome in the towns or villages we visited. We were harassed and confronted. We fled. We did not have the comfort or safety of home. In this regard, each of us faced the same predicament. It was grueling. It was also exciting.

DC: Was there anything unique to Thomas' character or personality that you confronted or addressed. What blocked him? What couldn't he see or appreciate?

JC: Thomas' intelligence and intransigence blinded him to his own narrow-mindedness. He thought he was free because he could think and see. He couldn't have been more wrong.

DC: When I ponder Thomas' predicament I can't help but think that you presented this dilemma to him. You would tell him something profound or something simple and he would reply, "I don't know if that is true, I have to see it to believe it. When it is shown to me then I'll know whether to believe it or not." Thomas' pessimism plagued him. He probably felt everything was fraudulent.

JC: Thomas' preconceptions influenced how and what he saw, which in turn influenced what he did.

DC: That is a disease common to all of us. You said it eloquently: "Can the blind lead the blind? (LK 6:39)

JC: He called my miracles unreal and invalidated the supernatural. He was prone to dismiss and minimize my ministry, and discount what his eyes saw.

DC: You had the ability to see the magic and mystery in everything. The greatest mystery is love. Thomas could not, yet you challenged him and that must have either intrigued him or irritated him.

JC: I would say both. He waited for the day to come when his propensity to doubt would change. He wanted to experience the Father as I knew him but, try as he might, he could not. His disappointment festered. He was willing, but throughout my ministry he was incredulous, disappointed, and mistaken. When I went to Lazarus at the behest of Mary, Lazarus' sister, "… Thomas said to the rest of the disciples, 'Let us also go, that we may die with him.'" (JN 11:16)

DC: One does not always put one's best foot forward. You knew there was more in the world. You could see reality for what it was instead of having an opinion about it. You intimately knew what it meant to live the life of the Father and to live the Kingdom of Heaven. That was the primary difference between you and the disciples.

JC: Thomas' mind was filled with words such as "I have to feel it and see it to know it." (see JN 20:24-25)

DC: His disappointment turned into resentment. He needed physical connection. He required his hands to be placed on something to feel its density. He was confused. He didn't know how to merge the heart with the mind, which is what you did so well. He needed to personally confront and validate; that trait was distinct from analysis, at which he was clever.

JC: He couldn't embrace the grimy – the down and dirty – nature of the ministry. People needed help. They were sick and needed healing. They were hungry and needed food. They thirsted for knowledge and I offered wisdom. I addressed and provided physical and spiritual needs. It was important to sacrifice the violence in the heart and make it an acceptable offering to the divine through the operations of compassion, forgiveness, mercy, peace, gentleness and love.

DC: You felt compassion, you saw people as lost sheep without a shepherd, and you filled that void as a shepherd.

JC: I felt the anguish in their hearts and the confusion in their minds. People tried to be respectable Jews, but when a religion is under siege it struggles to provide for the most basic of physical and spiritual requirements. Philosophy at this level has no power to mend the brokenhearted, to offer hope, or to feed the hungry. Thomas couldn't see that, but he could understand abstract reality; he just couldn't experience it.

DC: Did you send him out with the other disciples two by two?

JC: If one wanted to be my disciple that part of my ministry was a requirement. I gave everyone the same set of instructions. He did it but he could not embrace it. His heart was not in it.

DC: He was just going along for the ride. I see a character type in him when he says, "Lord, we don't know where you are going, so how can we know the way?" (JN 14:5) He's confused and puzzled. He's not sure. He wants everything spelled out. And when it is it is still not enough.

JC: The heart and mind work in conjunction. Together they produce faith to do something and it shapes the attitude that "something" can be done. Thomas was heartless, others were fearful, but all were weak in faith. Thomas was not altogether fearful, he just happened to be of the mind rather than of the body.

DC: The day arrived when that changed.

JC: His doubt turned to anger, which after my death turned to understanding; my words finally grabbed hold of him. Then he set out on his ministry.

DC: The Gospel of Thomas is attributed to him. It is a very different gospel from the canonical gospels in that it does not tell a story; it does not have a narrative structure; it does not have the traditional motifs of virgin birth, John the Baptist, or miracles. Nor does it speak of your death, resurrection, and ascension, though it does mention a number of your disciples, your brother James and Mary Magdalene. It is very cerebral, which is consistent with

Thomas' mind. It doesn't embrace the messiness of life and being with people. In spite of the differences you are at the heart of it with one hundred and fourteen enigmatic sayings just as you are at the heart of the canonical gospels.

JC: Of all the disciples, he had experiential knowledge of the Father and of the self. It was a brand of wisdom I rarely shared unless someone was absolutely capable and ready. He could grasp and understand this hidden knowledge.

DC: He doesn't seem to embrace the meaning of your death as did the other disciples. Resurrection is not a concept found in his gospel. In fact, the Gospel of John actually turns him into Doubting Thomas just for that reason – he doesn't believe in resurrection.

JC: Thomas preserved another facet of my ministry; it was a small facet but it was a facet nonetheless. Faith is not believing or worshiping in the concept of God. He knew otherwise. He had a direct experience of the divine.

DC: A near-death experience?

JC: No. Enlightenment!

DC: This is different than your message.

JC: Not necessarily. The Father is closer to enlightenment than the Jewish jealous Creator God. This was a source of confusion and why I spoke of the Kingdom of God in the manner I did. The Father is not about holiness or righteousness. Neither is the Kingdom of God. I was routinely misunderstood on this point. The Kingdom of God is about divine mystery, emptiness and the energy of life. It is divine energy flowing through and merging with creation without separation or distinction. Thomas kept that knowledge intact.

DC: The Gospel of John explores this deeper mystery and explores a deeper spirituality, but in the end it personifies you as the divine mystery.

JC: John depicted me as "the way and the truth and the life," (JN 14:6) along with "the Word became flesh." (JN 1:14)

DC: He portrayed you in a divine light which, I believe, you would not accept. I appreciate the reason for John's point of view and its necessity but I do not agree with John because his perspective overstates your divinity and downgrades your humanity. I take exception to this Christian formula. They regularly use exaggeration on one hand and minimization on the other. Either divinity is everywhere, is in all things, animates all things and provides everything with the breath of life or it does not. You are not the exception; you are not the only begotten one. Either we are all begotten or no one is.

JC: Can't you imagine something between those opposite poles? Can one, through an active participation with the divine, be transformed and achieve divinity?

DC: That is a Gnostic concept and it argues that inside each person is a napping divine spark waiting to be awakened by God's kiss. When received, the person awakens as a foreigner in a foreign land whose sole purpose in life is to journey back to God. I don't disagree with the awaken state. Simply, I know we already exist in and are of the divine; there is no going anywhere since we are already in it and it is us.

JC: I like the way you think.

DC: I'd like to move on and discuss your most controversial disciple – Judas Iscariot. He is enigmatic, infamous and the most vilified of your disciples for selling you for thirty pieces of silver. (MT 26:15) His betrayal gravely affected your life and the evolution of your ministry. Oddly, John's gospel account doesn't have him selling you for money or betraying you with a kiss in the Garden of Gethsemane. (JN 18:5)

JC: Hmmm!

DC: I gather Judas didn't fully appreciate the intent or meaning of the parable of the talent. (MT 25:14-28) Apparently he misapplied it, taking blood money and investing it unwisely.

JC: You're being facetious again.

DC: It's a hard habit to break, especially when I see such blatant irony and glaring inconsistencies. What can you share about Judas? Sometimes I wonder if he were a spy or an agent for the High Priest.

JC: Let me start by talking about agents and spies. The Romans, our powerful religious institutions and Herod had them. The authorities wanted to know what a person or group was doing at all times. Groups were infiltrated and any prophet, messiah or alternative leader was under suspicion and watched.

DC: It was a volatile time and the authorities didn't want to be surprised. The canonical gospels recount that the Jewish religious and political authorities questioned you. Did the Roman's ever question you?

JC: I was warned.

DC: That shouldn't surprise me. I wonder if the Roman centurion whose servant you healed warned you. (MT 8:5-13)

JC: The Romans knew of me and news about me spread into their camps. They watched from afar and concluded I was neither an immediate threat nor was I plotting a revolt or insurrection.

DC: I would imagine any group that questioned the status quo would be considered a threat.

JC: The Romans wanted peace and taxes. I was not a threat to them in that regard. At the same time they didn't want to intervene in each inter-Jewish rivalry.

DC: Yet groups and people sought alternatives to counter the regrettable and entrenched conditions.

JC: Some were disgruntled by the existing Hasmonean royal dynasty, others felt they were the rightful heirs to the Temple priest lineage, and still others wanted to revolt against Roman occupation and taxation.

DC: This situation is remarkable given the fact that people were motivated to identify with something new or look for a savior.

JC: We were under stress, which we've already spoken about.

DC: I'd like to discuss your screening method, given that spies were prevalent. Did you screen your disciples? Did you try to determine who was with you or who was against you?

JC: I knew it was possible for my ministry to be infiltrated, but I was not willing to vet or interview anyone. I saw the divine potential in every person. I also had a built-in test to determine one's loyalty: one had to do everything I did. Hardship was the norm. We didn't have a roof over our heads. We didn't always have food to eat, money was in short supply and we went without.

DC: As mentioned earlier. What inspired you, given these hardships?

JC: I was delighted in the small effects because I offered an antidote from the ravages of guilt, shame and sin. I saw people come alive. I saw a new light in people's eyes. I saw a frown turn into a smile, worry turn into hope, and agitation turn into peace. I felt burdens lifted, hearts relieved and minds cleared. When people gave money to the ministry I saw the hand of God giving back to me. When I was given food, I experienced the love of the Father. As I ministered everyone had the opportunity to experience these things. One has to have eyes to see it and an open heart to feel it.

DC: What can you tell me about Judas in this regard? Did he have eyes to see, a heart to feel or ears to hear?

JC: He was shortsighted, struggled with commitment and didn't appreciate my intentions. He saw money wasted when Lazarus' sister Mary poured perfume on me. He couldn't welcome her gesture when she wiped my feet with her hair. (LK 7:37-38, JN 11:2) But he wasn't the only one. (MK 14:4)

DC: Yet he saw it as empty and pointless. He failed to see the outpouring of love. Mary's act of faith was a healing and restorative agent. In a divine way, her devotion re-established her heart in God.

JC: Faith has many hands and feet. It is not about belief, although conviction is wrapped within it. Faith is active, in motion and dynamic. It is an interaction between the heart, the mind, the physical world and the Father.

DC: Your ministry was an act of faith. You went out and did something. You believed and were convinced it was possible. The more you did the more your faith moved the proverbial mountain. The Our Father prayer details the manner in which you conducted your ministry and reveals the character of your faith in action.

JC: That prayer was my guiding light. As I sacrificed my life to the Father, I knew my needs would be satisfied. I had to overcome insults with love, and did not want to be led into temptation.

DC: I want to point out the finer detail of Mary's gesture. She poured perfumed oil on your feet and wiped it off with her hair.

JC: Yes.

DC: This exchange has two parts – her devoted gift and your serene response. She freely gave and you gladly received. This act is spirituality in motion operating like a circuit.

JC: She acted in love and I received in love. Each of us gave a divine gift to the other. She gave her expensive perfume and I received it without judgment. When our hearts connected, she was healed.

DC: Did Judas appreciate and understand this dynamic?

JC: This divine movement was misunderstood by everyone at the time. "Give, and it will be given to you. A good measure, pressed down, shaken together and running over, will be poured into your lap. For with the measure you use, it will be measured to you." (LK 6:38) They couldn't experience that truth even though I pointed it out many times. Peter questioned and tried to refuse me when I washed his feet during the Last Supper. He thought it undignified of me and resisted my attempt. (JN 13:5-8)

DC: In your ministry, the foot is a small repeating theme/motif. John the Baptist felt unworthy to untie your sandals and carry them. (MT 3:11, MK 1:7) Mary poured perfume on your feet and washed them with her hair. (JN 12:3) Your disciple's feet are ceremoniously washed by you during the Last Supper while Peter's response to your act is consistent with John the Baptist's - both aggressively declined and felt unworthy. (JN 13:5-17) Two incidents show compliance and two show resistance and discomfort. Though easily overlooked, the foot theme is charged with significance which makes me wonder if it was customary in your time to touch another's foot.

JC: No! But it had unspoken cultural connotations I wanted to address. The foot is the lowest and one of the dirtiest parts of the human body and bowing down or touching another's foot was a submissive act. It expressed the relationship "I am great and worthy, you are not and therefore you must submit to and obey me. Kiss my feet."

DC: How did you subvert this practice and infuse it with new meaning?

JC: We discussed Mary's perfume gesture previously and it was her way of acknowledging me and my ministry. She needed to pour expensive perfume on my feet for healing. Peter and John the Baptist recognized me and my authority but were overcome by the feelings of unworthiness, guilt and disqualification. In Peter's case, his reaction was inappropriate and revealed his obstinacy instead of his acquiescence.

DC: What about the Last Supper foot washing ceremony?

JC: This is where I flipped tables once again. I did not accept the prevailing attitude inherent in our society.

DC: Which was?

JC: That the ruler was invested with absolute authority and everyone else was subject to him. Observing this practice went against everything I knew about the Father and I saw no merit in this top-down relationship. My foot washing ceremony was a gentle sign of my willingness to submit to my disciples. The ceremony does not ask any of them to acknowledge and to honor me. Rather it conveys that I am no better, stronger, or elevated than any of them and that I recognize, respect and see each for who they are. I had the eyes of the Father and I knew He loved everyone equally and unconditionally. The intention of the ceremony was to flatten the ego, minimize self-grandeur and reduce pride. It reversed the cultural norm by saying, "in order to be great, one must serve another."

DC: This is a difficult lesson to live by.

JC: It is but I did it.

DC: If you don't mind, I'd like to get back to Judas.

JC: We are speaking about ideas he, along with many others, failed to see.

DC: Then why did you make him the treasurer? That position holds a unique responsibility. (JN 12:6, JN 13:29)

JC: That was my gift to him, and the position embodied the manner of his salvation and growth. Again, he failed to see it as such.

DC: He was also a thief who stole from the purse. (JN 12:4-6) The lack of sympathy toward Mary and his stealing was characteristic of him and demonstrates his dismissive and backhanded attitude toward your ministry.

JC: Judas was a thief. I knew he occasionally dipped his hands in the money bag. He was dishonest and took advantage of his position. He couldn't allow the Father to provide him with his needs.

DC: What did you want him to learn as treasurer? How was it a gift?

JC: I gave him an important position and felt he needed to own that position and be responsible for it. I wanted him to accept and administer it and by doing so contribute to the whole of the ministry.

DC: In general, the Romans were known for taking money by dipping into the Temple treasury. They were considered unclean Gentiles, so the act of stealing sacred money was sacrilegious and potentially upsetting.

JC: It was.

DC: Did you think the money given to you on your ministry was sacred money?

JC: I considered it necessary to conduct the ministry. I knew its purpose and intention.

DC: Since you knew Judas was a thief, why didn't you confront him on it?

JC: This part of my ministry is overlooked. I wanted people to see their faults and shortcomings on their own terms. More is gained when they see it for themselves. I thought Judas would be able to see himself in light of me, to see the contrast and draw his own conclusion. I wanted him to see his lack of compassion, to turn from his thievery and make lasting change on his own. I was his mirror.

DC: But he didn't; at least not until the end. Judas is plagued by his halfhearted commitment and his dark personality.

JC: He was passionate, complicated, impatient and impulsive. He needed to belong and be surrounded with like-minded people who were dedicated to a mission. At first, my ministry conformed to his ideal, but he was naturally uncomfortable with my ideas and efforts to address the conflicts of the heart, the pain of poverty and the hopelessness of hate, which he considered beneath him. He soon lost interest. He couldn't see or embrace the necessity of healing or the quiet change of internal hope and restoration. These were foreign to him. Instead, he was enamored by enormous political and religious structural change.

DC: Judas' commitment to your ministry near the end might have been halfhearted, but his betrayal and suicide were not; they were wholehearted. Many disciples were emotional and headstrong rather than calm and clear.

JC: The allure of political and religious success enamored them more than the persistent and quiet engagement of the ministry; even up to the very end of my life. (LK 22:24-25) Judas was no exception. Like our ancestors wandering forty years in the desert, Judas grew weary. He grumbled, complained, and became frustrated and tired.

DC: You practically made it mandatory to cultivate the way of the heart and the presence of the Father.

JC: One had to learn patience and couldn't react impulsively. My ministry was a systematic engagement of liberation – liberation from the normal needs and demands of the ego and body.

DC: You desired humility and a life filled with the Father. Your Beatitudes speak of this as does your saying, "Consider how the wild flowers grow. They do not labor or spin." (LK 12:27) Another states, "Don't be blinded by the pursuit of food, clothing, and possessions. Only those who lack spirit and soul pursue them." (Q53)

JC: Judas lacked eyes to see the seeds we planted or the small shoots growing in people's hearts. He was quick to judge and he couldn't experience the renewed mind; he couldn't see the delicate effects of spiritual nourishment or the softer workings of the Father. He wanted power, big results and dramatic bloody events. He wanted a powerful sect where his ego could shine, where he could bark a command and jab a stiff finger in somebody's chest and feel important. My ministry did not allow him that comfort. My striking miracles were not enough to satisfy his power-driven cravings.

DC: Yet he responded to your call to follow you.

JC: He heard the news about me and saw a glimmer of hope with the ministry. He was devoted to Israel's restoration.

DC: He thought you and your ministry would overthrow the corrupt institutions and expel the Romans from Judea. He wanted to be close to the change, so he invested in you knowing he would have a place in your new regime after Israel was restored.

JC: That was the allure. Unfortunately, the reality was different than his imagination, and after a while his heart grew weary and he sought revenge for the wrong he thought I perpetrated against him. His loyalties were closer in alignment to the Sacarii than to me.

DC: Did he feel you misled him?

JC: He did. He felt his time and efforts were wasted. When we entered Jerusalem for Passover his mind and heart had already turned. He knew what he wanted to do. The straw that broke the camel's back occurred with Mary's perfume incident. (MK 14:3-11) I could see it in his demeanor; it radiated in his spirit. He was resentful.

DC: He became an agent for the chief priest and he betrayed you for thirty pieces of silver.

JC: At the time, there was no bounty on me. I was a nuisance. I questioned Jewish sacred history and practice. I was not well received by the authorities and they threatened my life, but there was no bounty on my head. But Judas felt thirty pieces of silver was the measure owed him for the wrong he felt I committed against him.

DC: "The measure used is the measure used on you." He misapplied this piece of wisdom.

JC: He was incapable of overcoming his pettiness and jealousy.

DC: Judas couldn't appreciate the consequences of his actions.

JC: That is correct. He was blind, overly emotional and prone to violence. He plunged down the path of violence and was filled with an uncontrollable zeal for revenge.

DC: He "went to the chief priests and the officers of the temple guard and discussed with them how he might betray" you. (LK 22:4) His decision was resolute, willful, unwavering and angry.

JC: Afterward he understood the extent of his action and knew he committed a grievous mistake.

DC: When he realized you were "condemned, he was seized with remorse and returned the thirty silver coins to the chief priests and the elders. 'I have sinned,' he said, 'for I have betrayed innocent blood.'" (MT 27:3-4)

JC: The irony is that Judas had a secret desire to make his mark in history and thought one swift and bold act would make a difference. It didn't cross his mind that the darkness in his heart would usher in the new age and that the violent revolution he wanted would be directed at me in my bloody flogging and crucifixion. He couldn't live with himself when he realized that occurred.

DC: He reacted impulsively and violently and failed to appreciate that your message of forgiveness and compassion extended to him in his black moment. You offered the path of nonviolence and internal renewal.

JC: He felt his only choice was to commit suicide. He learned nothing from me.

DC: Something is out of place with Judas' suicide account.

JC: How so?

DC: The Book of Acts states, "Judas bought a field; there he fell headlong, his body burst open and all his intestines spilled out. Everyone in Jerusalem heard about this, so they called that field in their language Akeldama, that is, Field of Blood." (Acts 1:18-19) Why would a person buy a field to kill himself? The transaction alone would take days if not weeks. Also, how does one fall down and his body burst open so that his intestines fall out? Did he fall from a very high cliff or tower? The force of a natural fall can't produce the aforementioned result. The circumstances in the Gospel of Matthew are completely different. Apparently, after accepting the money, turning you over to the chief priest and Temple guards and then realizing his deplorable action, Judas went back to the chief priests and elders to return the money. But they wouldn't accept it. He "threw the money into the Temple and left. Then he went away and hanged himself. The chief priests picked up the coins and said, 'It is against the law to put this into the treasury, since it is blood money.' So they decided to use the money to buy the potter's field as a burial place for foreigners. That is why it has been called the Field of Blood to this day." (MT 27:5-8) Two different parties buy the field, two opposing reasons are given for naming the field, even though the name remains the same, and Judas commits suicide in two entirely different manners. These discrepancies are astonishing given the fact that Judas was one of the twelve disciples and of your inner circle. Why couldn't the New Testament writers get this right? Aside from these anomalies, it is hard to reconcile the fact that the chief priests couldn't accept blood money for the treasury when sacrifices to Rome persisted and Pontius Pilate took money from it regularly. These stories don't add up. They also seem hypocritical and suggest, in the case of the priests and elders, a case of situational ethics.

JC: If I may suggest, Judas has many faces and many followers. It is a sad commentary for anyone who betrays themselves, their closest friends, their family and loved ones, or their ideals and God over a dispute, grievance or discrepancy. I was betrayed more than once. Many came to me, received something and left giving me nothing in return. Others accused me of crimes I did not commit or of making statements I did not say. Others who walked with me and left the ministry came back, but I could not receive them into the fold again for one reason or another. I'll leave it at that.

DC: I understand. I have one more disciple I'd like to discuss. She was one of the "women of means" and another controversial figure. I'm speaking of Mary Magdalene. What can you tell me about her?

JC: Why is Mary Magdalene controversial?

DC: Her role in your ministry doesn't coincide with traditional Jewish culture, and ambiguity about her role and function within your ministry persists.

JC: Mary's conviction matched her aspirations. Her mind was filled with ideas, her heart with hope, and her soul with purpose. From the outset and to the bitter end she was passionate, loyal and dedicated to me and my ministry.

DC: Did you consider her a disciple?

JC: I did.

DC: Mary is sprinkled throughout the New Testament gospels but there is some confusion about whether the gospels are talking about her or another Mary. Is that deliberate? Mary's portrait is sketchy at best. The gospels state she watched your crucifixion, is the first person to see the empty tomb, and is present during your after-death appearances. Other information about Mary Magdalene comes from the Gospel of Thomas, the Gospel of Mary and the Gospel of Philip. In the Gospel of Thomas, you tell her secret information, which makes the other disciples jealous. In the Gospel of Philip your disciples question you about your love for her, since it is more than you have for them and you kiss her on some undefined location. Is it on her lips, face or hands? That piece of information is missing. I'd like to know what role she played in your ministry.

JC: I consider her, along with other women, full disciples. All of them supported me in some capacity during my ministry.

DC: How did they serve your ministry?

JC: My disciples and followers traveled, ministered, ate and told stories together. The women listened to and applied my teachings; they witnessed my miracles and some even performed their own. I believed in the equality of women and that they should be treated with the same respect and honor as the men.

DC: Did you send them out two by two?

JC: No. There were limits that were reasonable. I had vision; I wasn't foolish.

DC: I bring this up because a legend records that the Apostle Paul traveled with a female companion named Thecla. Also, historical sources record the magician Simon Magus, possibly born in a Samarian village, traveled with his wife, whose name I believe was Sophia or Helena. I'd like to quote from Paul: "Do we not have the right to take a believing wife along with us, as do the other apostles and the Lord's brothers and Cephas?" (1 Corinthians 9:5) Hebrew culture consigned women domestically to stay at home, tend to the needs of the family, wash clothes, prepare meals and be midwives, but your example and the examples mentioned above show this was not always the case.

JC: My female disciples substituted the role of child rearing and tending to the family for my ministry. Not completely but generally.

DC: Many times you used the phrases "eyes to see" and "ears to hear."

JC: They had both, at times more so than the men.

DC: Did the women in the various towns and villages come to you directly or did they first approach your female disciples?

JC: Interaction between men and women was governed by unwritten rules of etiquette and customs. A woman was not supposed to approach a man, but some were brave and sought healing or bread from me. If a woman wanted clarity or advice they approached my female disciples first, who then presented them to me.

DC: Your ministry embodied a feminine element. It was nurturing and loving as a mother. It cared. It healed and taught by example.

JC: Other sects within my society lacked a strong female component. I felt compelled to include women and allowed them a greater role than was otherwise appropriate for our society. That was another facet of my vision – inclusion. I saw women and men equal in the eyes of the Father. One was not greater than another, but equal.

DC: How did the men respond?

JC: It was mixed. Some felt I set a table, cooked a bittersweet meal and served it to them but they would not eat. Others were more responsive and accepting.

DC: What about Peter?

JC: Peter grumbled at first, came around grudgingly with a halfhearted acceptance, but later rejected Mary's role and her contribution. The two fought. Many men were incapable of holding the heart of my vision. One primary lesson I taught was service to each other, not who was the greatest, who had authority or who was my successor. Service to others in relation to women was not fully accepted or continued because they were not seen or accepted as equals.

DC: It was customary to exclude deep and profound teachings from women because this, too, was the province of men. You thought differently. Examples exist that you confided in Mary. I say this because extra-biblical texts and gospels make this assertion. It is seen in the Gospel of Philip, Gospel of Mary, Gospel of Thomas, The Dialogue of the Savior, and Pistis Sophia. Did you tell Mary secrets that you did not tell your male disciples?

JC: I confided in her. Why shouldn't I? She was more capable than most of the men. I'm hard pressed to understand the purpose of these questions.

DC: Mary Magdalene entered our mainstream popular culture with an international bestselling book which was turned into a blockbuster movie. Afterward a Mary Magdalene niche industry developed, and the market was flooded with documentaries, television shows and books. Even an ancient manuscript titled The Gospel of Mary was recently discovered. Mary's popularity and notoriety drives these questions, and this isn't the first time. Her mystique stretches back to your ministry and runs straight through the first and into the fourth century. Disciples, apostles, Gnostics, mystics, saints, monks, Church Fathers, Popes and theologians were swayed, either negatively or positively, by her.

JC: I didn't have such speculative fascination because another fire drove me.

DC: Sometime after your crucifixion your disciples continued the ministry. New voices and opinions entered the dialogue, as did historical changes and events, and the ministry took on a life of its own. Your message and vision were readdressed and honed to meet a new shifting landscape, and this proved complicated to manage and control. Real people, with real needs and real opinions had real influence. I'm reminded of the German philosopher Georg Wilhelm Friedrich Hegel's thesis, antithesis and synthesis equation. There is a thesis which moves out. Its antithesis enters the frame. The two sides don't exist in isolation and they develop a dialogue that forces them to mix together and form a new synthesis. I see this working in this case. I also see Mary's importance and influence whitewashed, minimized and written out of the historical record because of this new synthesis.

JC: Maybe I shouldn't be surprised by this.

DC: Why?

JC: I tried to change the direction of my culture. I tried to change its heart and vision. I tried to change the manner in which it operates and knows itself. I tried to point to the Father. I tried to change the content of people's character. All of this required effort and willpower, both for me and my followers. I taught them to see what I saw. I wanted them to embrace the vision of wisdom and compassion and carry the torch. I showed them the way. They had to be the change and take that change into the community. Some of my intentions succeeded, others did not; some things lay beyond the scope of their ability, some were not.

DC: In regards to women's equality, I think the change didn't last long and reverted back to the patriarchal starting point.

JC: I was afraid of that.

DC: Inferences and whispers suggest Mary's role in your ministry was more than a disciple. The Gospel of John states "the disciple whom he loved standing nearby." (JN 19:26) Historically this was interpreted to refer to the disciple John, son of Zebedee. Some recent scholarship points in another direction to Mary Magdalene. In any event, something strange transpired with her story. Her real relationship with you is obscured and her importance is minimized or deliberately expunged from the historical narrative. Why did Mary Magdalene follow you?

JC: She recognized the purpose of the ministry and knew its importance.

DC: What was she like?

JC: She was fearless and bold; she knew the risks yet followed nonetheless and she did what she had to do without asking or needing direction. She was naturally inclined, free from doubt, and treated the ministry as a mother cares for her child. This was more than the men who consistently asked inconsequential questions, failed to appreciate the nature of the ministry, did not know what to do, and repeatedly needed direct and specific guidance. They were slow in that respect. She was not.

DC: What is her background?

JC: She was a "Jewish woman from the city of Migdala." (*The Gospels of Mary*, p. ix)

DC: Where is Migdala?

JC: On "western shore of the Sea of Galilee" and it "was well known for fishing and fish salting." (*The Gospels of Mary*, p. ix)

DC: As I understand, "salted fish" was a Roman staple. It was as common in your day as pizza is for us today, and that makes that industry highly lucrative. Putting two and two together, it seems to me that as a "woman of means" Mary and her family could have been merchants and involved with the salted fish industry.

JC: One could draw that conclusion.

DC: Where does Magdalene come from?

JC: It was the nickname I gave her.

DC: How did you two meet?

JC: What I'm about to share was concealed and buried. Mary and I knew each other as children. We were close childhood friends and grew up together. As we grew older our love for each other grew stronger. (See *The Book of Heaven for a Brand New Day*, p. 233)

DC: Was Mary born into a well-to-do family?

JC: We shared that in common.

DC: What else did you share in common?

JC: A strong sense of the divine. We were also frustrated by our society and the manner by which, in our eyes, it unraveled.

DC: Did you do anything together?

JC: We sailed on the lake.

DC: Tell me about that.

JC: We felt particularly free while sailing. When the wind was still we basked in the silence; when it blew, we delighted in the thrill of the moment. We laughed, played and had fun. We were content; we could forget the world and be ourselves. We didn't have to live according to our families' expectations. We could just be because nothing else mattered.

DC: Is there anything else you can tell me about her?

JC: She had beautiful dark brown eyes and they were filled with wisdom and love for me. When she looked at me I felt the love of God. I felt her love. It was unique.

DC: She loved you?

JC: She did and I loved her. My heart quickened at her gaze. Her passion consumed me. Our love for each other was rare; I considered it a gift from God. It reminded me of King Solomon's Song of Songs. We noticed that other couples could not match the kind of love we had for each other. We loved being around each other. At times we couldn't be separated.

DC: I have to catch my breath.

JC: I want to reveal this part of my life that has been hidden.

DC: I have to ask, were you married? Was Mary your wife?

JC: What do you think? That is more important than my actual marital status. Remember, the path of the heart is critical. Understand that the heart is a source of wisdom which originates with the divine, and returns back to the divine. It goes from here to there and back again.

DC: It loops around like a circuit.

JC: This was the mystery I came to realize and became the essence of my teaching. Mary had a significant role to play in my development.

DC: It was a powerful lesson.

JC: Follow the path from the personal to the divine. Ponder on that for a moment. Now ask yourself, "What does David gain by understanding Jesus' marital status?" Ask yourself that. What will it do for you?

DC: All right. I like history. You are an extremely important world figure. You helped shape the Western world. People want to know what you did and who you are. At least I think they do. I know I want to know your history and your motivations, and the more details I know the sharper the picture becomes. You were shaped by many forces. Your marriage is an autobiographical detail that was missing and now fills a gap in your biography. The implications are enormous. Let me work through this and accept the position you were married to Mary Magdalene.

JC: Let's assume I was married. What are the implications?

DC: Initially, I'd have to say that the Son of God position comes into question.

JC: Why does that come into question?

DC: The Apostle Paul says you were the Second Adam, redeemer of the world who was without sin, and an unblemished lamb acceptable to God. If you were married, then you weren't pure; you had sexual relations. Paul's theology unravels with your marriage; that is one lynchpin.

JC: Go on.

DC: And the theological nature of your divine status unravels and collapses like a house of cards.

JC: If that is the case then the concluding answer is that Paul's theology is inherently flawed.

DC: All of Paul's pieces have to line up in proper sequence. For you to be a God you could not be married; marriage implies sexual relations. For you to be a pure sacrificial lamb you could not be blemished. For you to take away all the sins of mankind you had to be divine and could not know sin; sin is foreign to the holiness and purity of God. For you to accomplish such a divine act you had to transcend your humanity, and according to Christian theology you did just that. You could not be of this world but you had to be in it to accomplish that single most defining act of God – the removal of the barrier that separates God from man. Someone or something had to pay the price of debt.

JC: Do you really imagine my life was as simple as Paul's logic?

DC: No I do not.

JC: I was not interested in that kind of symbolism or theological logic. It was too abstract and inconsequential for the task at hand. It was important to me to join together the heart of the divine with the heart of man. I wanted my wisdom to shed light on that relationship. As I have said before and I'll say again: my ministry was about the heart and not about holiness or righteousness. I never used those terms. I was opposed to them for various reasons as we already discussed.

DC: Let's get back on point.

JC: If Mary and I were married what did I have to go through during my ministry? Likewise, what did she have to go through?

DC: Okay! Let me work through Mary's dilemma. It raises questions about her reaction throughout the course of your ministry; from the beginning, through the middle, and to the end. Before I start let's take a step backward.

JC: If that helps.

DC: You started your ministry of the Father because you were compelled.

JC: I "began to hear the Father's roar" in my ear. (*The Book of Heaven for a Brand New Day*, pp. 209, 227) The Father beat in my heart and it wouldn't stop. I couldn't sleep; I was restless and without peace. I had to do something. The only way to keep from losing my sanity was to conduct my ministry.

DC: You must have talked with her about the Father and your vision of his kingdom.

JC: We had many discussions. From the beginning, she was informed of my religious understandings and experiences. I was open with her; I never kept secrets from her. She was the first to know of my NDE and she was the first to know of the Father. She knew every intimate detail of my transformation. I would tell her. But Mary was smart and observant and she could see things happening to me. She could see something new in my eye. She could see something new in the way I stood, in the way I talked and in the way I acted.

DC: How did she react?

JC: When it came to the Father and immortality it was difficult for her to understand, at least in the beginning. When I spoke of the heart she had an instinctive appreciation. Since our marriage was rooted in love she understood the concept that love could radiate out to everyone. It's also important to remember that each of us was raised in a devout family. I was saying something new and contradictory about Judaism. She was intrigued and stunned by my insights, but the conviction in my voice convinced her of the truth. She knew I wasn't imagining things.

DC: How did she respond to your decision to leave and conduct your ministry? I guess I could also ask: if you loved her as passionately as you say, then why would you leave her?

JC: The answer is obvious. The desire was too strong. I knew I could not continue with my life in the manner in which it unfolded. I felt I had to do something. Previously I had stepped into the unknown and had numerous objectionable experiences, but I learned from them. I didn't want to repeat or carry them into my ministry.

DC: How did compassion affect your decision?

JC: I saw it universally. I didn't make the distinction of loving one more than the other. My heart was open; it was just love – love of me, love of Mary, love of the Father, love of the stranger and love of my enemy. Love flowed in all directions. Because of this I felt the world needed a light because it was covered in a blanket of darkness.

DC: I would surmise you knew you would never be the same when you stepped away from your current life.

JC: I did.

DC: Mary must have been surprised and upset.

JC: I'll let you think this through. Go on.

DC: She was happy with her life and content to be your wife. She didn't want the disruption your ministry would cause. I'm trying to understand her anguish, trying to empathize with her. Her heart was broken. Yes. Her heart was broken. Just as Israel was a house divided so too was your house. Your family must have been concerned and divided as well.

JC: My decision cut through my entire family.

DC: She could see in your eyes that something had changed and that your demeanor had shifted. Maybe you paced in agitation and were moody. She knew she could not change your mind because you were set. Now is the moment of conflict. She must have been pulled in two directions – letting you go or putting her foot down and making you stay.

JC: Now you are seeing it. Continue.

DC: Oh! I'm having an epiphany. Now I see. Yes! She had a change of heart before your ministry and your disciples had it afterward. I should have seen that earlier. When she finally accepted her fate she probably made it conditional.

JC: On what?

DC: There were two conditions. First, you could not conduct your ministry from your home. She didn't want people over, which is partly the reason why you conducted it in another region of the country, and second, she would not be a part of it.

JC: Impressive!

DC: She changed her mind, however, and she joined you. Probably she couldn't be without you. She needed to see your face, and yearned for the caress of your hand and a kiss from your lips. She wanted to receive your gaze and know she was still the one for you. She wanted the warmth of your smile. She wanted to be by your side, and then everything would be fine. You were her world. She sensed danger and wanted to share that with you rather than be separated. She couldn't stand being apart. When John the Baptist was murdered, she feared for your life. When you were alone she pleaded with you to stop and come home, but you met that plea with the gentle caress of your hand as you wiped away the tears of sorrow streaming down her soft cheeks. The sound she heard flowing from your mouth was "shhhh," which was not reassuring, rather disheartening and not what she wanted to hear. She clutched you tighter, knowing the man she loved was fulfilling the purpose of his life and there was nothing she could say or do that was going to change your mind. She was ecstatic about the revelations of the Father but fearful you might be killed. It is the same unsettled feeling women have when their men go off to war. There is a certain inevitability.

JC: We were torn. The need to continue the ministry outweighed the demands of the marriage.

DC: Women came to you for healing, they touched you and you spoke with them. Mary, Lazarus' sister, wiped your feet with her hair and poured perfume on them, (JN 11:2) while another woman wept at your feet and her tears spilled on you. (LK 7:37-38) Was Mary jealous of the attention you received from other women?

JC: How would you respond if you were in love with me and witnessed these other women, both Jews and Gentiles, touching me and wanting my attention?

DC: She was jealous but learned to manage that emotion for the larger purpose.

JC: Mary was challenged by her fears and had to face them. We all did. She allowed herself, however, to be transformed so others could experience the love of the Father. I ministered to the needs of the downtrodden and dispossessed. My ministry was for them. I could do something for them, which I did. Unfortunately, what I did was not always what Mary wanted. But she went through a change. She learned to be more accepting and honest; it was beautiful to watch and it brought tears to my eyes.

DC: It is written that she was possessed by seven demons and that they were cast out of her by you.

JC: Mary's passionate and burning heart fueled the confrontational side of her nature. She challenged the disciples as much as I challenged the religious authorities, and she too was not afraid to speak her mind. This upset the disciples and made them uncomfortable. I assume this "demon motif" derives from that aspect of her personality.

DC: It was a deliberate smear against a confident and proud woman. I'm reminded of Queen Jezebel.

JC: Women who challenged social norms and expectations were not viewed kindly. To imagine she was demon possessed couldn't be further from the truth. If anything, her demons were sorrows, fears and a sad heart.

DC: Your disciples needed healing. Did Mary?

JC: Each had their own demons. Each was unique in that sense. Mary's healing, unfortunately, was recorded in the manner you speak of.

DC: She was demon possessed? That is a metaphor.

JC: Yes. When she overcame her demons, she was renewed and made more alive – more so than the men. She found the courage of a lion, the wisdom of Solomon, and the heart of God long before the men. They never found it and were cowards at the time of my death. She was not. That came later for them.

DC: On a slightly different note, this involves the argument during your time among the religious establishment regarding life after death. Did Mary appreciate immortality? Did she imagine life after death? Also, you experienced the living presence of the Father. He was alive, potent and active here on earth. Did she experience it also?

JC: Mary and I knew life was mysterious, that a part of us exists in the Father, and that life does not perish with the body but continues on. She came to know, as I came to know, the Father and his kingdom are active. One knows this truth by loving passionately, living compassionately and embracing wisdom. We also knew the other side of the Father and the Kingdom of Heaven as silence, and we experienced it through prayer and quiet meditation.

DC: I apologize for this beforehand. I feel I should ask, so please forgive me, but was Mary a harlot as written by Christians?

JC: I won't dignify that allegation with an answer.

DC. My deepest apologies. I'd like to move on. Again, empathizing with Mary and thinking of the end of your ministry, I can't imagine how she felt when you said you were going to Jerusalem for the Feast of Unleavened Bread. Terror must have gripped her. Was Jerusalem the heart of darkness for her?

JC: I like your heart of darkness metaphor. Mary learned to live with her fear. Even though she was courageous and her love and devotion were encouraging, she was scared and reluctant. I see the rain clouds are back and it started raining again. Before we continue, I'd like to go outside.

CHAPTER 10

LITERATURE AND THEOLOGY

JC: I just saw a hawk gliding overhead searching for prey.

DC: I heard its faint shrill. I'm enchanted by the birds nesting in the yard, the wild animals roaming the property, and lizards striding up to the glass sliding door peeking into the house. I'm captivated and soothed by the natural rhythms of the desert and feel connected to the expression of life. I receive blank stares from my friends living in the big city when I tell them about this; they fail understand the meaning of my words. Shall we continue?

JC: Yes.

DC: I'd like to conclude our conversation about Mary later in the interview, but for now, I'd like to switch subjects and explore Christian literature and theology. Do you mind?

JC: That's fine.

DC: I know these are sensitive subjects and potentially controversial, but any conversation involving you must also include Christian literature and theology. This is the place the world knows you or thinks it knows you and, as you know now, I find it difficult to find Jesus the man within this literary and theological context. For sure, a portion of your history exists within it but mostly it is shrouded in theology. Rather than seeing you, I see the reflected hopes, expectations and ideas of your followers. This discrepancy between you and them is starkly contrasted.

JC: What is on your mind?

DC: To begin, I question the veracity of the New Testament gospels, especially in regard to your final days and your decision to celebrate Passover in Jerusalem. I feel the historical accuracy and facts during this period are limited by the reservoir of theology.

JC: Why do you say that?

DC: Theology is presented as history. The Christian writers had an unwavering agenda in depicting you as the fulfillment of the Jewish End Time Messianic and Sacrificial Lamb prophecy. We touched on some of this earlier. It's difficult to see the chain of historical events and how your decisions affected them, because actual events are mixed together with Christian theology, Jewish Midrash and Jewish pharisaical interpretation. The New Testament writers wrote their literature and shaped their theology to make me, the reader and believer, see what they wanted me to see. They had definite goals in shaping your story and presenting you in a specific light. I see an intentional theologically driven bias rather than a historical one.

JC: Explain this further.

DC: A reasonable explanation of your life cannot be reconstructed and analyzed completely because the New Testament narrative is symbolic, metaphorical and theological. Your life, teachings, sayings and miracles get intermingled with the Son of God imagery and salvation theology. Your humanity is minimized while the symbolic and salvation message is maximized.

JC: Because of this you can't fully appreciate my motive to go to Jerusalem to celebrate the Feast of Unleavened Bread and Passover? Is that what you are asking?

DC: To answer that specifically, yes; I cannot determine your true motive to celebrate Passover before your crucifixion. I have to deduce from the only sources I have, which are the New Testament gospels. But generally, I'm pointing out that the Christian motive in telling your story and the conclusions they draw are manufactured, narrow and biased, making the truth hard to see. At every stage in your life they invent symbolism and metaphor and fail to portray you as a person living a life and making tough and grueling decisions. Now, I face a series of perplexing questions.

JC: Which are?

DC: Which events are accurate and true and which aren't? Are you portrayed accurately or approximately? What motivated you? What was your purpose to go to Jerusalem? What did you wish to accomplish with your sacrifice? What did death and its significance mean for you? Why does the Gospel of John depict Passover and your sacrifice a day earlier than when it should have occurred? How could the elders and priest see you after your arrest when they would have been preoccupied with the logistical details of the festival? I receive no accurate or truthful answer to any of these questions. Instead, I get a Christian, theologically driven answer.

JC: I lived a committed, truthful and honest life and conducted my ministry similarly. I did not want to propagate doubt or hypocrisy. I did not say one thing and then do another. My words, actions and deeds were consistent with my message and with the Father. I could not control what others thought or said about me because I had no way of controlling that.

DC: There is another issue that concerns me. The New Testament is regarded as the actual Word of God. This position is entrenched and hard to get around. The internal logic of the argument states "God can't lie." If God can't lie and the New Testament is the Word of God, then everything written in it is fact, historical and, therefore, true. I discovered the canonical gospels are not history; at least not in their entirety, and this undermines the God can't lie argument. Now, I have to wonder who's telling the truth and what truth is being told.

JC: Do you believe in the truth of the divine?

DC: I am convinced of a mysterious reality involving potential, substance and no-substance, and existence and nonexistence. Whatever it is, it is highly abstract and hard to see; we are interconnected and intertwined with it. People simply call it God.

JC: Can you know it?

DC: Because I am a part of it, I can know something of it, if only in a small portion.

JC: My people were convinced of the divine reality. I was convinced of it, even though I saw it differently than they. I was a storyteller as many other people were. The Jewish people believed one can glimpse and appreciate the divine through story and it is story and the truth of story that connect us together.

DC: You also knew something different.

JC: What was that?

DC: You knew you could live in the divine and you called this the Father. By living it, you knew something about it.

JC: My teachings point to and my life demonstrated that.

DC: That is how I understand it, but the gospels present a different story. The writers expect their audience to believe that you were the Sacrificial Lamb of God, and that you were the long-awaited Messiah whose salvation work as the Son of God redeems mankind from the ravages of sin.

JC: My life and teachings point to the truth of the Father. What you describe points to something else altogether.

DC: Christian theology and End Time prophecy assemble on one side of the ledger while the Kingdom of Heaven sayings, the Beatitudes, the parables and the Our Father prayer stand on the other. I concluded that many of your sayings are incongruent and inconsistent with and do not include the Son of God salvation theology.

JC: Let's step back for a moment. After examining the New Testament you drew new conclusions about Old Testament influences.

DC: I did.

JC: Explain them to me.

DC: The Gospel of Matthew has thirty-eight quotes to prove you fulfilled prophesy and that you were the Jewish Messiah. Several stories and incidents in the gospel narrative mimic the prophets Isaiah and Jonah, while the Apostle Paul – a trained Pharisee – quotes the Old Testament verse after verse in his letters to support his claim that you fulfilled Jewish law. Incidentally, he uses other nonscriptural sources.

JC: Which are?

DC: The *Book of Enoch* and the Egyptian *Book of the Dead*.

JC: I was familiar with the *Book of Enoch* and *The Wisdom of Solomon*.

DC: Paul, with missionary zeal and thinking himself the Christian Moses, traveled throughout the Roman Empire starting new churches and instituting a new moral code, all the while claiming you were the Messiah and the Son of God who was raised from the dead. But Paul was not the only one quoting scripture. Aside from the gospel writers, other New Testament writers were just as generous and liberal. Curiously, these men used different verses to advance their claims. For example, the Book of Hebrew presents you as a High Priest from the Melchizedek lineage.

JC: Melchizedek came from an ancient priestly caste.

DC: Also, the Gospels of Matthew and Luke present you as a king from the royal Davidic caste of kings.

JC: My followers tried to make sense of me any way they could. Jews were keepers of the genealogy and drew straight lines from the present to the past; this begets this, which begets that and so on. Christians used genealogy to connect me to the bloodline of King David.

DC: They exploited the plaque above your cross which stated you were "The King of the Jews." (MK 15:26) The Gospel of John said the chief priests protested to Pilate the error of this statement but Pilate dismissed them outright. (JN 19:21-22) The Gospel of Mark does not quote you saying, "I am the rightful King of the Jews," nor do your sayings suggest you were a king. Rather, you practiced humility and service. There is another title I find curious, one more elevated than King of the Jews.

JC: And that is?

DC: Christians assert you are the "King of Kings."

JC: King of Kings derives from the Persian King Cyrus. He is the only Gentile king the Jews considered anointed by God and as such was considered a messiah.

DC: He receives that title because he allowed the exiled Jews to leave Babylon, return to Israel, and rebuild the Temple of David. Incidentally, this initiates the Second Temple Period. In any event, Old Testament verses were collected, catalogued and presented to various communities to prove a particular point.

JC: Different verses were used to make particular assertions.

DC: Which tended to conflict with one another. The Christians tried to create a uniform theology and history but weren't always successful. They created inadvertent inconsistencies and conflicts. Later Christians realized the errors and attempted to remedy and smooth over the conflicts.

JC: From your perspective Christianity emerged from scripture rather than history, the bulk of my life is excluded from the accounts and substituted with theology and Paul and other writers of the New Testament were involved in this trend.

DC: That pretty much sums up what I believe. Again, that is not to suggest there is no historical accuracy but it is overshadowed by other factors. Paul's letters are the oldest existing Christian documents; maybe others exist but the world does not possess them. It is safe to assume he is the first Christian writer to quote avidly from the Old Testament and that he initiated the "quoting trend." Ironically, he never met you, he did not know you and he was antagonistic to your followers at first. He persecuted them and possibly killed them on orders from the Jewish religious establishment. He got to know you through a supernatural experience. It is said that you came to him in a powerful vision and spoke to him directly. The experience knocked him off his horse, blinded him, and flipped his life around; it was another one of those quick turn-around events I described earlier.

JC: From his account my alleged appearance started him on his path to ministry.

DC: His mystical experience redirected him off the path of persecution and onto a path of reconciliation, recognition and allegiance. Apparently, he went to one of your followers for help. After his eyesight returned and after many years of processing and digesting the meaning of his mystical experience, he went to your followers, including Peter and your brother James. Somewhere and somehow he learned the "Hymn of Christ." Perhaps it is the earliest piece of Christian writing, and he quotes it in his letter to the Philippians.

JC: I would like to quote it.

DC: You know it?

JC: I do. It states, "Who, being in the form of God, did not consider equality with God something to be used to his own advantage; rather he made himself nothing, taking the very nature of a servant, being made in human likeness. And being found in appearance as a man, he humbled himself and became obedient to death – even death on a cross! Therefore God exalted him to the highest place and gave him the name that is above every name, that at the name of Jesus every knee should bow, in heaven and on earth and under the earth and every tongue acknowledge that Jesus Christ is Lord, to the glory of God the Father." (Philippians 2:6-11)

DC: What is your response?

JC: I'm stunned by this hymn and I don't think I can formulate the correct words to respond. I'm flattered by the hymn's regard but it is unnecessary and counterproductive. It shows the importance of my ministry and my accomplishment, but I never thought of myself as so elevated nor did I conceive of myself in the manner that every knee should bow to me. That is foreign to my conception and to my desire to do something I felt necessary. At all times I tried to downplay my personal importance so much that it was difficult for me to use the personal pronoun *I*. I felt and I knew God was powerfully moving through me. I considered I was married to Him and that I was His devoted servant. The more I gave of myself, the more I emptied of myself, the more He gave Himself to me.

DC: I see your disregard of the demands of your ego in the desert test and temptations. You dismissed the temptation to rule the world.

JC: One has to have a large ego to rule the world. I chose a more humbling path and that path continued to quiet and erase my ego.

DC: When I read Paul's letters I notice he is not aware of the Q Document. He doesn't quote it and he never quotes you. He never says to his churches, "This is what Jesus said. Listen to his words." I find this puzzling.

JC: Explain to your audience the Q Document. What is it?

DC: Q is short for Quill. It is a theoretical collection of your sayings that were neither edited nor embellished by later Christian writers.

JC: Another way of saying what you just said is that the Q Document is a more accurate version of my original sayings.

DC: That is the assumption. Mark, who wrote the first New Testament gospel, uses the Q Document extensively. Of course, he uses other sources as well. He stitches together your deeds and walking–event stories with your spoken words. The structure of his gospel is simple. You walk to a place, you speak, you perform a deed, you leave on foot or by boat to another place where you say something else, maybe a lot or maybe a little; when you are finished you move to another place and say something else. Walking, sailing or riding a donkey and placing you in a landscape setting are narrative props intended to give you a three-dimensional life. Paul's depiction of you is archetypal and symbolic; it is flat and theological. Mark, on the other hand, was the first to give you a flesh and blood description. In essence, his gospel says Jesus is real and this is what he said, this is what he did, this is what he wore, and these people are his friends while those people are his enemies.

JC: Mark never met me and Paul never met me. Neither man ever talked to me. They never witnessed my ministry, they never listened to one of my sermons and they were never present at one of my miracles. That which they knew of me was hearsay. They heard stories on top of stories; some were accurate and some were not.

DC: Mark was a second- or third-generation Christian. He was not an original.

JC: You say Mark used the Q Document, Old Testament scripture and oral traditions to write a theological narrative about me?

DC: He was the first to write about your ministry in detail. He creatively and seamlessly blended history, Jesus sayings, oral tradition, Jewish Midrash and the Torah. Like Paul, he methodically searched for verses in the Torah that appeared to resemble your ministry, and when he found them he strung them together like pearls on a necklace. He developed a symbolic portrait of you and made it appear that you fulfilled Jewish Messianic prophecy, in a manner somewhat similar as Paul.

JC: And that is the reason why you question his motive.

DC: Is he illuminating and detailing your life? Or is Mark following in Paul's footsteps and promoting his agenda?

JC: One has to ask that question.

DC: I envision Mark compiling his Old Testament verses in a manner similar to Paul and as he's doing this I can hear him say, "This fits, this one fits, this seems to fit – I can make it work – this doesn't, but I'll include it by inventing new characters and settings to make it fit. I'll do it with this one, this one, and this one."

JC: Mark wrote his gospel around the year 70.

DC: Nearly forty years after your death.

JC: Enough time had elapsed to forget the finer details and subtle nuances of me and my ministry.

DC: Many things were left out, and when Matthew and Luke wrote their gospels another round of mythic elements were introduced – like the Virgin Birth and Ascension – along with a few other details not found in Mark.

JC: My story was exaggerated and expanded from the beginning and end?

DC: And many personal details were left out. I want to mention that both Matthew and Luke didn't know you. Matthew, whom the gospel is named after, is not one of your twelve disciples, nor was Luke. Matthew's identity and history is sketchy and obscure, while Luke traveled with Paul.

JC: I had twelve disciples minus one, three brothers and a wife who could have written about me.

DC: They did not write about you. I have to stop and think about that for a moment. Maybe they didn't think it necessary or maybe their writing was lost to history. Maybe their writing was deliberately destroyed or not copied and circulated as Paul's letters and the four canonical gospels.

JC: Let's discuss the new and different details that come after Mark's gospel.

DC: Luke expands, reintroduces and embellishes. He uses Mark's gospel as a template but adds and subtracts from it. He speaks of your birth and the surrounding circumstances; Mark does not. He depicts the time when you are twelve at the Temple with the elders, he minimizes the forty days in the desert, he embellishes the Last Supper narrative, and he adds another dimension to the post-resurrection period – the Road to Emmaus being one story. Again, it is important to note that Luke was a close associate of Paul and as such was influenced by him.

JC: I know you have concerns about the veracity of the gospel accounts. What are your thoughts concerning the Last Supper? Do you believe I had a last supper with my disciples?

DC: I believe you were together with them one last time before your arrest. This seems to be a common and shared detail among the gospel writers. The Passover rite, the act of remembrance for what God had done, washing away sin, and sharing a meal with friends and family are consistent with Jewish festival practice. Likewise, sharing a meal with friends and followers was an essential feature in your ministry, as was listening to stories about the divine. I feel, however, that Luke's Last Supper depiction is too incredible to be true. Let me quote it directly: "And he took bread, gave thanks and broke it, and gave it to them saying, 'This is my body given for you; do this in remembrance of me.' In the same way, after the supper he took the cup, saying, 'This is the new covenant in my blood, which is poured out for you.'" (LK 22:19-20) Here is Paul's version: "The Lord Jesus, on the night he was betrayed, took bread, and when he had given thanks, he broke it and said, 'This is my body, which is for you; do this in remembrance of me.' In the same way, after supper he took the cup, saying, 'This cup is the new covenant in my blood; do this, whenever you drink it, in remembrance of me.'" (1 Corinthians 11:23-25) These accounts are nearly identical. The language is the same. The setup is the same. The meaning is the same. Luke is using Paul's letter, which means he either remembered it verbatim or possessed a copy when he wrote his gospel.

JC: I traveled to Jerusalem to celebrate Passover as I had done many times before. This was the first time I celebrated Passover in Jerusalem since my father Joseph's death. Instead of celebrating it with my immediate family I celebrated it with my closest followers, my mother Mary and Mary Magdalene.

DC: That's what I imagined. I'm also convinced you knew this was going to be your last Passover meal.

JC: Correct.

DC: I can accept that.

JC: I want to mention that consuming the flesh and blood of a god has Egyptian roots.

DC: Yes, I know. It is written about in the Egyptian *Book of the Dead*. Even though you are quoted as saying, "do this in remembrance of me" and it is a "sign of the new covenant," in actuality by participating in the Last Supper rite one is consuming a divine being, and when one consumes a divine being one subsumes the magical powers of the God. This idea is new to the Jewish religion and cannot be found in the Old Testament.

JC: One has to ask, "Why is it necessary to eat a God?"

DC: Exactly. After all, you said the Kingdom of Heaven is inside of you. That is another reason I take issue with the gospel narrative. It is one more story that obscures the historical Jesus with the theological Jesus. Examine the Kingdom of Heaven sayings and understand them. Realize that eating the flesh of a god is inconsistent and incompatible with the meaning and intent of the Kingdom of Heaven sayings. They cannot sit side by side and support one another because they are contradictory. There is no need for the Last Supper rite because it is outside the spiritual logic and mechanics you taught. However, I can accept sharing a meal, as you had done so many times before, as a way of remembering and acknowledging you and your ministry.

JC: Do you have the passage that comes from the Egyptian *Book of the Dead?*

DC: Let me find it in my notes. Oh, here it is. Quote, "In this way, having swallowed the magical powers and spirits of the gods, he becomes the Great Power of Powers among the gods, and the greatest of the gods who appears in visible forms. "Whatever he hath found upon his path he hath consumed, and his strength is greater than that of any spiritual body (SĀHU) in the horizon; he is the firstborn of all firstborn, and ... he hath eaten the wisdom of every god, and his period of existence is everlasting, and his life shall be unto all eternity ... for the souls and spirits of the god are in him." (*Egyptian Religions*, p. 200)

JC: This hardly sounds like Paul.

DC: It doesn't, but don't get lost in the rhetoric. Examine the purpose and the meaning and the rite. Granted, the significance for Paul is colored differently. What is not different is the rite of eating or swallowing a god, and your Last Supper is eating your flesh and blood. The above Egyptian passage describes the effects of eating or swallowing the flesh of the gods: one increases strength, one increases wisdom, and one experiences eternal life. Are these not the similar hallmarks of Christianity? One is supposed to believe in Jesus and partake in communion. So I ask why is a cannibalistic rite of eating or swallowing a god in Paul's letter to the Corinthians. Also, why is an ancient Mystery Religious rite appropriated by the early Christians? The Last Supper has all the trappings of an ancient mystery religion. To me, something is askew. I seriously doubt you started this rite unless you had Egyptian training, which then subverts your Kingdom of Heaven analogies and insights. As I said before it is reasonable to believe you had your last Passover meal with your disciples; after all they were with you, right? Your last Passover meal with your disciples seems plausible and accurate; the content and symbolic meaning of the meal does not. I believe this event was constructed to convey an alternative meaning and it is one of which you and your family would not approve.

JC: What other matter do you believe is inaccurate or construed?

DC: The entire passage and account of Judas Iscariot and the Garden of Gethsemane. It is written in the gospel that you turn to Judas and perform the same ritual specifically for him. You break a piece of bread, dip it in red wine and hand it to him. He accepts it and then dashes off to inform the authorities of your whereabouts. After you finish the feast you and your disciples inexplicably leave the special room for the Mount of Olives. It's your "usual place" – I don't know how this place can be so usual unless you visited it often, which suggests a familiarity with Jerusalem and specifically this location which the gospels fail to mention – and after some time Judas conveniently arrives with a contingent of soldiers and guards, and you are led away.

JC: It's hard to appreciate this account in the manner in which you describe. I want you to know my arrest was very real.

DC: I'm not discounting that. I accept its authenticity but not in the manner in which it is told in the gospels. I'd like to move on to another facet of the story I find difficult to believe in relation to the Garden of Gethsemane. This too makes me question the veracity of the narrative.

JC: The place of my arrest?

DC: The setting and story are graced with a polished and beautiful yet unnatural symmetry.

JC: What do you mean by symmetry?

DC: It is symmetrical to the Garden of Eden. Again, this is symbolism rather than history, unless you planned it in that manner.

JC: Elaborate on this.

DC: In the creation story Adam and Eve are tempted by the serpent with the fruit from the trees saying, "For God knows that when you eat from it your eyes will be opened, and you will be like God, knowing good and evil." (Gen 3:5) Both Adam and Eve fall for the trap and bite into the apple. Mankind falls and is forever changed, cursed and banished from the Garden. Man and God are separated. In contrast, you are tempted in the Garden of Gethsemane. It's not unlike your forty days in the desert; it's another temptation, but the difference is that you don't fail or fall. When put to the test you stay true to the course. You do not run away when the authorities come. You do not scatter in fear like your disciples. Rather you accept your destiny to save mankind from Adam's curse. That is why you were born: to rectify Adam's failure and correct the ravages of sin through your Paschal Lamb sacrifice. That was God's will for you. You couldn't run away, otherwise the sin that separates man from God would remain. Man would not be saved; he'd be eternally lost to his Fate. With Judas' kiss your Fate is sealed and your demise is set in motion. You are arrested and led away to your trial, flogging and crucifixion. Where Adam failed, you succeed. That is symmetry.

JC: For you this story is poetic but symbolic and as such inaccurate.

DC: It's logical to believe the Christians searched for rites that set them apart from other existing religious practices, yet not too far apart. The Last Supper and the baptismal rites became identification markers that gained traction and made Christianity distinct. The other part was to create a metaphor like the Garden of Gethsemane and link it to the Torah and to End Time prophesies. I'm making a blanket statement here and going out on a limb, but I see the birth of the Christian religion not according to you, your ideas and practices as much as the appropriation of prevailing religious ideas and practices. You are then reinserted and reintroduced into the mix as the foundational figure; you are the God-man who died and was resurrected from the dead. That particular piece is the special ingredient to the package.

JC: I was the hub, not as a man but as the Son of God.

DC: You are the hub around which everything revolved. They needed a face and you became that face. You were unique, odd, unusual, smart and coura-geous. I believe your followers really didn't know how to deal with you after your crucifixion. They could neither embrace nor reject you. I imagine they thought you were strange; a cross between an astonishing peculiarity and an exceptional man of God.

JC: Why do you say I was the face? You know I acted, taught and lived according to the wisdom of the Father. I neither imagined nor intended to create a new religion. If I was the face and inspiration, then Christianity grew from me. I was the first cause, not the other way around.

DC: The Christians were Hellenistic inventors blending Judaism, Mystery Religion, and Jesus in a new and innovative manner. They created belief, creed, literature, practice, rites, Midrash and theology. They created a complete package and presented you to the world as the Son of God who became mortal. You are one part divine and one part human; you were the God-man walking on earth. This concept derives from the Mystery Religions and harkens to the Greek Eleusinian Mysteries and to the Osiris-Dionysus Myth. According to these myths, the God-man dies, descends into the underworld (Hades) and then is resurrected on the third day. These are the tenets of Christianity and they are too mythological and coincidental to be historical.

JC: They applied my "new wine and new wineskins" saying into their new religion.

DC: The Christian writers crystallized their position through Midrash and literature and circulated it within the various communities throughout the Roman Empire using oral tradition, Q, gospels, acts, letters and the Book of Revelation. When the gospels were written the Christian followers got to peek into your life. You were given a face, a heart, a personality and, to some extent, a family. Paul and the early writing traditions – I'm thinking of Q – neglect to mention most of your humanity and relied either on the mythic and symbolic content or your sayings. Maybe the oral traditions supplemented the missing and more personal elements of your life.

JC: My life and my face were used to promote the emergence of Christianity. According to them I was the fulfillment of Jewish eschatological prophecy and I was presented as the Son of God, Messiah, Lamb of God and Savior of the World.

DC: Would you have wanted this?

JC: I detect an ounce of cynicism. I was cognizant of Jewish prophecy. To believe I adhered to or fulfilled it doesn't take into account my motives to follow the divine voice I felt guiding me.

DC: The Christians didn't take your personal motive into account. Instead, they incorporated an extracurricular dimension into your story.

JC: I want to comment on story since we are discussing literary traditions. Entwined in Jewish culture is story. We were literate, learned and precise storytellers. Scribes, sages and priests spring from this tradition. We nurtured and cultivated learning and wisdom, developed a system of theological principle, and created rites, rituals and practices in the manner in which we understood the world and related to our God. It was a unique tradition with a long history, each consistent and interlocking. Sacred scripture was at the heart of this. It carried a lot of weight and meant a great deal to most Jews. Our society revolved around it. In one sense, scripture is its own sacred world. I can appreciate the Christian tendency in harnessing the Hebrew literary traditions.

DC: Sacred scripture reinforces its own internal logic, rhythm, cadence and theology.

JC: It is how we know and experience the world. Scripture contains hope; it contains stories of people following God or not following God and it peeks into the world of the divine. One knows something of the divine because of it.

DC: Scripture contains an internal knowledge to explain external, real-world conditions, and as you point out it has the power to dictate and shape perception and experience according to its vision and end. Scripture acts as a filter and guide; it confines and interprets reality accordingly. Anything outside its scope is vigorously opposed or rejected, and its boarders are narrow and restrictive rather than spacious and expansive. This is the literary and scriptural tendency. When the world and its influence enter scripture, however, it is reluctantly and grudgingly accepted or is looked upon with disdain and suspicion.

JC: Explain that further.

DC: Let me break this down. From the monotheistic perspective, the external world is not to be lived; rather, it is to be known as a teacher or guide. History and the world are insertion points for God to respond and interact with mankind's infidelity and sin. In one sense, it is the place of comparison, the arena where our faults and limitations sit in stark contrast to God's holiness and righteousness. In another sense the world is a place of judgment and wrath. At the heart of monotheistic reality is God's moral universe, a hidden reality of strict moral and ethical rules governed by an ultimate morality tale – God is the Creator, you are the creation; you are bad, God is good; you are fallen, God is not. But ironically God is here to help you after the fall. He wants us to become good and to conform because the only reality to be known is obedience to God's dictates and compliance to his moral universe. This underpins the Jewish Creation and Fall story. God established the behavioral moral code not out of goodness, but out of His essence and nature. If one doesn't abide by it one is destroyed or annihilated simply by the rational logic of the God essence. Any reality outside of God cannot exist; it cannot live side by side with God;

it cannot coincide with God; it cannot be this and that simultaneously. It can only be one infallible nature and it is to that we are held to account.

JC: You assert God is an ultimate moral code. Is that your belief?

DC: I see the logic of monotheism. I see its operation. I see its story and its dualistic essence. One is either on the inside or outside, one either believes or does not, and one is either obedient or disobedient. According to the monotheists all are fallen and only a select few are chosen. We see this dualistic tension in the relationship between words and ideas – chosen and Gentile, believer and unbeliever/infidel, saved and sinner, heaven and hell, God and Satan. These are powerful ideas that imply life is nothing but a fierce battle between two opposing forces. If one stops and asks, "Which side is going to triumph?" one would be hard pressed to see an obvious victor. Apparently, you – Jesus – came to turn this equation around. The Christians invented an entire theology around the Fallen World and Savior of the World premise. Unfortunately, the world is the same yesterday as it is today – chaotic, unruly and messy.

JC: I navigated my way out of that relationship, and when I did I offered a heart of compassion, spiritual wisdom and a blood sacrifice.

DC: You broke the pattern before you started your ministry. You first became the change you wanted to be and then you went out into the world to make the change you became.

JC: That is why I conducted my ministry. I was no longer attached to ideas and practices I thought were obstructive and perpetuated chaos and blindness. I wanted the peace inside me to spread out into the world.

DC: You were calm, clear, peaceful and compassionate.

JC: I was.

DC: As you can see, I'm suspicious of the theological tenets of monotheism. I prefer the Hellenistic mythology and its participation in divine energies rather than strict worship and obedience to a single deity.

JC: All right. I appreciate your disagreement with monotheism.

DC: I believe you did as well. There is more than a hint. When I understand your authentic Wisdom Sayings and examine your actions, I conclude you transmuted and transcended sacred literature. Once you did you gave birth to the new and with that the oriental and European world were renewed, refreshed, and reinvigorated. You did not have to live according to the old world of scripture; that was behind you. You were audacious to live your life according to your personal inspiration and convictions, not the dictates of others or of society. That was new. You learned that from the heritage of Jewish prophets. You knew that was the future. You did not connect with scripture as much as you connected with heart. You experienced one-on-one relationships with people. That was real and those relationships were not governed by the law or morality; they were based on love and compassion. It was tangible not theoretical, dogmatic or narrative.

JC: I discovered ecstasy in life and in the Father. To know it was to live it, experience it and enjoy it.

DC: I found the same truth. When I finally came to the conclusion that the New Testament was heavily biased I felt liberated, and not just from the New Testament but from the entire scriptural tradition. I knew the divine of my own accord and did not need intercession from others. Nor did I need someone saying, "The divine is this and that, and you need to do this and that." Physically and intellectually I stepped out of that a long time ago but, unfortunately, my heart was not in step. My mind was ahead of my heart, but when the two aligned I entered into a new world of possibility with new conviction, new knowledge, and a new set of eyes.

JC: The Kingdom of Heaven is all around you and in you. You don't need an author to tell you that or anyone one else for that matter. Open your eyes. Open your ears. Open your heart. The divine is known through experience, not through the head.

DC: It sounds as though I dismiss scripture. I do not, at least not in its entirety. I reached a point in my life when scripture no longer acted as a guide or teacher. It had served its purpose and I got what I needed from it. At that point scripture lost its appeal and it neither fed nor nourished me. I saw it as a hindrance to my progression. I grew out of it as I naturally grew out of a pair of pants. In one sense, I shed old skin and moved on. That was an interesting moment. I look back at the road I walked and notice the distance I traveled. When I gaze upon my new path it is dark and uncertain, but I know as I move forward that I am spiritually mature with divine knowledge and insight. Now I have to ask, "What am I going to do with my knowledge and wisdom?"

JC: Your first task is this interview. You might not know where it will take you or what it will do for you – you'll have to wait to find out. But be certain it will take you into the unexpected and will test all your wisdom and character. This same process occurred to me. When my time arrived, I conducted my ministry and brought something new to my people.

DC: I see it in your "new wine and new wineskins" saying.

JC: Yes, new wine and new wineskins.

DC: You had faith that your actions, words, and deeds would have positive effects on you, your followers, disciples and society. You had faith that your sacrifice, both in your life and in your ministry, would effect profound changes. That is faith as I know it and it is similar to investing. One prepares the ground, plants the seeds, watches over it, and cultivates and waters it. When the season arrives, it is time to harvest the fruit.

JC: I agree with that.

DC: I want to move on and explore another tenet of Christianity.

JC: I can guess because I know how you think. You want to talk about immortality and the afterlife.

DC: I do, but from another angle. Christianity closely ties your death and resurrection together. They go hand in hand. As such there is a connection to the afterlife. I would like to explore the role immortality played in your society.

JC: We pondered and thought about it; we considered it.

DC: A number of other societies recognized immortality but your society came late to the stage, but when it did immortality became a topic of heated debate.

JC: We weren't exactly sure of its nature but the idea gained momentum. Different opinions held sway. It was discussed and positions hardened into camps; one group thought this, another that.

DC: The Sadducees – who were a part of the aristocracy, the privileged, the wealthy, and some were High Priests – did not recognize resurrection, angels or spirits (MK 12:18, LK 20:27, ACTS 23:8) but the Pharisees did. Can you present the general argument?

JC: The argument evolved from "God gave us the Promised Land and we are asked to keep and abide by His law. That is enough; that is the covenant" to "If we are faithful to God's law and covenant yet are tortured and killed because of it, surely we must receive a reward for our faithfulness because God is just and merciful."

DC: When I surveyed the spiritual and religious literature during the Jewish Second Temple period – when the Jews returned from Babylonian exile in sixth century BCE until the destruction of the Temple by the Roman in 70 CE – I noticed instances and discussions pertaining to resurrection, immortality, soul and sheol. As I read further I discovered that each of these topics was in a state of flux. In other words, as the ideas emerged, there was discussion; as that discussion became more substantial a counterargument appeared to dispel the original argument and that created two fiercely entrenched sides. By the time you were born these ideas were organized into hardened camps. Lines were drawn and territorial boundaries fortified. Then you inserted something new into the argument with your sayings and your ministry. Some people think you did not exist. I say otherwise. When one examines the bulk of the Second Temple Period religious literature, one notices an explosion in the early-middle to late first century literature, and curiously a man named Jesus is at the heart of the explosion. Again, your ideas influenced many writers and followers.

JC: Each Jewish group and sect understood each of these ideas differently. Each idea contained meaning, significance and nuance. The ideas either coincided with one's beliefs or they didn't, so they were either accepted or rejected depending on the group.

DC: Let's look at a few.

JC: The points of contention involve a sharp question. For example, if there is a soul what is its nature? Is it good or evil? Another involved immortality and entrance into the divine realm to live in divine time with the divine being. In other words, who is qualified? What is the standard of qualification? How does one obtain immortality? These questions raised a further question: if there is a soul, how does it move from this world to the next?

DC: The mechanics of transportation?

JC: You have a way with words.

DC: When I contemplate this topic, especially as it relates to your people and your society, I notice an underlying subtext. It involves tribal distinction and inclusion – who is a member and who is not. To be a member certain precepts and obligations had to be accepted and abided by. This argument extended into the afterlife. Immortality wasn't a birthright; it was earned in some manner. One had to be of a particular moral character, one had to embody and embrace a set of moral standards and ethics, and one had to make a choice that had eternal consequences.

JC: The Jewish experience involves a stratum of identity. We had a common religion that revolved around a covenant relationship. This was a common and shared experience for us.

DC: There is a sharp line of distinction between a member of the chosen and a person who is a Gentile. The chosen were obligated to live, participate and believe accordingly. They had responsibilities. If a Gentile desired to become a Jew, then he or she was required to adopt Jewish beliefs and practices.

JC: The God of our fathers had duties and obligations. He was to be our God, provide for us, be with us, shepherd us and reveal Himself to us. He gave us our Promised Land so we could worship Him without outside interference. For our part we were obligated to live according to His rules, regulations, rites, practices and favor. He gave, we received; we gave, he received. The relationship was dynamic and reciprocal. Each side had duties and obligations. This is what it meant to be in a covenant relationship.

DC: The Greeks and Romans organized their society differently. They did not have a covenant relationship like the Jews. Instead, the Greeks embraced a representative government with a voting citizenry, while the Romans had Caesar, a Senate that was elected, a standing army and layers and grades of citizenship. There was an array of tax and military obligations depending on one's citizenship and status. At one end of the Roman spectrum there were full rights and privileges, while at the other end there were no rights and no privileges.

JC: You are speaking of slavery, which was at the bottom end of the spectrum while Caesar was at the top.

DC: The first among equals versus the multitude of slaves.

JC: Slavery also carried spiritual significance. It was a metaphor and model of the self.

DC: One was either a slave to destructive forces or alive in the active and creative forces.

JC: The Christians adopted this model. For them, one was a slave to sin and the consequence of sin is death. To counteract this perpetual death sentence one had to be made alive in Christ. This required a second birth which they termed *born again*.

DC: The new birth initiated a new process of life and of knowing.

JC: I'd like to explain the relationship between the big and small in this new birth. There is a personal new birth as the Christians and Gnostics claim. Inside each of us is the divine lying dormant. This is the small part and it has to be called upon and activated. Next requires the big part: something – the hand of God, an announcement, or a shove from the divine – activates the unformed mystery inside us to move. The Greeks coined the term *unmoved mover* and it applies here. One is like an unborn universe waiting for the divine to call out and get the process of creation started. When that takes place the individual moves from being dead to being alive, from being unknown to being known, and from being held captive by the material world to being liberated by the immaterial world.

DC: The proverbial ball starts in motion. In Genesis God spoke the words, "Let there be light." (Gen 1:3) After these words everything was created to know and experience the divine.

JC: Either way the concept of getting things started is similar. Contained within the new birth are potential processes, knowledge, wisdom, becoming, destiny and Fate. In any event, we were speaking of the Christian view of slave to sin and alive in Christ. A war rages within each person, but within this personal battle of life and death there is a greater dualistic tension between opposing cosmic forces. Christianity affirms this as the real battleground. We, as the individuals, are pawns in a much larger battle, and the fight is as much about our soul as it is about the cosmic winner between good and evil. For Christians the conflict pits the world, the flesh, and the devil against God, the Son of God, the Holy Spirit, archangels, saints and the faithful. They mixed dualism, like leaven and yeast. There is the war between believers and nonbelievers, God and the devil, heaven and hell, saints and sinners, life and death, and the groans of the old creation and the hope in the new creation. All of this got blended into their theology.

DC: I also see in these components the elements and creation of a mythology and in this new Christian mythology a person becomes the battleground between the forces of good and the forces of evil. One had to be on guard at all times. One had to put on the "full armor of God" as Paul encourages and exhorts. (Ephesians 6:13-18) One was forced to make hyper-critical choices annually, monthly, daily, hourly. The internal questions scream within a person: Am I doing the right thing? Am I sinning against God? Is this action drawing me closer to God or closer to the devil? Is this pleasure sinful? Is this suffering from God? Am I afflicted with God's disfavor because I am sick, or am I out of favor because I enjoyed the pleasure of that? Am I saved or am I not? Am I going to heaven or hell? How come my choices here on earth have eternal and cosmic consequences for my soul? What am I supposed to do? The internal dialogue is noisy and deafening. Where is the silence? Where is the calm? Where is the vision? Much of this stems as an offshoot of your Father experience and wisdom teachings. Both were appropriated into Christianity but both were understood and applied in a different manner from your original intention and meaning.

JC: Even though I understood the concepts I tried not to be guided by them. I didn't want everything unseen to be clear and defined. I didn't explain it; rather, I pointed to it. One cannot hold the mystery in the palm of one's hand and parade it around for all to see and say, "Here it is!" I wanted people to envelope the mystery, not argue its merits rationally or logically.

DC: To be clear, the Father is also mystery.

JC: The Father is mysterious. I wanted people to be compassionate, and if they embraced and acted compassionately then the forces inside us that move to tear us down, ravage us and separate us would be nullified.

DC: I believe your words and deeds were misunderstood, misinterpreted and misapplied, and this created unintended consequences that you neither wanted nor meant.

JC: Before we got on this we were discussing immortality. Let's circle back to it.

DC: All right. I want to understand what you meant. From your sayings regarding the Father and the Kingdom of Heaven important questions about immortality are raised or implied. Again, it goes back to: What is it? What is its nature? Who is allowed entrance? What are the requirements?

JC: Those are important questions and my experiences of the Father informed me of a living presence that was available to any one today right now. One did not have to wait for death to experience or know something about it.

DC: This runs counter to the concept Paul propagated. He had a definite idea about entrance. He believed that one had to believe in you and your salvation work, and one had to perform good works to enter heaven. Your sayings and Beatitudes do not support his premise. I'd like to explore immortality from the point of view of entrance, and I want to look at this from three historical perspectives.

JC: From three historical perspectives?

DC: The Egyptians understood immortality as a journey in the netherworld. They had a book titled *Book of the Dead* that describes this process. Upon death one entered the murky netherworld. The prospective candidate had to navigate a tricky maze, overcome obstacles and, if successful, enter the Hall of Judgment. The Hall housed a scale and on that scale sat the feather of truth, Maat. This was the final test. Standing beside the scale was the god Anubis, the god with a jackal head and body of a man, and Thoth, the god with the ibis head and body of a man. The seeker's heart was placed on one pan and weighed against the feather, which rested on the other pan. Anubis "adjusts the plummet while Thoth writes down the verdict.... Whilst the weighing takes place the deceased recites the Negative Confession, addressed to the 42 gods who sit in the Hall, denying all sorts of heinous crimes as well as some more mundane ones. Upon a satisfactory verdict the deceased is then led by Horus before Osiris who sits in a pavilion at the end of the Hall of Judgment.... The deceased is presented as one 'true voice, justified' and a suitable candidate to be admitted into the joys of the netherworld." If the candidate failed his heart was thrown to the Eater of Hearts demon. (*An Illustrated Dictionary of The Gods and Symbols of Ancient Egypt*, p. 128)

JC: Very serious and grotesque business.

DC: The Christian judgment day is just as serious and grotesque except the soul is hurled into the "lake of fire," as is Satan. The Greeks had a very different understanding.

JC: They had an odyssey.

DC: It was sort of a life trial. One was severely put to the test and had to navigate a tricky maze and use their wit and strength to overcome obstacles. But the test did not take place in the netherworld like the Egyptians; rather, it was in the here and now. Their epic poems *The Odyssey* and *The Iliad* are illustrative. Their trial was a test of endurance and skill; it could have occurred on the battlefield or in some far-off land. It could be a heroic stand or a heroic triumph. It could be a difficult and obligatory quest in order to bring something new or important back to the community because the community was in need of that particular something, like the Golden Fleece or Medusa's head.

JC: Don't forget it was imperative for the Greeks to make a name for oneself. It was about terrestrial triumph either on the battlefield or on the quest. Then one's name would be immortalized in the historical record and remembered.

DC: There was no immortality in the afterlife, for that was the realm of the gods. But one's name could be remembered throughout history. This part reminds me of your Last Supper, "Do this in remembrance of me." (LK 22:19)

JC: Hercules and Achilles are names we remember. I was surrounded by different concepts of immortality. To the north and west there was the Greek version, which the Romans' adapted, to the south there was the Egyptian version and to the east was the Babylonian version. Explain the Babylonian version to your audience.

DC: The Babylonian *Epic of Gilgamesh* also explores immortality through journey and odyssey, though the story drew a different conclusion. Gilgamesh, the protagonist of the story, overcomes heroic odds as he fearlessly faces one trial and tribulation after another in his search for the wise old man who could tell him the secret of immortality. As a side note, the Greeks adopted the same quest structure and format. Gilgamesh discovers that a wise old man, who was born before the great flood, could be found on a mountain top and provide him the answer he seeks. Gilgamesh finds the mountain, navigates his way to the top, and is given an audience with the wise old man; but then the unanticipated happens, making the story all the more tragic.

JC: What was that?

DC: The wise old man tells Gilgamesh something he could not bear to hear, and it dashed his hope in disappointment and horror. Because Gilgamesh's father was divine, Gilgamesh thought he should be granted immortality. But the wise old man informed him that he could not because his mother was human. This part of the story reminds me of you. In the eyes of the Babylonian poet Gilgamesh was sixty percent divine and forty percent human.

JC: Sixty percent divine and forty percent human?

DC: There is no explanation as to why Gilgamesh is not fifty percent divine and fifty percent human. In any event, in spite of his quest, overcoming great odds and being a divine–human hybrid Gilgamesh did not receive divine favor nor was he granted immortality. He could not enter the divine realm and be with the gods because he simply was not one of them. He was mortal and mortality cannot transform into immortality. His optimism was dashed and ultimately his quest failed. It is a tragic and sour tale. The wise old man told Gilgamesh he would die, and then he told him to drink more wine and enjoy his wife.

JC: These stories and ideas, and those like them, circulated throughout the Mediterranean and Roman Empire. I was aware of them.

DC: To what extent did you know them?

JC: They were not as prevalent in the Galilee and my hometown as the stories of Hebrew patriarchs and prophets, for it is these stories that captivated and inspired me. These stories are at the root of the Torah. That is not to say other stories from the other parts of the world did not exist or that I was unaware of them. To be sure I was curious and wanted to have insights into them. They suggest, whether real or imagined, whether solid or poetic, that a world different than ours existed somewhere.

DC: And this concept of different worlds extends into immortality. Two worlds exist; one right here and one over there.

JC: Now I want to speak what I know and understand. The world we know and the world of the divine are not as separate as imagined. I experienced the divine realm and I knew the dividing line between it and us was not as real or as solid as it seems. It appears that way but it is not.

DC: Is it an illusion?

JC: Let me say this: knowing it, seeing it and participating with it requires an extra eye and an open heart, but it is not as different as it seems. It is perspective. Each one of us is in it and of it.

DC: There is a saying, "I am that." When I experience a moment of love I seriously doubt that it is fundamentally or intrinsically different here than it is over there. I seriously doubt a musical note to an angel is different than a musical note to a human. They are not two separate things; they are the same thing here as they are the same thing there. If this illustrates the truth of love and a musical note, then I stop and contemplate what else is equivalent or similar – maybe a little or maybe a lot. Maybe everything here is a mere shadow of everything there. Maybe it is all one and the same.

JC: I want to expand on this idea and ask you something.

DC: What?

JC: Do you believe the light of the divine is always shining?

DC: That seems so simple but I'd have to answer yes. I can't imagine it any other way or that it ever turns off.

JC: Is it the same here in this house as it is on the other side of that mountain over there?

DC: Yes.

JC: So I can experience it here as I can experience it over there?

DC: Yes. That means space is not a factor.

JC: Was the divine light shining this morning when I arrived at your front door?

DC: I'd have to say yes to that as well.

JC: Is it shining now?

DC: Again, I'd have to agree that it is.

JC: Then time is not a factor.

DC: I see your point. If God's light is always shining, and neither space nor time affect it, then space and time are not factors in God's light and by implication an intermediary is not necessary.

JC: That sharpens the point: it comes down to you. How come you are not seeing it? How come you are not experiencing it? How come you don't know it? How come you are not acting on it?

DC: I'd say we act as a dimmer switch.

JC: There you go again! What is a dimmer switch?

DC: A dimmer switch controls the flow of electricity to a light. When fully open the light shines brightly, when it is turned down low the light shines dimly, and when it is turned off the light doesn't shine at all.

JC: As you say, and to use your metaphor, each one of us acts as the dimmer switch. We can turn it to high, medium, low or off. It is up to each of us to determine the amount of light we want to experience and to shine. After I came to know this I felt compelled to share that vision and truth.

DC: I'd like to quote one of your sayings because it encapsulates this perspective. Your disciples ask you, "When will the kingdom come?" To which you reply, "It will not come by looking for it. Nor will it do to say, 'Behold, over here!' or 'Behold, over there!' Rather, the Kingdom of the Father is spread out on the earth, but people do not see it." (THOM 112)

JC: I wanted people to wake up to this. By implication the divine does not reside in the Jerusalem Temple in the Holy of Holies. The divine is in us and all around us.

DC: The divine is not located in one specific place. There is a backhanded reference to this in your saying, "Let the dead bury the dead." (MT 8:22)

JC: The Father is not just a story that captures the imagination of mind, and the Father is not dead.

DC: The Father can capture the imagination and sway the heart.

JC: I knew the Father as a living presence, not as a philosophical idea. The Father is not to be worshiped in the historical religious context; rather, he is to be known and experienced. For me, worship was participation in the divine and applying the wisdom of the heart and mind in society. The more I did the more I received of the Father.

DC: You faced many obstacles in your ministry that you navigated and overcame. You brought something new to the community that was needed, and you were willing to weigh your heart on the scale as a sacrifice.

JC: I accepted my burdens and responsibilities to the very end. I was willing to carry my cross as I knew and understood it. I brought love, compassion and peace; I brought a new understanding of the divine to a world in desperate need of it; and I introduced an awakening of spirit that is a cogent and a necessary operation.

DC: This discussion is flavored differently than the Christian assertion of resurrection.

JC: I knew the divine was everywhere. I knew it was inside me. I knew it was outside of me. I knew where to look and how to look. I knew its silence. I knew its prayer. I knew its voice. I knew how to be still and to focus my mind. I knew how to harness the divine and bring it into the world and to share it.

DC: "Split a piece of wood, and I am there. Pick up a stone, and you will find me there." (THOM 75)

JC: I have to clarify that statement. It points to a truth I understood, but the personal pronoun *I* is foreign to me. I am not in the piece of wood. I am not under the stone in the literal sense, but the divine is. It can be discovered in the smallest of things, or it can be discovered in the largest of things. The divine is present in all things and I am present in the divine. I just don't appreciate the personal pronoun *I* in relation to that saying. The reality I knew was not just of the mind. It was of the heart, it was in the doing, it was in the application. I mixed this together like leaven and yeast.

DC: I believe the "split the wood" phrase points to an Egyptian god story.

JC: Osiris.

DC: In the story, the god Seth commissions a sarcophagus to be built. He presents it to the Egyptian pantheon of gods and says it belongs to the one who fits in it. One god after another jumps in, but it doesn't fit anyone until Osiris leaps inside. Then the trap snaps shut on Osiris. He is duped. While lying inside, the lid is maliciously nailed shut by Seth, and the sarcophagus, with Osiris in it, is taken down to the Nile where it is set adrift. The sarcophagus sails down the river, into the open Mediterranean Sea and washes ashore on the coast of Lebanon. There a large cedar grows in and around it. The goddess Isis, Osiris' sister and wife, is distraught by Seth's deception and searches long and hard for her husband. Finally, she finds the sarcophagus wrapped within the cedar tree. She speaks magical words given to her by Anubis and miraculously Osiris resurrects from the dead. I believe this is where the phrase "split the wood" originates. The story shows a mythic truth and it corresponds to unconscious and psychic processes.

JC: You believe that somewhere in this mythic story is buried truth?

DC: I do.

JC: I discovered buried truth requires careful observation and some fair amount of digging to find it.

DC: I agree, but there is another way. It is a matter of knowing the secret.

JC: What is that secret?

DC: One can know the truth by living it. As I carefully read your sayings and compare them to your actions I realize resurrection, which is not specifically related to the living presence of the Father, has little to do with you. For the dead to come alive an outside agent is required. In the case of Osiris, Isis has to find him and then she must speak the magical words given to her by Anubis.

JC: It meant that a dead body would be reanimated by God, made alive once more, and allowed to walk about the earth but animated rather strangely, like stinking rotting corpse.

DC: Paul circumnavigates this dismal and unsettling image by painting a glowing picture of the risen body. He makes a particular case when he says, "If there is a natural body, there is also a spiritual body." (1 Corinthians 15:44) "And just as we have borne the image of the earthly man, so shall we bear the image of the heavenly man." (1 Corinthians 15:49) "Listen, I tell you a mystery: We will not all sleep, but we will all be changed – in a flash, in the twinkling of an eye, at the last trumpet. For the trumpet will sound, the dead will be raised imperishable, and we will be changed. For the perishable must clothe itself with the imperishable and the mortal with immortality. When the perishable has been clothed with the imperishable, and the mortal with immortality, then the saying that is written will come true: 'Death has been swallowed up in victory.'" (1 Corinthians 15:51-54) "But our citizenship is in heaven. And we eagerly await a Savior from there, the Lord Jesus Christ, who, by the power that enables him to bring everything under his control, will transform our lowly bodies so that they will be like his glorious body." (Philippians 3:20-21)

JC: This is very complicated and reminds me of the Pharisees' argumentative style.

DC: You had problems with them.

JC: We did not see eye to eye. They were always willing to provide a theological answer to everything or an argument as to why this is this and that is that, why this is right and that is wrong. They sorted everything out in their minds. Everything meant something other than what it really was. Everything had a symbolic or metaphorical meaning. I lost interest in their tedious connections. I was interested in the here and now and what I could do about the problems of the day. I knew death was not the end but a transition. I didn't concern myself with the particulars because they had no bearing on my ministry and what I attempted to accomplish.

DC: Paul quotes directly from the Egyptian *Book of the Dead* when he writes about the natural body and the spiritual body and switching from a mortal body to an immortal body.

JC: Now I need to take a break.

CHAPTER 11

CRUCIFIXION

JC: You make a strong cup of coffee.

DC: I like coffee and coffee talk; conversations tend to be more personal and philosophical. Prior to our previous discussion we were talking about Mary Magdalene.

JC: I remember.

DC: Your marriage to Mary Magdalene was a tragic love affair, and when I put myself in her shoes I find myself sympathetic to her anguish and anxiety.

JC: She knew danger lurked at the outer edge of my ministry and out along the horizon. She couldn't always see it but she could feel it.

DC: Little did she know that danger was also at the center of your ministry; I'm thinking of Judas Iscariot and to some extent Peter. I also surmise she was terrified with your decision to celebrate Passover in Jerusalem. That fateful decision set in motion the end of your friendships, ministry and marriage and marks the beginning of your demise. Everyone you knew, from your followers and disciples to your family, understood the danger in that decision.

JC: I would argue they knew it from before, at the moment I decided to conduct my ministry. Heading to Jerusalem was a continuation of my promise and sacrifice to the ministry and the Father.

DC: I can envision an ominous air circulating in the shadows of your heart and in the back of Mary's mind.

JC: I still felt compelled despite my feelings of anxiety and dread.

DC: At one point your brothers chided you to make a name for yourself and to be heard and seen. Jerusalem was the place to make a reputation and to define one's character. Yet your name had preceded you there. The authorities wanted you dead. Maybe you secretly wanted to shock your disciples with your bloody sacrifice. When you decide to leave for Jerusalem to celebrate Passover the mood seems rather dire and gloomy. The Gospel of Mark states, "They were on their way up to Jerusalem, with Jesus leading the way, and the disciples were astonished, while those who followed were afraid." (MK 10:32)

JC: My followers, gripped by fear, continued to look over their shoulders to see who was watching and who was coming after us. I did what I needed to do, and I did it with conviction and passion without thinking of the consequences. I was free from fear and the normal responses to it.

DC: How did Mary feel? She must have been scared and concerned.

JC: She was overcome by those feelings, along with anger. She didn't want me to go. Of course, she wanted me to be safe, what wife wouldn't, but she knew the dangers before I started my ministry. We knew this day would come and it arrived.

DC: Was she resigned?

JC: Can one ever be resigned in a situation like this? She had some comfort though. In the back of her mind she felt she could call upon friends in Jerusalem if I got into trouble; she would go to them for help.

DC: Who?

JC: The Pharisee Nicodemus or Joseph of Arimathea.

DC: I'd like to mention that, according to tradition and legend, Nicodemus was not treated well by the Jewish leaders and paid a high price for following you and for asking for your body. They considered him a partner with you and wanted him dead as well. He had to run for his life.

JC: Safety was a concern for many who associated with me.

DC: When you went to Jerusalem, the proverbial deck was stacked against you. Even Caiaphas the High Priest that year "advised the Jewish leaders that it would be good if one man died for the people." (JN 18:14) For the leaders, any other choice could not be entertained or considered.

JC: I was a threat and thorn to the authorities and elders.

DC: I'd like to explore this Jerusalem stage of your life in more detail, and I'd like to start by saying it is significant to Christianity.

JC: You mean my death carries the most weight for Christianity?

DC: The Christians refer to this period in your life as the Stages of the Cross or The Passion. I don't want to discuss every detail but I do want to say that it is here that your death transforms from local nuisance to cosmic significance. It is the place where the heart of Christianity beats and where the seeds of the future religion get planted.

JC: This particular time was an indispensable and final ingredient to my ministry.

DC: It was an extraordinary sacrifice.

JC: I told everyone who wanted to follow me to sell everything they owned. (MT 19:21, LK 18:22) If they did, it was a telling sign of their commitment. Now I was faced with a similar obligation and was following my oath to the Father to the very end.

DC: I don't want to be crass, please don't take it the wrong way, but your death has the appearance and feel of a suicide. You wanted to die at the hands of another.

JC: Suicide was not in my vocabulary. My death was a sacred and solemn but horrifying event.

DC: I must admit that I see something different in your death than do Christians.

JC: That seems apparent, given your last statement.

DC: It's not intended to sound disrespectful or tactless. Where Christians see salvation and the sacrifice of the Son of God I see a man making a terribly onerous decision. You didn't have to make it, but when you did you accepted Fate and you accepted the consequences to the bitter end without complaint.

JC: I agonized over that decision but it was not the first time I had to make such a momentous choice.

DC: Agonizing decisions carry the most weight because the risks and rewards are so high. This kind of decision has considerable impact and ramifications, not just for the one making it but for all those around. Decisions ripple out into the world and have lasting effects. Deciding to leave the Galilee and go to Jerusalem was an impactful decision. Ultimately, it led to your death and the inception of a new religion.

JC: One cannot always know how a decision will affect the future or what that decision will set in motion, because that which transpires lays hidden in the "womb of time." Eventually it reveals itself.

DC: The point is to make a decision and be willing to live with the consequences.

JC: Choices are hard even if you know the potential outcomes.

DC: I discovered a relationship between choices and their effects: the more difficult the decision the greater the impact, and the greater the impact the greater the opportunity to grow and mature. We don't know the full extent of the future, what it contains or what we will gain or lose. All decisions have outcomes. Maybe some things can be fully appreciated, but I think the best we can say is that something will happen; hopefully the outcome is what we anticipate.

JC: When I was younger I was brash and made decisions impulsively. Some consequences were disastrous. As I matured impulsiveness turned to calculation. I could see possible outcomes and see the potential of a decision. I also realized doing nothing had consequences just as much as doing something. Seeing possible outcomes was the gift, a gift of wisdom and of the Father. I enjoyed the gift and used it to the best of my abilities. Having said that, I could not see the outcome of every decision I made. I just knew something would happen and that I wanted to be a part of it. I did not know my life would be the inspiration of a new religion. I didn't see that possibility or that it would have the impact that it did.

DC: Again, I'm reminded of the Our Father prayer. It was your guide. You acknowledged the Father in all things, and you asked for your daily bread, not to be put to the test, and to forgive. The rest is out of your control.

JC: The prayer resonated more prominently with my decision to go to Jerusalem. I was already guided by it. This moment was no exception but Jerusalem happened to be my most extreme test.

DC: Your third feat of endurance.

JC: As you say.

DC: Let's go through a few events that defined the end of your life. I'm sorry if this sounds morbid and callous. I don't mean it to be.

JC: I understand what you want. Let's discuss it. It's important.

DC: Let's start with the number of your followers and disciples.

JC: That's curious. What do you want to know?

DC: The gospel writers were in the habit of saying large crowds followed you. That's hard to tell because they exaggerate the point. My mind keeps thinking about logistics. What would they gain by following you into Jerusalem? When you decide to leave the Galilee for Jerusalem it appears only a handful follow you.

JC: People came and went. My ranks swelled and dwindled throughout my ministry. Some fell away due to obligations. Others were disconcerted and worried but faced their concerns and followed me nonetheless. My ministry disrupted preconceived notions and expected outcomes. I'd say it was characterized by the unfamiliar and the unexpected. Surprises were normal. One had to accept that. When we went to Jerusalem it was difficult to predict the future because there was also the hope of a miracle. While some journeyed with apprehensions others anticipated the unexpected.

DC: The Synoptic Gospels agree with your decision to leave the Galilee and travel to Jerusalem for Passover. One states you were resolute. I find your decision puzzling.

JC: Why?

DC: You had an effective ministry in Galilee. You inspired your disciples and followers. You had an audience whose lives were changed on account of you. Why would you want to go Jerusalem? Galilee was your home. It was the place of your ministry. It was the place of friends, family, followers and listeners. You had everything you needed; you didn't need anything else. Or so it appears. What did Jerusalem offer?

JC: I wanted to celebrate Passover.

DC: It's that simple?

JC: Why wouldn't it be?

DC: I want to look at this from another perspective and then circle back. I wonder if you weren't motivated to go to Jerusalem because you felt your days were numbered.

JC: Numbered?

DC: On numerous occasions the gospels mention the Jews wanted to kill you and in one case a Pharisee, of all people, warned you: "Leave this place and go somewhere else. Herod wants to kill you." (LK 13:31) Maybe the noose was tightening around your neck.

JC: I was not afraid to die. Why should fear dictate any of my moves? I wanted my ministry to last as long as possible. Did it ever occur to you that maybe I simply wanted to celebrate Passover? I enjoyed Passover and the Feast of Tabernacles and wanted to experience them again in Jerusalem. After all I grew up celebrating them in Jerusalem with my family. (LK 2:41-42) This was nothing new.

DC: I suspect when you left for Jerusalem the number of your followers was significantly reduced. Maybe they were fearful. Maybe they had had enough. Maybe they wanted to celebrate Passover with their families. I can't piece this part of your story together, but when you leave it appears your twelve disciples, Mary Magdalene and your mother Mary follow you into Jerusalem. Suddenly, though, when you get to the outer gate a crowd greets you enthusiastically. How did they know you were coming? Did your disciples enter the city and announce your coming? Did they whip a crowd into a frenzy? Did they prepare the way for you?

JC: I sent my disciples ahead of me numerous times.

DC: Tell me about Jerusalem. What did the city mean to you? Did you identify it as the City of God?

JC: Jerusalem was the City of David and the navel of our world, uniting Jews together. Jerusalem was the heart of Jewish life, in the heart of every Jew and the center of the Jewish religion. At the heart of the city was the Temple, which King Solomon built and which dominated the city and its life. The Temple was the place of God, His heavenly dwelling on earth, and the place of sacrifice, purity and restoration. The light of Jewish history revolves around Jerusalem and the Temple. On a darker note, the Seleucid king, Antiochus, desecrated the Temple through the sacrifice of a pig in the Holy of Holies.

DC: Jerusalem was the axis-mundi for the Jews.

JC: Purity radiated out from Jerusalem like concentric circles. The closer one was to the Holy of Holies the closer one was to God, while the further one was from Jerusalem the further one was from God's holiness and righteousness.

DC: What more can you tell me about Passover and the Temple, and what did each mean to you?

JC: Passover was an exciting and sobering festival filled with hope and expectation, and it was a time of remembrance and personal accounting.

DC: When you celebrated Passover in Jerusalem with your family, what kind of arrangements did you make?

JC: The journey to Jerusalem took many days. We had to prepare and pack accordingly. We brought food and water, an assortment of clothes, tents, and our one-year-old, unblemished sacrificial animals.

DC: Did you caravan with others?

JC: We did.

DC: What do you remember about Passover?

JC: I remember in my youth my enthusiasm and joy in seeing the Temple Mount. My heart would lift and fill with awe. The Temple was white, large and impressive. When I'd see it from afar I'd wonder what lay in store, and when I climbed the Temple courtyard I felt close to the presence of Yahweh. It was awe inspiring and possessed a particular atmosphere. There was a mysterious air that made me think, "Here I am in the house of the God." My mind would race. The entire experience made a lasting impression on me.

DC: It is said the Temple was a massive structure that took forty-six years to remodel and rebuild, and that it was completed near the time of your birth.

JC: Herod the Great struck a deal with the Sadducees and Jewish elders in exchange for certain rights. The religious community would not allow impure hands to build a pure and sacred building and avoided all such relationships.

DC: The Roman historian Tacitus claims the Temple was rebuilt as a Jewish defensive fortress, with ramparts, strongholds, an underground food storage facility and a water system. Within the complex Herod built the Antonio Palace to live in while he was in Jerusalem and named it after his Roman benefactor, Mark Antony.

JC: That was a sore spot and rubbed people the wrong way.

DC: Passover was a sensitive time of the year and the Romans were particularly suspicious. They allowed the celebration with trepidation. They didn't want trouble. They didn't want Jews filling their heads with revolt and disturbance, and they especially didn't want someone acting like Moses and confronting them.

JC: There was always the possibility that a disturbance during the festival would initiate a chain of events, and some Messianic prophets hoped it would occur and force God's intervention.

DC: The Romans were in force and their presence was everywhere – on the rooftops, in the streets, along the avenues, on the Temple Mount, and positioned around the Temple.

JC: They had spies as well and we believed they had a contingent of soldiers stationed inside the Antonio Palace. We were watched carefully. Their suspicious eyes were keenly searching for agitators, conspirators or disrupters.

DC: Despite the Roman presence, you enjoyed this festival. Is there anything else you can say about it?

JC: I enjoyed the sites, running my hand across the surface of the large stone walls, listening to the cacophony of sounds – trumpet blasts, the priests reciting prayers and psalms, the groans of animals, the clamor of people talking, the sandals striking the stairs, and water splashing. I liked bathing in the ritual baths, finding our temporary house and preparing for the sacred meal. I liked mingling and talking with other Jews who came throughout Judea and the Diaspora. I got to listen to stories from other parts of the world. I liked watching people purchase their sacrificial animals; I liked walking the route and climbing the steps with all the other Jews who were offering their unblemished animal to the priest. I remember the smell of the animals, the odorous sweat of men, the perfumed fragrance of women, the smell of blood, the baking of unleavened bread, and the roasting of the meat. The time was dynamic and the Passover festival was in my heart. That feeling didn't diminish as I grew older.

DC: Explain the purpose of Passover.

JC: It is a commemoration of the Passover sacrifice and a time of remembrance. It celebrates the beginning of our freedom from Egypt.

DC: Explain it further. What happened at Passover?

JC: While the Jews were enslaved in Egypt, God commanded each Israelite to sprinkle sacrificial blood on their door posts the night before the Exodus. That night the Angel of Death looked at every door post for blood. Since the Israelites brushed blood on their posts the Angel passed over them. When the Angel came to an Egyptian house, which did not have blood on the door post, the first-born was slaughtered. Passover commemorates God's judgments and God's hand in liberating the Jews en masse from Egypt. It is also a time of cleansing, a time of blood sacrifice to wash away sin, and a time to recommit one's life to God and follow Him.

DC: Explain in more detail the history of the Exodus event. The Angel of Death was the final plague leveled against the pharaoh.

JC: Passover is an exceptional moment in the history of the Hebrew people. While in Egypt we grew large but we were not free to worship or live as an independent people; we were Egyptian slaves. God, in His mercy and love, delivered us from that bondage by directly intervening on our behalf. The death of the first-born was the last of the ten plagues. Afterward, we left en masse following Moses, who was now our leader. We headed northeast toward the Red Sea. We reached the shoreline but could not cross. Our scouts warned us the Egyptian army was in full pursuit. We didn't know what to do and Moses walked to the water's edge raised his arms out high and asked God for help. Miraculously, God separated the waters, holding them back long enough for every Israelite to safely cross from one side to the other. The Egyptian army pursued us into the Red Sea. As we safely arrived on the other side, God once again intervened and allowed the walls of water to fall upon the Egyptian army, sweeping them away. Since then we commemorate the date with a celebration of sacrifice and a sacred meal with our family.

DC: We have a holiday I think is comparable to your Passover, not exactly the same but similar. We call it the Fourth of July and it celebrates our Declaration of Independence from British tyranny. We also have another special holiday in the dead of winter.

JC: Christmas.

DC: It honors and celebrates your birth and the moment of the world's redemption. It's quite beautiful when thought about more deeply. I have to ask you a direct question. Is there anything else you wished for or hoped to accomplish in Jerusalem during Passover?

JC: Other than participation in the festival?

DC: Your primary goal was to celebrate Passover? You didn't have an ulterior motive?

JC: It was a time of cleansing, anointing, and washing away sin. Why should something else motivate me?

DC: Those ideas and practices were old-world and old-school thinking. You brought a new vision to the world that is fundamentally different from them.

JC: Even so, my heart remained invested in the festival and this time of the year.

DC: I sense you are deflecting my question, so I'll move on. Maybe we can circle back to it. There is something you did often I'd like to discuss.

JC: What is that?

DC: You led by example, and I would say your decision to go to Jerusalem had an internal lesson for your followers and disciples.

JC: While conducting my ministry I taught by example. That technique was equally important as my words.

DC: Your ministry embodied moral integrity and personified wisdom.

JC: Why do you drag it down that way? I taught not because I was right but because I knew the Father and I wanted to share that knowledge with others. I could not keep it to myself. I did. I spoke. I showed. I taught. I healed. I could do nothing else and could not think of any other way.

DC: That is my point. You must have known Jerusalem was your death sentence. The gospels again are consistent on this point. You tell your disciples you must go to Jerusalem to die. I don't agree with their theological perspective, but a kernel of truth lies at the heart of your decision. I wonder if your decision was another lesson for your disciples.

JC: I wanted people to know what it meant to be committed to the divine, to know and experience both the costs and the rewards. I loved my life, my family, Mary, my followers, fellow Jews and the Father.

DC: Was your last defining act a choice you wanted?

JC: My heart sensed it was necessary and essential. I felt I was following God straight into the lion's den. I knew what I had to do even though I didn't know exactly what I was going to do when I got to Jerusalem. I learned to allow the Father to guide and inspire me in such cases. I learned to follow my heart and feel my way through the obscurity. I had gut feelings. I sensed I needed to do something and I had butterflies flapping in my stomach.

DC: You relied on a gut feeling?

JC: That too is a way of knowledge. Clarity was not always present. It's murky. As events unfolded, I adjusted and reacted accordingly. Sometimes I was in front directing the outcome; at other times I was directed by unfolding events. I tried to stay in front of circumstances but that was not always the case.

DC: I have a saying in relation to this: "Is life playing you or are you playing life?"

JC: To think we can control life or force the divine to bend to our will is supremely arrogant and prideful.

DC: I read a saying once, I can't remember the exact words but it goes something like this, "A powerful king of a large empire strides confidently up to the seashore, gazes upon the sea and exclaims, 'Bow down to me. I decree that your tides shall never again rise or fall.' When the sea ignores him, he turns away saddened and depressed."

JC: There you have it. The mystery of life and the divine is all around and we cannot control it, but we do need eyes to see it and a heart to feel it.

DC: Pain, suffering and death are woven into the fabric of life and we are subject to it whether we like it or not.

JC: Yes, I know.

DC: The human mind fears such issues; curiously, the mind also knows it is alive and conscious. The thought of death makes the situation all the more dreadful. The mind simply can't compensate for its own oblivion.

JC: I did not want to be governed by death, pain or suffering. I was alive in the Father and that knowledge flattened those concerns.

DC: You did not make choices according to fear's voice.

JC: I was liberated from that voice and was not afraid of pain or death.

DC: I want to ask a sharp and directed question. What did your death mean to you? I know what it means to Christians but I don't know what it meant to you.

JC: Before I tell you what it means to me, first tell me what it means to Christian's.

DC: Your sacrifice and death were the fulfillment of Jewish law and prophecy. You were the suffering servant who took away the sins of mankind. You were the Paschal sacrificial lamb and that is the only reason for your trip Jerusalem at Passover. From this perspective, you lived an archetype – the Messiah, Son of God, and Son of Man.

JC: I know you don't agree with this symbolism.

DC: Or its intent. I once did but not anymore. I've evolved and have new insights into your death.

JC: What do you see?

DC: The story the Christians tell is captivating and grabs one's immediate attention. During the first century, when it gained traction, an apostle didn't need much time setting up the story, delivering the punch line, or explaining the meaning. The story gets to the point quickly. Immortality is a gift from a loving God and anyone who believes in Jesus, is baptized, eats his bread, and drinks his wine is saved from God's wrath and allowed entrance into heaven.

JC: You're being sarcastic again. Besides, the love of God was scarce as water in the desert on a hot summer day.

DC: For that time it was. I agree. I want to venture again into delicate territory but be forthright. What did your death mean to you? What did you hope to accomplish?

JC: You make it sound trivial and matter of fact. It's more nuanced and complicated.

DC: I don't mean to be dismissive or trite. I don't in any way wish it to appear as if your death should be viewed loosely or flippantly.

JC: I didn't want my life to end and I was nervous and disturbed about it. My ministry was a divine gift and I was true to that calling. I received many blessings and riches.

DC: What made you feel it was necessary to die?

JC: Every person is faced with their mortality. One cannot escape it. I was filled with driving conviction. I asked, "Am I willing to die for my truth?" At the beginning, I said yes, but later I faced its actuality. Then everything changed. Death was no longer hypothetical or speculative. It was real and heavy as a large stone.

DC: You faced death figuratively and literally. When you began your ministry in service of the Father and for others you died figuratively. When you were arrested, flogged and nailed to the cross you died literally in the service of the Father and of others. Did you accomplish what you set out to do, or were your goals cut short?

JC: I moved quickly knowing my time was short. Moving from town to town and village to village was an effective technique in my ministry. It allowed me to teach and to heal around Galilee, Tyre and Sidon.

DC: That tactic extended the life of your ministry.

JC: I'm going to let you in on a secret. I did not always know my next move. Neither could I predict or determine where I was going or what I would do when I got there. I felt my way through. I had gut feelings. I sensed when it was time to stay or when it was time to leave. The silent inner voice of the Father guided and directed me.

DC: Did your disciples understand and appreciate your motives or concerns?

JC: To some extent. I want to point out that they had definite ideas. I brought something new into their lives that they had to accept and process. You also have to take into account that speaking one's mind and contradicting prevailing attitudes and customs is not tolerated in a strict theological society. Eventually my disciples discovered and understood what I taught all along. I overcame fear, suffering and pain. I was devoted, committed and dedicated to them and the divine. One can teach only so much; my ministry showed the way. At some point, they had to embody my wisdom, take responsibility, and do something with it. When they did, they conducted their own ministry.

DC: The Parable of the Talents comes to mind. In the parable, several people are given money to invest. Some invest to various degrees; another doesn't invest at all and buries the talent.

JC: That sums up the wisdom I taught. One is required to make the necessary investment. One cannot simply bury the talent and expect the divine to be cultivated. One must do and use the tools that are given.

DC: In a theological society obedience dictates life. In your case, you chose to undercut and challenge the laws and customs of your society to bring into focus another divine reality. You were subservient to that end.

JC: I stepped out in faith to conduct my ministry. I faced the stiff and relentless opposition. I felt I had no choice; I simply had to do it time and again. When I felt otherwise I sought quiet and lonely places to gather myself. Once rejuvenated, I ministered again. I knew my time was limited so I acted with purpose.

DC: Was there something in the air when you chose to go to Jerusalem for Passover? What did you sense?

JC: Opportunity. I felt an urgency to face my deepest concern, which was fear. I didn't want to be persuaded or moved by it. I wanted to be fearless.

DC: I thought you overcame your fear.

JC: Fear has many layers. When I peeled back one layer and I got through it, I thought that was that until I came face to face with another. To my surprise, each layer required more determination and grit than the previous. Jerusalem at Passover was another layer.

DC: At this moment, you explored a deeper layer of fearlessness? That was your underlying motive?

JC: Death is a battleground. I cultivated the heart of the warrior. Even though I had the heart of compassion I had this one last test – fearlessness – in the face of the grueling and cruel death I knew awaited me.

DC: The story in the Garden of Gethsemane speaks succinctly to this point. You prayed, "Father, if you are willing, take this cup from me; yet not my will, but yours be done.... And being in anguish, he prayed more earnestly, and his sweat was like drops of blood falling to the ground." (LK 22:42, 44)

JC: The moment before my arrest was upsetting and terrifying.

DC: You were willing to drink from that cup and face your deepest fear? Did the Father direct you?

JC: Yes.

DC: I believe it was your final gift to the disciples.

JC: How so?

DC: You shocked them.

JC: They were shocked and terrified.

DC: I wonder if your trip to Jerusalem on Passover was calculated religious theater for maximum shock value. You went into the lion's den and got mauled. That was the point. You knew what was in store, as did your disciples. They followed you to Jerusalem despite their concern.

JC: They were suspicious but were willing to see what would happen next. During my ministry, we got into trouble and we got out of trouble. It was a part of our routine.

DC: You played them and you knew your actions and sacrifice would buy an exhilarating story. Each of your disciples, followers, and family would have been stunned and shocked by the horror of your death. That was the point. You gave them a story to tell, it seared in their minds and they told it over and over.

JC: I felt it was time to offer my last gift and I did it in the most profound possible manner. My disciples needed to know there was nothing to fear in death and that it was a transition from one realm to another. Even though I knew this, I still felt ambiguity.

DC: At times, shock and awe are constructive tools to get one's attention.

JC: Passover in Jerusalem proved to be the most dangerous place for me and became the final stage of my earthly ministry.

DC: It also held the greatest source of notoriety and visibility. As your brothers said in the Gospel of John, Jerusalem was the place for impact, to create a name for yourself and become known. Hundreds of thousands of people from all over the Diaspora attended the Passover celebration. They would have heard about you or seen you.

JC: The stakes were high and I paid heavily in pain and sorrow.

DC: Going in you suspected the religious establishment. You were dangerous to the peace and to Roman rule, and they hated you for challenging their authority on the forgiveness of sin, breaking the Sabbath, and speaking of God as a Father.

JC: They did.

DC: As we discussed earlier, Messianic hope and expectation were in the air. You used the title the Son of Man during your ministry. It got people's attention.

JC: I used existing concepts to further my ministry and facilitate change.

DC: The way I see it you happened to be the right person to bring a new version of the divine at a time pregnant with Messianic and End Time expectations. It was a perfect storm. People read what they wanted to read at precisely the wrong time for the wrong reason.

JC: I knew those ideas were potent. They captivated people's attention. That was the time. It was in the air. I also knew Passover was symbolically charged and I used it to my advantage.

DC: You were being coy with me before. Now the truth comes out. What do you mean that it was symbolically charged?

JC: One animates the holy Passover festival by participating in the practices, rites and meals.

DC: How were you persuaded by its symbolism?

JC: I calculated the sacrificial facet to my advantage.

DC: You had the knack for seeing opportunity where others could not. You branded yourself with a charged sacrificial Passover symbol.

JC: I knew I had to elevate my ministry head and shoulders above every other man, and there were many who claimed to be the Messiah or End Time prophet.

DC: Jerusalem was the biggest theatrical stage for your final offering. Many people from all walks of Jewish life would witness your final devotion and sacrificial commitment.

JC: That was also in the back of my mind when I decided to go to Jerusalem.

DC: I can see that now.

JC: Death was an objective. I couldn't be certain it would unfold as I imagined but I didn't want this one-time event to be arbitrary and without symbolic meaning. I had only one chance to get it right.

DC: You knew your death was on the horizon?

JC: Yes. In the back of my mind I was thinking of John the Baptist.

DC: John was beheaded alone in a dungeon, and his severed head was placed on a platter as a gift to Herod's stepdaughter for her erotic dance.

JC: It was undignified and demeaning. The manner of his death was anticlimactic to his ministry. I didn't want to be remembered in a similar light. I couldn't imagine my head being given to anyone as a cynical gift in private.

DC: People were sickened and outraged by Herod's atrocity.

JC: It upset and disgusted people, but not enough to act and make a difference. It didn't have the power to persuade or cause lasting change. Many of John's followers then came to me.

DC: Now that I think about it, I see you recalibrating your assessment. You wanted your death to be visible and in public, not in private. You wanted it to be meaningful, to be inspiring but at the same time to shock and horrify. That appeal was electrifying, captivating and intriguing.

JC: Now you are seeing.

DC: If I were a disciple and had to summarize your life story to an audience as a man who healed and taught a new version of God and was silently taken away by the authorities and killed privately, my audience would quickly lose interest. If, on the other hand, the story was told as the God-man who the Jews handed over to the Romans to brutally torture and execute for his new vision of the divine, my audience would be mesmerized and would want to know more.

JC: That is how I saw it. I told you I learned to calculate my decisions.

DC: Flipping the money-changers' tables in the Temple courtyard was for show. It was deliberate, provocative and intentional. You knew money had to be exchanged and was a necessary process. You knew people did not bring a sacrificial animal and needed to purchase one. At first, I imagined the flagrant materialism of the Temple upset you or that you were disgusted with the Temple priests – as were the Essenes – and wanted to confront the Temple authorities for their alliance with Rome.

JC: The Essenes believed the priests were illegitimate and bogus because they were not of the proper bloodline and for making daily sacrifices to Caesar and Rome. Both facts were unorthodox and both disturbed and upset the Jews.

DC: That may have bothered you, but it is not the primary reason to flip tables and make a scene. Metaphorically, you did that throughout your entire ministry.

JC: Many things bothered me. People felt ritual was the path to God but I knew otherwise. Even though I had already made up my mind and was inspired to face my death, this discrepancy upset me. Anger surged in my veins. Jews reduced the love of God to a financial transaction and an empty sacrificial gesture. I couldn't stand it. People acted as though all that were true and effective. It was all too much for me. I was about to face a grueling death and people went about their daily business inside the Temple area. It seemed ridiculous.

DC: It would appear as if your actions had the hallmark of Essene opposition, but I think you wanted an audience with Pontius Pilate.

JC: Why do you suppose I would want an audience with Pilate?

DC: To "look the devil in the eye" without flinching. You knew he would be in Jerusalem during Passover. You figured your arrest would place you in the presence of the High Priest or Pilate. The consequence of your actions provided you a high-profiled audience.

JC: As you imply, that kind of audience would legitimize and publically announce my ministry. I hoped for that audience but I couldn't be sure I would get it.

DC: Let's slow this down for a moment and talk about Pontius Pilate. I would guess you knew of him. He was notorious and his reputation preceded him.

JC: Yes, I knew of him. He succeeded Valerius Gratus and was the fifth Roman Prefect.

DC: He was prefect of the Roman provinces of Judea, Idumea and Samaria from 26 to 36 CE. The previous procurators were respectful of Jewish religious custom and practices but he was not. He was belligerent, antagonistic, cruel and vindictive, fueled by a vicious temper. He insulted, robbed, committed outrages and executed many without trial. His first act as prefect was controversial and nearly caused an insurrection.

JC: Pilate allowed his army to bring the Roman eagle standard and effigies into Jerusalem at night. That was his first act as prefect. When the Jews found out, crowds descended upon Caesarea Maritima, where Pilate resided, and demanded the sacrilegious images be removed.

DC: I'll let you tell the events. You were there after all. What happened next?

JC: Heated objections and discussions that lasted for five days.

DC: Heated as in protests, or heated as in militant action?

JC: I heard people were very upset and vocal, but not violently provocative.

DC: How did this get resolved?

JC: Pilate ordered his soldiers to surround and kill the petitioners, but when the petitioners said they would rather die than allow the standard and effigies to remain, Pilate withdrew his order.

DC: In other words, he yielded. I suspect the standard and effigies were removed.

JC: They were. Pontius Pilate was not the first to act in such an appalling manner. Herod the Great had a golden eagle erected at the entrance of the Temple prior to his death. This incensed a group of loyal and religious Jews who conspired to remove it, which they did. Both the planners and perpetrators were caught and executed.

DC: How did Pilate's first act make you feel?

JC: Like many I was upset and surprised. It was brazen, arrogant and obnoxious. It said, "I am the Roman prefect. I can do anything I want. I have the power and right to exercise my authority whenever and however I want." The Seleucid kings acted similarly.

DC: You came in direct contact with him.

JC: Yes I did.

DC: That meeting proved disastrous. Or maybe not? Maybe it played into your hands.

JC: Do you believe God's plans are linear and that they unfold systematically and sequentially?

DC: I don't think that anymore. Anyway, prior to speaking of Pilate's first act as prefect we were talking about your motive to flip tables in the Temple courtyard in order to have an audience with the High Priest or Pilate. You got both. I can think of another motive that inspired you at this point and I can sum it up in one word: story! You turned your life and ministry into a captivating story. Your death became a topic of interest and discussion, like John the Baptist's.

JC: That is a private motive I thought would remain secret. I have to congratulate you on that insight. That was left unexplored for thousands of years. As you know, story is important to the Jews. It embodies a special reality that cannot be ignored. Scripture is considered the Word of God and the Jews were given the gift of being caretakers and guardians of divine revelation.

DC: You remembered stories of Judas the Galilean, Herod the Great and the first act of Pontius Pilate.

JC: Their acts, deeds and words made people remember and they were turned into stories. We spoke about them, learned from them and were inspired by them. These weren't the men to emulate or follow, but we talked about them nonetheless. They gripped us in frustration, anger and awe.

DC: We call those kinds of stories newsworthy. Like them, though your story is contrary to political power and abuse, you wanted your story told throughout the land. You wanted people to remember you and talk about you. The story about your death was a catalyst.

JC: That was my hope.

DC: Death became the means for your life to become your story. You were turned into Midrash and I would even venture to say that you were the story of your time and it hasn't diminished for two thousand years. One thing you didn't calculate, though, was the effect of the written word and that you would be turned into a divine being, the Son of God, for your actions. You gained more traction as a story rather than as a man who taught compassion, forgiveness and wisdom. This aspect of your life was secondary to your gruesome death and sacrifice.

JC: I could only control so much. It didn't turn out as I envisioned.

DC: I'd like to ask you what you were feeling or thinking when you were led to Pontius Pilate. His reputation for being brutal, cold and callous must have concerned you.

JC: I hid my nervousness. I knew my time with him wouldn't bode well. It never did for most Jews. He liked executing people without trial.

DC: What was it like when you first met him?

JC: I was roughed up by the Jews. My lips were bloody and my face was bruised. My injuries caused me physical pain, but when I saw Pontius Pilate my pain disappeared. I was in the presence of a man whose eyes were as cold and lifeless as his demeanor was cruel and compassionless. I had to swallow my fear and curb the alarm in my eyes. I had to detach myself and focus on my breath. I wanted to be as clear as I could when I looked him in the eye and answered his questions.

DC: When I read his biography, there is nothing of his humanity that engenders warmth or sympathy, and nothing that would crack his stern, cold bearing. One couldn't connect to him. He wasn't a man as much as he was a monster who personified Roman merciless business. He was proud and arrogant, obsessed with power, rule and authority, and indelicate and insensitive to Jewish sensibilities. He also placed the Roman standards in the Temple a second time. When he did he didn't negotiate with the Jewish protestors; instead he commanded his army to slaughter everyone present.

JC: He was efficiently ruthless in collecting taxes, maintaining peace and dispensing judgment. He was a man who wanted to be known and praised, who thrived when people bowed and cowered to him. I didn't give him that luxury.

DC: Roman privilege consumed him as he desperately tried to move up in the elite Roman society. His infamous quick judgments and swift death sentences induced fear, but in the end that ruined him. He was called back to Rome for his treachery and was never heard from again. Your parables are filled with men who were blinded by lust, power, prestige, authority, clothes and fine food.

JC: He was such a man who could have learned something from me.

DC: There is something subtle during your trial that perplexes me. I want to quote from the Gospel of Luke because I think it is important. "Then the whole assembly rose and led him off to Pilate. And they began to accuse him, saying, 'We have found this man subverting our nation. He opposes payment of taxes to Caesar and claims to be Messiah, a king.'" (LK 23:1-2) Several accusations are leveled against you. At your kangaroo trial your actions and reputation preceded you. The assembled chief priests, elders, and teachers of the law insisted, "He stirs up the people all over Judea by his teachings. He started in Galilee and has come all the way here." (LK 23:5) Other accusations are leveled against you: that you were the Messiah and the Son of God, and that you forgave sin which is God's province.

JC: Some charges were trumped up, others were not.

DC: One bothers me the most and I can't reconcile it with the various accounts.

JC: Which one is that?

DC: You are accused of opposing taxes to Caesar. That is hard to believe since one of your well-known sayings is, "Then give back to Caesar what is Caesar's, and to God what is God's." (LK 20:25) This statement is presented immediately before your arrest, but the opposite is articulated at your trial.

JC: It wasn't a trial. I confronted the authorities and challenged Jewish traditions and religion. My teachings were disagreeable to the establishment and many ran counter to their understanding. Everything I did was an affront to them. That is why I was on trial.

DC: A commandment from Moses states, "You shall not give false testimony against your neighbor." (Exodus 20:16) Is this a case of false testimony?

JC: To them I was already guilty regardless of the charge and I was to be shown no mercy. They already knew what they wanted to do with me.

DC: You were guilty of a capital offense. You opposed and challenged Roman authority and your punishment of flogging and crucifixion fit the offense. You were considered a common criminal and the plaque on your cross reads, "Jesus, King of the Jews." This is not a religious matter, it is political one.

JC: In Judea religion and politics went hand in hand.

DC: I'd like to turn around and explore this last phase your ministry on a more personal level.

JC: Go on.

DC: I want to talk about Mary Magdalene. While you are in Jerusalem for Passover she is not mentioned until your crucifixion. I find this hard to believe. Why is she silent? Why is she invisible? Why is she in the shadow of the narrative?

JC: Where do you want to start?

DC: When you decided to go to Jerusalem, did you consult her?

JC: I let her know before I informed my disciples.

DC: How did she take the news?

JC: Not well. She hid her feelings and concerns. She liked Passover as well and wanted to celebrate it, but she knew Jerusalem would be dangerous and wanted us to stay in the Galilee.

DC: Did she know your true intentions?

JC: No. I didn't want to upset her. Traveling to Jerusalem was hard enough. It seemed as though we were heading to the executioner. She put on her best face, with hope, but in the back of her mind she knew that was overly optimistic.

DC: When you flipped the money-changers' tables in the Temple, how did she respond?

JC: I saw the shock in her eyes and read the words coming from her lips.

DC: Which were?

JC: Something to the effect of, "How could you?"

DC: You know I question the validity of the Garden of Gethsemane because of its metaphorical analogy, but it goes without saying you were arrested in a particular spot. If truth is to be found in this story it is your tendency to seek a quiet place to pray and meditate for divine guidance and direction. This story is consistent to that end. Did you receive a divine gift or insight?

JC: I received many divine insights during the period when most people are asleep.

DC: What did your gut tell you while you were praying in the Garden of Gethsemane?

JC: It was balled up and churned like milk when making butter.

DC: You knew something was wrong.

JC: Yes. A feeling came over me that death was coming. It was eerie. I can't describe it.

DC: You have no words.

JC: It was a new sensation. I had to accept the Father's will and Fate at this point. Everything was set in motion and there was no turning back.

DC: Where was Mary?

JC: She didn't want to leave my side. She also felt something ominous. It's rather curious knowing that another force is acting on you and nothing is going to counteract it. Neither Mary nor I could say anything or do anything to stop Fate. It unfolded as it unfolded. To be sure I always felt I was in the hands of the Father, but during that long night we both sensed something dire.

DC: You sensed a threshold was crossed and nothing was going to intervene to alter the course.

JC: Nothing. It was a long grueling night for everyone. When the contingent of guards and religious elders came for me I went willingly and was taken away. I did not speak a word. Many, if not all, of my disciples fled in fear, thinking they were the next to be arrested. The next day after my trial and flogging, Mary saw me carrying my cross to Golgotha. She barely recognized me. I was horribly beaten and bloody and my head was pierced with the crown of thorns. I struggled with my last measure of strength to manage the torment the wooden cross inflicted on my back.

DC: What the two of you had to endure! It was the culmination and focal point of terror in contrast to all the amazing things you experienced. When I close my eyes I can feel her heart ripped out of her chest screaming in agony. What more can you tell me about this moment?

JC: I was in utter misery. I could barely focus my mind as she could barely withstand her grief. She was horrified, but tried to be strong even though that was difficult. Her grief turned to doubt; she wondered whether the ministry was worth the cost of my torn and bloody body. That moment of realization came later for me.

DC: Are you referring to the words you cried out loudly, "My God, my God, why have you forsaken me?" (MT 27:46, MK 15:33) Your experience of darkness must have been incomprehensible in order for you to utter those words.

JC: I was delirious with pain from head to foot. It was unbearable and try as I might I couldn't stop it or put it out of my mind. The worst was the dark silence in my mind and the anguish in my heart. I looked out upon the hilltop. Of the thousands of people I healed, touched and taught, only a few were courageous enough to stand at the base of my cross and watch my death. All were women, except John. That is testimony to their spirit and heart.

DC: The men, on the other hand, were afraid and gave into fear.

JC: That broke my heart. I gave everything. I could have stopped my ministry mid-course and returned home to live a quiet domestic life with Mary, one we both wanted. But I chose not to.

DC: I sense something dreadful when I contemplate your words, "My God, my God, why have you forsaken me?" (MT 27:46) I have to ask myself what motivated you to say them. I know you were in agony; that was the point of Roman flogging and crucifixion. Your body was not the only thing screaming in pain. I sense you were overcome with a horrible anguish both in your heart and in your mind. I also sense that your connection to the Father was severed.

JC: It is hard to remember all that transpired and what I felt. I was delirious.

DC: This is hard to bring up but I also wonder if at that moment you questioned the effectiveness of your ministry, whether you had a profound sense of doubt. As I visualize this scenario I can see you gazing upon the few who remained true. I can see and hear your detractors taunting you, and I can see the Roman soldier's uncaring gestures. When I think about this and put myself into your position, I wonder if maybe you were plagued with the thought that your ministry was for nothing. To imagine that you did so much and endured so much for so few seemed incongruent and disproportionate to the amount of pain you suffered.

JC: It was then that Solomon's words bit into my mind furiously like the horde of bandits who robbed and beat me earlier in my life. "Everything is meaningless. What do people gain from all their labors at which they toil under the sun?" (Ecclesiastes 1:2-3) Those words stung as the dark silence descended on me and I became terrified. Why did I conduct my ministry? Doubts filled my mind. It was too late to reconsider the choices in my life. I could not go back and change them. I knew the love I experienced was real, and so too the Father and his kingdom. Yet at that moment the only reality I knew was the pain in my body, the anguish in my heart and the darkness in my mind. In an ironic twist, I relived the time when I returned home from that first serious adventure. Empty feelings flooded me once again. Had I invested everything in another failed venture? Was wisdom the only thing I could show for my life? Did I really accomplish something? Did anyone really listen to me? Did anyone even care? I felt shame and humiliation. I felt the jagged iron spikes smashed through my feet and wrists. I felt the hand of Roman oppression and religious intolerance pressing down on me; I could not move freely, I could not go where I wanted to go. I could not eat what I wanted to eat, visit my home where I felt safe, or be with friends and laugh. I was nailed and suspended naked on a splintery wooden cross for the world to see and not many were there to see me die. Few kind words greeted me; few comforted me. Where was everyone I healed? Where was everyone I fed? Where was everyone

I taught? Where was everyone I greeted with a smile? I recalled Job's agony. It was the agony of a solitary man without hope. The Father's presence completely vanished. Everything tormented me and I was moments away from death. I had trouble breathing, swallowing, seeing. I could not scratch the itch on my nose or wipe the blood from my face. I was thirsty. My mouth parched. The entire experience was unbearable. The women cried and wailed. Mary was inconsolable. Was she in more pain than I? Or was it the other way around? I offered words of encouragement but by that time my words were whispers and carried little weight or strength. They were incoherent. Dark clouds gathered and I got cold. I closed my eyes. I didn't want to gaze upon the landscape any longer; I didn't want to look at the sun or the clouds; I didn't want to see my blood dripping from my body; I didn't want to see another human face. I closed my ears to the viscous mocking words and the wailing cries of mourners who came to witness the other two who were crucified. I tried to listen to the wind rustling through the bushes. I couldn't. I was miserable in every manner possible.

DC: This upset me. The entire episode is very solemn and I am without words and my heart is heavy.

JC: It's a powerful event that can transform a pleasant and gripping mood into a morbid one.

DC: I'd like to move to the next phase of your story and discuss the tomb and resurrection.

JC: David I'm exhausted. I can't continue.

DC: Let's take another break; get a glass of water and a bite to eat.

JC: I'd like to leave that part of my story for another time. David, look! Look at what I am seeing. Turn around.

DC: It's beautiful. A double rainbow!

JC: It is a sign of God's double blessing.

DC: Jesus, my heart has been deeply touched. In all my days, I will never forget our time together, nor will I discount the importance of this interview. Thank you from the bottom of my heart.

JC: May the blessings of the Father fill your heart, His wisdom enlighten your mind and His strength quicken your feet. Peace be upon you. May it always be upon you. Until our next time.

MYSTERY SYMBOLS STATEMENT

"I'm drawn to the phenomenon of the mysterious; the place where magic and poetry comes alive." We swim in a sea of millions of symbols and signs; some as old as mankind. What's revolutionary? What's new on the horizon? The Mystery Symbols explore innovative graphic imagery that lay hidden in the ocean of my unconscious waiting for me discover and embrace them. They were shaped by my intuition, my spiritual sensibilities and my artistic aptitude for geometry, pattern and design and find inspiration from the past but point to the future. Like Jesus, who bridged the old world with the new, we hover on the brink of bright possibilities waiting for divine insights and original symbols to capture our imagination.

David Collis

BIBLIOGRAPHY

Borg, Marcus, Mark Powelson and Ray Riegert. Editors. *The Lost Gospel: The Original Sayings of Jesus*. Berkeley, California: Seastone, 1999

Borg, Marcus and Ray Riegert. Editors. *Jesus and Buddha, the Parallel Sayings*. Berkeley, CA: Ulysses Press, 1997

Boulding, Maria. *The Coming of God*. Third Edition. Conception, Missouri: The Printery House, 2000

Budge, Sir Wallis. *Egyptian Religion*. New York: Citadel Book, 1991

Churton, Tobias. *The Gnostics*. New York: Barnes and Noble Books, 1987

Crossan, John Dominic. *Jesus: A Revolutionary Biography*. New York: HarperSanFrancisco, 1994

Crossan, John Dominic and Jonathan L. Reed. *In Search of Paul: How Jesus' Apostle Opposed Rome's Empire with God's Kingdom*. New York: HarperSanFrancisco, 2004

———— *Excavating Jesus: Beneath the Stones, Behind the Text*. New York: HarperSanFrancisco, 2001

Ehrman, Bart D. *The Battles for Scripture and the Faiths We Never Knew*. New York: Oxford University Press, 2003

Eisenman, Robert. *James the Brother of Jesus: The Key to Unlocking the Secrets of Early Christianity and the Dead Sea Scrolls*. New York: Penguin Books, 1997

Eusebius. *The History of the Church; From Christ to Constantine*. Trans. G.A. Williamson. New York: Penguin Books, 1981

Fideler, David. *Jesus Christ, Sun of God: Ancient Cosmology and Early Christian Symbolism*. Wheaton, Illinois: Quest Books, 1993

Fredriksen, Paula. *From Jesus to Christ*. Second Edition. New Haven: Yale University Press, 2000

———— *Jesus of Nazareth: King of the Jews.* New York: Vintage Books, 1999

Freke, Timothy and Peter Gandy. *The Jesus Mysteries: Was the "Original Jesus" a Pagan God?* New York: Three Rivers Press, 1999

Funk, Robert W. *Honest to Jesus: Jesus for a New Millennium.* New York: HarperSanFrancisco, 1996

Funk, Robert W., Roy W. Hoover and the Jesus Seminar. Trans. *The Five Gospels: What Did Jesus Really Say? The Search for the Authentic Words of Jesus.* New York, HarperSanFrancisco, 1997

Gaffney, Mark H. *Gnostic Secrets of the Naassenes: The Initiatory Teachings of the Last Supper.* Rochester, Vermont: Inner Traditions, 2004

Goodman, Martin. *Rome and Jerusalem: The Clash of Ancient Civilization.* New York: Vintage Books, 2007

Goodspeed, Edgar J., Trans. *The Apocrypha.* New York: Vintage Books, 1989

The Holy Bible. New International Version. Grand Rapids, Michigan: Zondervan Bible Publishers, 2011

Hopper, Richard. Editor. *The Essential Mystics, Poets, Saints and Sages.* Charlottesville, Virginia: Hampton Roads Publishing, Inc., 2013

Howard, Michael. *The Occult Conspiracy: Secret Societies – Their Influence and Power in World History.* Rochester, Vermont: Destiny Books, 1989

Hurtak, James J. *Gnosticism: Mystery of Mysteries: A Study in the Symbols of Transformation.* Los Gatos, California: The Academy of Future Science, 1999

Jewish Encyclopedia. www.jewishencyclopedia.com

Josephus. *The Jewish War.* Trans. G.A. Williamson. Revised E. Mary Smallwood. Middlesex, UK: Penguin Books, 1959, 1970, 1981

King, Karen L. *What Is Gnosticism?* Cambridge, Massachusetts: Harvard University Press, 2005

The Lost Books of the Bible and the Forgotten Books of Eden. Author Unknown. New York: Meridian, 1974

Lurker, Manfred. *An Illustrated Dictionary of the Gods and Symbols of Ancient Egypt.* New York: Thames and Hudson, 1980

MacCulloch, Diarmaid. *Christianity: The First Three Thousand Years*. New York: Viking Penguin, 2009

Mack, Burton L. *Who Wrote the New Testament? The Making of the Christian Myth*. New York: HarperSanFrancisco, 1995

Meyer, Marvin. Trans. *The Secret Teachings of Jesus*. New York: Vintage Books, 1986

Meyer, Marvin and Esther A. De Boer. *The Gospel of Mary: The Secret Tradition of Mary Magdalene the Companion of Jesus*. New York: HarperSanFrancisco, 2004

Mitchell, Stephan. Editor. *The Enlightened Mind: An Anthology of Sacred Prose*. New York: Harper Collins, 1991

Pagels, Elaine. *Beyond Belief: The Secret Gospel of Thomas*. New York: Vintage Books, 2003

———— *The Gnostic Gospels*. New York: Vintage Books, 1989

Robinson, James M. Editor. *The Nag Hammadi Library: The Definitive New Translation of the Gnostic Scriptures*. Third Edition. New York: HarperSanFrancisco, 1988

Roukema, Riemer. *Gnosis and Faith in Early Christianity*. Trans. John Bowden. Harrisburg, Pennsylvania: Trinity Press International, 1999

Rudolph, Kurt. *Gnosis: The Nature and History of Gnosticism*. New York: HarperSanFrancisco, 1987

Shanks, Hershel. Editor. *Understanding the Dead Sea Scrolls: Reader from the Biblical Archeology Review*. New York: Vintage Books, 1992

Shanks, Hershel and Ben Witherington III. *The Brother of Jesus: The Dramatic Story & Meaning of the First Archeological Link to Jesus & His Family*. New York: HarperSanFrancisco, 2003

Shantananda, Swami and Peggy Bendet. *The Splendor of Recognition*. South Fallsburg, New York: SYDA Foundation, 2003

Smart, Ninian. *The Religious Experience of Mankind*. New York: Charles Scribner's Sons, 1969

Spong, John Shelby. *Resurrection: Myth or Reality?* New York: HarperSan-Francisco, 1994

Stark, Rodney. *The Rise of Christianity: How the Obscure, Marginal Jesus Movement Became the Dominant Religious Force in the Western World in a Few Centuries.* New York: HarperSanFrancisco, 1997

Stillwagon, JoAnne N. and The Foundation of Heaven. *The Book of Heaven for a Brand New Day.* LaVerne, California: Foundation of Heaven Publishing, 2007

St. John of the Cross. *Dark Night of the Soul.* Trans. and Edited by E. Allison Peers. Third Revised Edition. New York: Image Book, 1959

Tacitus. Trans. Kenneth Wellesley. *The Histories.* London, UK: Penguin Books, 1995

Van den Broek, Roelof and Woulter J. Hanegraaff. Editors. *Gnosis and Hermeticism: From Antiquity to Modern Times.* Albany, New York: State University of New York Press, 1998

Vermes, Geza. *The Authentic Gospel of Jesus.* New York: Penguin Books, 2003

———— *The Changing Faces of Jesus.* New York: Penguin Compass, 2000

———— *The Complete Dead Sea Scrolls in English.* New York: Penguin Books, 1997

Wikipedia. https://wikipedia.org

Williams, Michael Allen. *Rethinking Gnosticism: An Argument for Dismantling a Dubious Category.* Princeton, New Jersey: Princeton University Press, 1999

Wroe, Ann. *Pontius Pilate.* New York: Modern Library Paperbacks, 2001

ABOUT THE AUTHOR

David Collis, a native of Southern California, is romanced by exploration and invention and driven by curiosity and creativity. He characterizes his life as a living odyssey and vision quest combined. As a young man, Collis sought to become a commercial airline pilot but after a life altering crisis at nineteen, he dove wholeheartedly into the world of art, religion, philosophy and history. The writing of Thomas Merton, the Christian mystics, Joseph Campbell, J. Krishnamurti, Paramahansa Yogananda and Rumi inspired and guided him like a compass "through the maze of the world's religions and mystic traditions."

He earned his BFA from the Otis Art Institute and his MFA from the Claremont Graduate School; made a living as a Studio Art Assistant; rose through the ranks of carpenter, foreman, supervisor and inspector in the construction industry; traveled the world and conducted pilgrimages to sacred sites, temples and Cathedrals.

He says, "I spent decades wading through unknown spiritual territory, years unwittingly digging into Christianity and Gnosticism and, in one fell swoop, every one of my endeavors came together in *Interviewing Jesus*." Christianity and the life and sayings of Jesus of Nazareth allowed him to center his creative energies and insights on a single subject "in order to bring a new and fresh insight into an ancient living tradition."

He currently lives in the Sonoran desert where he writes, conducts lectures and creates art. Interviewing Jesus is his first book.